Revolutionary Ride

On the Road in Search of the Real Iran

LOIS PRYCE

NICHOLAS BREALEY
PUBLISHING
London · Boston

First published in 2017 by Nicholas Brealey Publishing
An imprint of John Murray Press
An Hachette UK Company

1

© Lois Pryce 2017

Map drawn by Rosie Collins

Although the events described are all true, in order to preserve anonymity some
names and identifying characteristics of individuals have been changed.

A CIP catalogue record for this title is available from the British Library

ISBN 978-1-85788-657-3
Ebook ISBN UK 978-1-85788-929-1
Ebook ISBN US 978-1-47364-489-2

Typeset in Bembo MT by Palimpsest Book Production Ltd, Falkirk, Stirlingshire

Printed and bound by Clays Ltd, St Ives plc

Nicholas Brealey policy is to use papers that are natural,
renewable and recyclable products and made from wood grown in
sustainable forests. The logging and manufacturing processes are expected to
conform to the environmental regulations of the country of origin.

Nicholas Brealey Publishing
John Murray Press
Carmelite House
50 Victoria Embankment
London EC4Y 0DZ, UK
Tel: 020 3122 6000

Nicholas Brealey Publishing
Hachette Book Group
Market Place Center, 53 State Street
Boston, MA 02109, USA
Tel: (617) 523 3801

www.nicholasbrealey.com
www.loisontheloose.com

For Austin-*jan*

Contents

TURKEY

IRAQ

Tabriz

I

Qazvin

TEHRAN

Kashan

R

Isfahan

A

YAZD

Persepolis

SHIRAZ

Caspian
Sea

SAUDI ARABIA

Persian Gulf

miles

0   50   100   150   200

Journey to Shiraz

AFGHANISTAN

PAKISTAN

N

'I have no reason to go, except that I have never been, and knowledge is better than ignorance. What better reason could there be for travelling?'　　　　　　Freya Stark

I

A Curious Invitation

I N THE FIRST week of December 2011, in London, I was
approached by a stranger with a proposition that would eventually lead me on a journey of thousands of miles to a land of
secrets, fear and an irrepressible lust for life.

The incident occurred in the exclusive district of Kensington –
not an area I frequent often, but I had a lunch date nearby and
with a few other errands to do, I rode my motorcycle into town
and parked in a bike bay in the consular district, close to the Royal
Albert Hall and Hyde Park. Above me, the spectrum of embassy
flags brightened the wintry sky while around me a glossy stream
of diplomatic cars slid in and out of coveted parking spaces. But
on that day there was one embassy that definitely wasn't open for
business, although its green, white and red flag still hung limply
above its locked doors. Black-clad figures in bulletproof vests stood
guard, silhouetted against the white stucco building, but there was
nothing to see here. Everyone at the Embassy for the Islamic
Republic of Iran had gone home – not to their diplomatic London
residences but all the way home: 4,000 miles away, to Tehran.

A few days earlier, on the 29 November, the British Embassy
in Tehran had been stormed and set on fire in a protest over sanctions imposed by the British government. Hundreds of protestors
had scaled the walls, ransacked the buildings and thrown firebombs
into the embassy compound. The British staff were commanded
to leave Iran and two days later William Hague, then Foreign
Secretary, took his revenge, ordering the closure of the Iranian

Embassy in London and expelling its staff from Britain, giving them forty-eight hours to leave the country. All diplomatic and financial relations between the two countries were severed with immediate effect. The British papers featured images of angry, bearded men in Tehran burning the Union Jack; solemn newscasters delivered fear-laden prophecies and the Foreign Office declared Iran unsafe for travel. The ever torrid Anglo-Iranian relationship had hit an all-time low, with accusations that the Tehran protest had occurred with the tacit support of the Iranian authorities.

I had followed the story with the curiosity of a traveller who keeps an interested eye on world affairs. Iran featured somewhere on my to-do list and I was acquainted with a few British Iranians in London, but that was about the extent of my involvement. Or at least it was until I returned to my bike after lunch and found a handwritten note tucked behind the speedo. It was in English, in an untidy script, from someone called Habib.

I didn't know anyone called Habib and, judging by his opening line, he didn't know me either. But he had an invitation for me, or was it a challenge?

Dear Sir.

I have seen your motorbike and I think that you have travelled to many countries. But I wonder, have you been to my country? That is Iran. It is very beautiful and the Persian people are the most welcoming in the world. Please do not think of what has happened here and in Tehran. These are our governments, not the Iranian people. WE ARE NOT TERRORISTS! I wish that you will visit Iran so you will see for yourself about my country. WE ARE NOT TERRORISTS!!! Please come to my city, Shiraz. It is very famous as the friendliest city in Iran, it is the city of poetry and gardens and wine!!!
Your Persian friend,
Habib

It wasn't so unusual to find a note on the bike. Riding in London you get to recognise certain motorcycles and in the small community of overland riders it is not uncommon to know someone's bike by sight, whether or not you are acquainted with the owner, and to make comradely contact. Mine had all the identifying marks of a well-travelled machine – large capacity 'desert' tank, sheepskin seat, scruffy panniers, a few foreign stickers and a general tatty, battered appearance, not to mention an oil leak that was currently soiling the streets of SW7. For a fellow motorcycle traveller to say hello in this way wouldn't be considered strange. But the mysterious Habib made no reference to his own motorcycle travels or ownership. I wondered if he was a member of the embassy staff, but as far as I knew they had all been bundled on to a hastily chartered Iran Air flight out of Heathrow a few days ago. Maybe he was just a regular Iranian living in London, distressed at the recent bust-up between his homeland and his adopted country. Although there was no official 'Persian quarter' in London, there were plenty of Iranians in this part of town, where those with the necessary funds had settled after fleeing the Islamic Revolution of 1979. They tended to be of the well-heeled brigade, more likely to inhabit the high-end boutiques and restaurants of Knightsbridge and Kensington than to be found sticking notes on random ratty motorcycles.

The discovery of this message added a certain air of mystery to an otherwise routine day. I enjoyed the oddness of it and told a few friends about it over the next few days; just another funny tale of biking in London. And maybe that would have been the end of the story if the newspapers and radio hadn't still been full of angry rhetoric about Habib's homeland. His note didn't just disappear into my 'peculiar incidents' file; his words kept coming back to me whenever I heard a politician denouncing Iran on the news or referencing George Bush's 'Axis of Evil' speech. What kind of man would be so distressed at how his home country is perceived as to make a written plea to a complete stranger to seek out the truth? Did he do this all the time? Was he an overzealous employee of the Iranian tourist board? Was there even such a thing as the Iranian tourist board? So many questions. All unanswered, and, it seemed, unanswerable.

Meanwhile, the UK was still reeling from the protests in Tehran and its subsequent tit-for-tat actions. 'A poll reveals the majority of British people believe Iran to be a negative influence and support military force to prevent their development of nuclear weapons,' declared the BBC World Service one morning.

The presenter didn't bother explaining why we all believed this; the reasons were taken as read. Somehow, our little island had reached the point where we considered Iran to be our greatest enemy and a genuine threat to civilisation. No wonder Habib had taken to writing messages to strangers. How else could he make his point? I began to acquire a sneaking respect for his grassroots approach to international relations. If you can't make the people at the top talk sense, then spread the word on the street.

Habib had me intrigued, and my growing interest saw me lurching between chilling reports of torture and executions, and alluring tales of an ancient, sophisticated civilisation. As Habib pointed out in his note, and as common sense will tell you, the citizens of a country and their government are two entirely sep- arate entities. After all, I wouldn't want a foreign visitor to Britain to associate me with my government. Why should it be different anywhere else? But, countered my inner doom-monger, maybe Iran was different; maybe it really was that bad. I didn't know what to believe.

This turn of events forced me to admit that, like most Brits, my impressions of contemporary Iran came entirely from the British and US media – and it wasn't pretty. A sinister mash-up of rogue nuclear physicists, inflammatory rants at the UN, women being lashed for adultery, chart-topping numbers of executions; the horrors of Iran seemed endless. The current president, Mahmoud Ahmadinejad, was not helping the cause; he seemed

intent on furthering Iran's pariah status with his outlandish statements on topics ranging from homosexuality in Iran (it doesn't
exist), to the Holocaust (it didn't happen), memorably dismissing
the crippling US sanctions as being 'annoying, like used tissues'
and even supporting a fatwa against the wearing of ties – a symbol
of western decadence, apparently. The British and US media
lapped it all up; Ahmadinejad made for tasty headlines – there
were even allegations that he had been involved in the taking of
American hostages in the 1979 US Embassy crisis. Whether this
was true or not, it further compounded the image of Iran the
western media liked to project – a bunch of ranting religious
lunatics that needed to be kept on a tight leash.

But as I dug a little deeper, seeking out reports from less
mainstream sources and asking British-Iranian acquaintances
about their families and backgrounds, I found there was another,
quieter story to be told – a story far removed from the shouty
business of international politics, sanctions and religious fundamentalists. There were tales of Iranian artists and film-makers
making a stand, underground musicians and bands putting on
illegal gigs, activist poets and lawyers risking their lives, and
young sportswomen standing up to the regime – stories on a
human scale that offered a glow of hope and a whiff of intrigue.
The internet, although strictly monitored and painfully slow,
had brought the world to the youth of Iran via illegal private
networks. Unsurprisingly, they liked what they saw and wanted
to be part of it. The sealed-off world of the Islamic Republic
could reign supreme when the only information was via state-
controlled media, but here was a new threat. With a vast youth
population – the result of Ayatollah Khomeini's state-sponsored
baby boom in the early years of the revolution – the kids of the
1980s had come of age in the internet era and were not impressed
with the restrictions imposed on their lives. Unlike their parents,
this was not what they had signed up for.

The more I researched, the more fascinated I became – and the more convinced I was that the only thing to do was to go and see Iran for myself. In London, the opinions on the ground were as you would expect. Iran was a dangerous destination, especially for female westerners, a view that was compounded by the official Foreign Office advice, which coloured the whole country in no-go red. Very occasionally, on the underground telegraph of overland travellers I would hear real-world reports from a few rare folk who had actually been to Iran, and the message was quite different. 'The Iranians are so kind and hospitable,' they would say, echoing Habib's words. 'It was my favourite country, the people are fantastic.'

But their travels had mostly been transient, a few days passing through on their way from Europe to India or the Far East. I never met anyone who had been to Shiraz, so they couldn't testify to Habib's claims about his home town and, although endearing, I suspected his statement had been fuelled by nothing more tangible than homesickness and patriotism.

But what did any of us in the UK really know for sure about life in Iran nowadays? There was a time when Britain and Iran had been inextricably linked, but the era of real British involvement in Iran's business was long gone, and the relationship could not be said to have ended happily. In my lifetime alone there had been numerous diplomatic spats, with our respective embassies being attacked, opened and closed, ambassadors being expelled back and forth, not to mention the infamous Salman Rushdie fatwa in 1989. But it went way back before that, most significantly, to the beginning of the twentieth century when Britain had taken control of Iran's oil. Even that wasn't the start of it; the British influence, or some would say, interference, dated back to nineteenth-century Persia. And in recent years Tony Blair had hardly helped, with his constant Iran fear-mongering. *I see the impact and influence of Iran everywhere*, I remembered him saying, his glassy, maniacal eyes staring out from behind a lectern at some international summit. Really, it was no wonder it was hard to get a visa.

For most of my lifetime Iran had been closed to the world. Over thirty years had passed since the 1979 revolution, when Ayatollah Ruhollah Khomeini had returned to Iran from exile and successfully overthrown the Shah, who was viewed as a puppet of the West. The Iranians had had enough of the Shah's excesses and brutality, and welcomed their new leader with open arms. Khomeini had turned plain ol' Iran into The Islamic Republic Of, had cut all ties with 'Great Satan' and 'Little Satan' – his names for the USA and Britain – and, unsurprisingly, the 'Visit Iran' ad campaigns had been a bit thin on the ground ever since. In my lifetime this ancient civilisation had become a mystery, our knowledge based on whispers and propaganda.

I had made my decision. I would take up what I had now termed the 'Habib Challenge' – I would travel to Iran on my motorcycle and have a look for myself. Destination, Shiraz, supposedly the friendliest city in the world's unfriendliest country. I would travel alone, not with the entourage of a guided tour, or as a journalist with a suspicion-arousing press pass, but just as me, a regular Brit, talking to regular Iranians. As a freelance travel writer, this was my preferred modus operandi – getting on the ground, to the heart of the action, making myself open to whatever came my way. My many thousands of miles on the road over the years had shown me that the combination of autonomy and vulnerability that is to be found by travelling alone on a motorcycle is the best way to achieve this kind of intense immersion. I wanted to know where the myths and the truth overlapped and, most of all, I had to admit that I had my own ingrained prejudices and fears about Iran that would benefit from a reality check.

Naturally, the naysayers were out in force when I announced my plans. It was hard to ignore them, despite knowing from my previous travels that what you see on the news isn't what you get on the ground. In my darker moments I got sucked in by the doom merchants and fully expected to be arrested and banged up by Iran's infamous 'morality police' upon arrival. After all, here

I was, a British female, with no religion and a fondness for gin and tonic, heading alone into an Islamic theocracy on a motorcycle, an illegal form of transport for Iranian women. It was hard to find anyone in the wider world who thought it was a good idea, but I did find approval close to home; my mum and my husband were right behind it. Mum had spent time as an international observer in Palestine, where she had acquired an interest in Islamic cultures and was currently learning Arabic. Her interest extended to all things Middle Eastern, and I think she was hoping I would bring her back a nice Persian carpet. My husband, Austin, as a fellow motorcycle world traveller, is a fervent supporter of my adventures, and his gung-ho approach to just about everything is one of his many endearing traits. At our wedding, back in 2005, we had persuaded the registrar to let us write our own vows. When we had exchanged rings and made the standard pledges of love, respect and friendship, the registrar had solemnly read to each of us in turn our own home-made one: 'Do you promise to embark on a life together of hair-brained schemes, crackpot plans and ill-thought-through adventures?' To which we had both replied, equally solemnly: 'I do.' It looked as though the time had come, once again, for Austin to let me come good on that promise.

Whenever I felt a bit wobbly, I also took inspiration from Freya Stark – the British explorer and author who had spent much of her life in the Middle East – and particularly from her adventurous travels in what was then Persia during the 1930s. Outspoken, wilful and not in the slightest bit concerned about doing things by the book, she had trekked through remote and dangerous terrain to map uncharted territory, often tackling hostile and doubting locals, battling serious diseases and regularly riling the British establishment, who disapproved of her unscientific, maverick approach to expeditions. A fluent speaker of Persian and Arabic, she immersed herself with the natives in a way that was considered distasteful by British society of the time, and wrote several brilliant and entertaining books about her adventures, which were hailed as instant classics. Her gung-ho approach meant that she was always ready to throw herself into the thick of the action with an exuberance not normally associated with the rather serious geographical expeditions of the era. I admired her rebellious spirit and the way she embraced indecision, solitude and vulnerability as well as risk and her fellow humans. Most of all, I liked that she was entirely unpretentious about the motivation behind her unconventional lifestyle: 'For my own part I travel single-mindedly for fun.'

But Freya Stark's snappy quotes and tales of derring-do could only get me so far. I lived in very different times. Her Iran had been wilder in some ways, but it had also been under the control of Reza Shah, who was actively modernising the country, while the British presence was still powerful, running Iran's oil industry as well as the railways and telecommunications. The ayatollahs of the twenty-first century wouldn't have had much truck with Miss Stark, and I doubted they would think much of me and my motor-bike. At night I would lie awake and wonder if I was making a terrible mistake, if this was one adventure too far. It wasn't as if I hadn't done this kind of thing before; in the last decade I had motorcycled the length of North and South America solo, and also through Africa, riding from London to Cape Town via the Muslim countries of North Africa, so I had some idea of what I was getting into. And I knew from past experience that there is a certain kind of person who likes nothing more than to predict a grisly outcome. But something about Iran brought out a different kind of response, even in people I considered worldly and open-minded. This time it wasn't the usual concerns of 'What happens if you break down in the middle of nowhere?' or 'What will you do if you crash and break your leg?' It was all about the locals, and primarily the men, and what they were going to do to me.

I had to admit that I was not immune to the insidious drip-feed of anti-Iranian, anti-Islam sentiments that had entered our collective consciousness over the years, and I couldn't always shrug off the concerns of the naysayers. This journey would be more than just an interesting road trip around a foreign country; it would be a painful test of some of my own deeply entrenched fears and opinions, the ones to which I didn't really like to admit. But if fear is a product of ignorance, then that in itself was a reason to go.

So I monitored the political situation over the next year, watching and waiting for news of the embassies reopening. But the freeze never thawed and Ahmadinejad continued to stir up trouble, so in 2013 I decided that hanging around for politicians to cosy up to each other was a mug's game. Would there ever be a 'good time', according to the Foreign Office, for a solo British woman to ride a motorcycle around Iran? Probably not. I took the plunge and applied for a visa.

With no functioning embassy or consular services in London, I employed the services of a specialist visa agent, a brilliantly efficient Lebanese woman. By coincidence, she had recently learned to ride a motorcycle, and therefore thought my idea of a solo bike trip around Iran was a great idea. It was refreshing to finally receive some positive encouragement, but it was soon countered during the second stage of the process – by the man behind the counter in Snappy Snaps who took the photo for my application.

'Iran?' he said, aghast. 'What d'you wanna go there for?' It was becoming something of a mantra. 'Well, whatever floats your boat,' he continued, not waiting for an answer and shaking his head. Then he read me the rules: three concepts that were all entirely alien to me. 'Right, you'll need your hair covered, no make-up and don't smile.'

The resulting photo may not have been my first choice for an online dating profile pic but, I decided with an objective eye, it was perfect for cosying up to an Iranian bureaucrat. With my bare, unsmiling face and tightly wrapped headscarf, I felt like a poster girl for female oppression. I sent it off along with a carefully

A CURIOUS INVITATION

constructed application and a large amount of money. But despite my best efforts to appear a reputable and unthreatening tourist, my application was returned a few weeks later with a request for further information. I had been singled out for some suspicious questioning by the Iranian authorities: What was the purpose of my journey? What did I do for a living? By what means was I travelling? I gave some creative responses that I hoped chimed with the ideals of the Islamic Republic, and waited.

Life went on hold. I couldn't make any plans. I was twitchy with nerves and sometimes, in the middle of the night, I secretly hoped my application would be rejected. After about two weeks the call finally came from the visa agent. This was it. My fate would be sealed: was I going to Iran or not?

Her voice was upbeat. 'The good news is that they have approved your visa, but . . .'

I held my breath. That 'but' didn't bode well.

'The bad news is that it has only been granted on the condition that you travel by public transport. They won't let you enter Iran with your own vehicle.'

A muddle of emotions was already coursing through me: excitement, fear, relief. And now, frustration. This news was a major blow. The autonomy afforded by having my own wheels was crucial to my plan.

'You mean I can't go on my bike? Does it mean I have to fly there? And travel by train or bus or. . .? What do they mean exactly?'

She interrupted my protestations. 'You know what? I've never heard of this happening before. They haven't given a reason, but to be honest, I don't think there will be anything actually written on your visa to enforce this rule. Maybe you could put your bike on a train or a truck in Turkey, just to get over the border? Once you're in Iran I'm sure you'll be fine to travel around on your bike.'

'Really? You think I can get away with it?' It seemed sketchy as hell, but I liked this woman's gung-ho style.

'Obviously I can't give you the official go-ahead to do this, but from what I know of the system, I don't think they will have this level of detail at the border post, so I don't think you will get challenged.'

'So you think I should just set off on my bike and wing it?'

This was all beginning to sound slightly weird, a bit risky and hugely exciting. I gave a thought to Freya Stark. I knew exactly what she would have done in this situation. My visa lady was speaking again and it seemed as though she too was channelling Freya Stark's ghost.

'Obviously, there's a risk and the decision is up to you, but my unofficial advice would be to give it a go.'

That was all I needed to hear.

2

'Go and Wake Up Your Luck'

Two months later I was riding my motorcycle across Turkey, heading east, following the classic hippie trail of the sixties and seventies – but in the twenty-first century this route was a whole different story. Only a few decades ago the standard itinerary of Turkey–Iran–Afghanistan–Pakistan had been the mind-opening rite-of-passage for thousands of wide-eyed British teens making their way to India. But now, a generation later, Iran stood isolated from the world; Kabul, once the swinging city of the Middle East, was reeling from war; the Buddhas of Bamiyan were blown to smithereens and Pakistan had become a no-go zone, only accessible with military escorts for the few overland travellers prepared to run the gauntlet.

I was born too late for that innocent era; my world travels had coincided almost exactly with the so-called War on Terror. In the spring of 2003 I had left the safe but tedious confines of my BBC office job to ride my motorcycle from Alaska to Argentina, just as George Bush invaded Iraq. The Stars and Stripes were flying high on the first leg of that trip. But as soon as I crossed the border into Mexico it was a different story. And by the time I reached Central America the graffiti was already appearing – BUSH GENOCIDIO, ENEMIGO DE LA HUMANIDAD. I spent a lot of time explaining that I was a UK passport holder, '*Soy Inglesa!*', not a war-mongering gringo from north of the border, and it seemed to help. But a few years later, while travelling through Muslim North Africa, that distinction had blurred;

our 'special relationship' meant that as far as the rest of the world was concerned, we were all in it together. Border guards saw my passport and spat Tony Blair's name into the sandy ground as they issued a grudging entry stamp. *Hey! I was on that anti-war march in 2003*, I wanted to tell them. But what good would it do? As much good as the march itself. In the intervening years London had been shaken by the 7/7 bombings, and in 2007, when I emerged from the Algerian Sahara to discover that Saddam Hussein had been killed, I knew that the days of chatting with immigration officials about David Beckham and Princess Diana were over. Now, taking my first foray into the Middle East, to a country famous for its hostility towards Britain, I felt a mixture of sadness, anger, regret and shame, albeit for actions for which I wasn't personally responsible but which still hung heavy on my shoulders. The great British passport had lost its lustre, and its pompous statement on the inside cover – 'Her Britannic Majesty's Secretary of State requests and requires in the Name of Her Majesty all those whom it may concern to allow the bearer to pass freely without let or hindrance, and to afford the bearer such assistance and protection as may be necessary' – seemed vaguely ridiculous. Good luck with that, Ma'am.

My first taste of the East had appeared in the shape of Istanbul, with its thrilling skyline of minarets and domes and the mighty Bosphorus Bridge shuttling traffic between Europe and Asia. But as I continued east my confidence in outwitting the Iranian Ministry of Foreign Affairs began to wane. Their mistrust surrounding my visa application was contagious; they were paranoid about me, and now I was paranoid about them. Ever since the embassy-storming episode of 2011, the granting of visas to UK citizens had become such a fickle business. I imagined it presided over by some demonic bureaucrat in Tehran, brandishing his all-powerful rubber stamp and laughing maniacally whilst burning the applications of hapless Brits in his wastepaper bin. I was surprised they had agreed to let me in at all.

The further I got from home, the twitchier I became. The long days in the saddle, across Turkey's lonely Pontic Mountains, allowed my imagination to concoct all sorts of dramatic stories which involved me being turned away at the border, arrested for spying, escaping from my cell and hitching a ride in a truck full of contraband booze, and making a midnight crossing via some obscure smugglers' route in the mountains.

My arrival in Ankara, the functional, if rather dreary, capital of Turkey, stilled my fevered imagination and offered an agreeable, if less theatrical, answer to my problem: the Trans-Asia Express, a weekly rail service between there and Tehran. Its first Iranian destination was Tabriz, the north-western city just over the frontier that I had planned as my first stop. For the price of a few kebabs I could put myself and my bike on the train across the rest of Turkey and be deposited just inside Iran, 1,000 miles away. Hopefully, once there, I could slip the bike out of the guard's van and be on my way, no questions asked. There was a time when my younger motorcycling self, who valued the notion of purism, would have been aggrieved by interrupting the ride like this, but purism be damned! Outwitting the Iranian authorities was my priority, and besides, as a secret railway fan, I was geekily excited about the idea of riding such a romantically titled train.

Much to the bemusement of Ankara's morning commuters, I pushed my bike through the busy station, over a level crossing and on to Platform 2, where it was heaved into the goods wagon by a gang of surly Turkish railway workers in greasy shirts. At the shriek of the guard's whistle, everyone climbed aboard and I found myself alone in a four-berth sleeping carriage. After a few hours rumbling through Ankara's outskirts, I flirted with the idea of contacting Turkish Trading Standards to point out that not only was the train just Trans a little bit of Asia, it was also seriously stretching the definition of Express. Not that I minded. I had a cosy cabin to myself, and as darkness fell and rain spattered the window, I knew I had made the right decision.

My solitary status was not to last long. At the next station a knock on the door brought the conductor with the news that I was to be joined by some fellow travellers. '*Bayan?*' I asked. It was the word that accompanied pictures of women on toilet doors. I had been '*Salaamed*' with a little too much interest by a couple of unctuous guys in the train corridor and hoped I was not destined to spend the next two nights in similar company. The conductor nodded and struggled in English,

'Yes, *bayan*, a woman and her—' he faltered, searching for the word. 'Her chick.'

I imagined a young lady and a baby, so was surprised when an elderly Iranian woman appeared at the door and her 'chick' turned out to be her middle-aged son.

My new companions greeted me like a long-lost friend and, after arranging their beds, wasted no time in laying out a tea towel on the table and barricading us in the cabin with a wall of Tupperware. From this came a steady supply of bread, cheese, tomatoes, grapes and a home-made spread of egg, potato, mayonnaise and dill.

'Please, eat with us,' they said with beaming smiles. I tried to imagine this happening on the 09.42 to Doncaster, and failed. I had vague childhood memories of strangers sharing food on trains in the 1970s, but the chances nowadays of my own countrymen and women offering to share their food with a foreign stranger on public transport were, sadly, almost nil. I wondered if this protectiveness of our personal space and possessions was a symptom of being a small, overcrowded nation; if there was an unconscious need to keep hold of something, anything, for ourselves.

The first course was followed by a cake of dates and nuts with tea brewed in a tiny electric travel kettle plugged into the train carriage socket. My new companions were from the Iranian city of Isfahan and the chick, as I now thought of him, spoke some English, while his mother spoke only a few words, but we muddled through with the help of my Persian phrase book, much to their entertainment. Meanwhile the food kept on coming and I eventually had the opportunity to use the crucial phrase an Iranian friend of mine in London had warned me I would need, '*Seer shodam, merci*' – I am full, thank you. I had the feeling this would become something of a catchphrase.

After the meal had been cleared away the mother closed her eyes and put her hands together.

'Now I pray.'

She began a high, keening wail that seemed to go on and on. I sat there in awkward silence, not sure how I was supposed to respond, wishing we could just talk about the weather or have a pop quiz, or something. I didn't know where to look. The carriage suddenly seemed very small and a little too intimate. Her son sat next to her, a beatific expression on his face, and when she finished he pulled out a small book from his bag and began reciting a prayer from it.

'We are followers of the Bahá'í religion,' he said when he had finished. I nodded a little too eagerly, glad that any kind of normal conversation had resumed. 'It is illegal in Iran,' he explained. 'I was two years in prison because I am Bahá'í.'

He was a jeweller by trade, with long, slender fingers and a gentle manner. His expression and tone of voice were so soft and open that this revelation came as a shock to me. I couldn't imagine him weathering the harsh environment of an Iranian jail. I had read a little about the Bahá'í religion, mainly that its followers in Iran were a persecuted minority, but often well educated and professional. The religion dated back to nineteenth-century Persia, originating in Shiraz. It had since spread throughout the world, picking up some well-known followers along the way, including jazz trumpeter Dizzy Gillespie and, more recently, the British-Iranian comedian Omid Djalili. But the celebrity endorsement had failed to convince the Iranian authorities, who still considered it to be some kind of sinister cult and took a heavy-handed approach with its followers. I asked him why it was outlawed in Iran.

'Because it began by breaking away from Islam. Mohammed says Islam is the last religion, there will not be another. But it's mostly because we believe in peace and equality for all people – men and women are equal in Bahá'ísm. But this is not true in Islam; they do not believe in this. We believe in unity, of all humankind.' I had to admit, it didn't sound like something the Iranian ayatollahs would be signing up for any time soon.

'Other religions are allowed in Iran; there are Zoroastrians of course, the original religion of Iran. But also Christians and even Jews in Iran, but the Bahá'í faith, it is the only one that is illegal. For our people in Iran, life is very difficult,' he went on. 'We cannot attend university, or work in government positions, our people are imprisoned, sometimes executed. They say we are a political organisation, that we are linked to Israel, they destroy our businesses, our homes . . .'

He fished around in his bag and handed me a Bahá'í promotional pamphlet. I read the propaganda, a vaguely woolly treatise on love and peace with a sprinkling of moon, sun and stars thrown in. It seemed pretty harmless as religions go, and these two gentle folk seemed about as kind and sweet as you could get, but the disseminating of literature and the loud praying made me uncomfortable. I wondered if this is what the rest of my trip would hold.

'What is your religion?' asked his mother. They both looked to me for my answer, all friendly, interested eyes. I sensed a cheerful proclamation of atheism might kill the mood but I hadn't prepared an answer and I found myself mumbling something about 'not really being religious'. I wondered if I should have made something up. Maybe any religion was better than no religion in this situation. There was a short silence.

'And do you work in London?'

'Yes, I'm, er, a secretary, at a school.' I decided to lie this time. It was an innocent lie but it tied in with my visa application, where revealing yourself as any kind of writer was a fast track to the DECLINED stamp. A school secretary seemed a respectable and innocuous job for a woman, I reasoned, unlikely to raise the suspicions of the authorities. I was paranoid enough to feel the need to keep my story straight, even with these embattled religious dissidents.

'Ah, so you will be returning to work soon. The summer holidays are finished, yes?' asked the son. Caught out! I made some rambling explanation about how I was allowed special leave for this journey.

'Are you married?'

The questions kept coming, but at least to this one I could give the right answer truthfully. They looked pleased.

'And do you have children?'

Their expressions turned to sympathetic disappointment when I answered truthfully on this count.

'But you will have children when you get home?' they said hopefully.

I heard myself agreeing to start breeding the minute my feet touched British soil. I had now concocted an entirely false identity but at least they were happy.

'We will pray for you to have good children,' said the son with another radiant smile.

'Thank you,' I said weakly.

He set about dismantling the Tupperware barricade and I settled back into my bunk to read while trying to maintain the demeanour of a broody school secretary. The chick left the carriage to wash the plates and cutlery and returned a while later, excitable and animated.

'There are many of us on this train!' he exclaimed, 'Many Bahá'ís, all travelling home from visiting family in Turkey.'

He was so happy to be amongst his people and had obviously designated our carriage as Bahá'í party central. For the rest of the evening his comrades were popping in and out, men, women, old and young, all dropping by for a snack and chat and to meet the woman from England with the motorcycle. They questioned me, invited me to stay with them in Iran, giggled and made jokes among themselves, which were half translated to me and seemed to be largely at the expense of the Iranian mullahs. We had occasional visits from a teenage student computer programmer who dressed like Ali G but spoke better English, and was therefore commandeered to translate long-winded religious reveries about the sun and moon reflecting God, which he did with exceptionally good grace and patience.

Despite our differences I felt entirely at ease with these people. They exuded a comfortable, human warmth and kindness that I could not claim to have experienced very often amongst complete strangers. I felt safe and welcome in their company but wondered if this was a Bahá'í phenomenon. Would I have the same experience with all Iranians? I would find out soon enough; in twenty-four hours we would transfer on to the Iranian train and I would enter the Islamic Republic.

At Lake Van, in the mountainous wilderness of eastern Turkey, the baggage car was uncoupled from the train, trundled on to a ferry with a section of railway tracks embedded in its hold, and I and the other few hundred passengers climbed aboard the ferry for a five-hour sailing across the lake. On the eastern shore the baggage car would be hauled out of the ferry and hooked up to an Iranian train, which we would all board and continue on our way. It seemed a strangely convoluted way of getting to the other side of a lake. Why didn't they just continue the tracks around its edge? True, the surrounding country was rugged and rocky, but the railway had been built as recently as the 1970s with British and American funding, so I assumed they'd had the skills and finances to lay a few miles of track on some rough ground. I couldn't understand it, but when I asked people the reason, nobody knew. They shrugged their shoulders, laughed and seemed unconcerned. I wondered, not for the first time when finding myself confronted with foreign illogicality, if my obsession with efficiency was a character trait peculiar to northern Europe. I decided

I needed to lighten up – what the heck if they want to waste loads of time and effort hauling trains on to boats? It made for an interesting diversion and meant I got to hang out with more of my Iranian travelling companions, most of whom seemed to be entertaining themselves by taking photos of each other shinning up a giant flagpole on the deck and clambering up and down rickety ladders. I watched them swinging off the top, whooping and laughing with apparently no concern for their safety; it was exhilarating to see and particularly refreshing that nobody tried to stop them fooling around. I stood on the deck, alone in the darkening evening, cheered by the clowning going on all around me. It made me feel at home; this was the kind of thing my friends and I would get up to. But I was surprised. My image of Iran was not that of a nation out for a laugh and a good time; I had expected Iranians to take a more solemn approach to life. My preconceptions were already unravelling fast.

Below decks, a fetid miasma of diesel and chemical toilets lingered and inside the cabin the woodwork was scuffed and the upholstery tatty, a stark contrast to the trim orderliness of the Turkish train. I guessed the boat belonged to the Iranian side of the Trans-Asia Express, as all the signs were now in Persian with a few attempts at English translations – 'In case of death do not lean on balustrades.' I found my Bahá'í carriage companions and attempted to buy them dinner and tea from the food counter, but they were having none of it, and insisted, once again, that the tea towels and Tupperware were deployed for another feast.

'You must eat with us,' said the son with his kind smile, 'you are like a sister now.'

On the eastern side of the lake the Iranian train was nowhere to be seen but nobody grumbled. In fact, it barely warranted a mention. So we all squeezed into a waiting room, furnished with nothing but a few plastic chairs, and did what the room was designed for.

Eventually, an Iranian railway official, dressed casually in an open-necked shirt, began herding us into some sort of line in order to allocate us carriages and seats. Next to me in the melee that passed for a queue was an elderly Iranian woman, dressed in the head-to-toe black chador, tightly wrapped around her neck and hairline with only the oval of her face visible, wrinkled and weathered from decades of Middle Eastern sun. She kept staring at me, her features large and expressive, although I was having trouble working out exactly what it was she was trying to express. Many of the other women were dressed in western outfits and some had their hair exposed as we were still officially on Turkish soil, but this woman's clothing suggested a devout Islamic faith and all the traditional values that accompany it. I felt nervous under her gaze, sensing her criticism. This was the Iran I had feared, disapproval from a nation of hardline Islamists, angered by the nerve of my infidel jaunt around their country. I shifted awkwardly, reluctant to lose my place in the 'queue' but fearing the situation that I sensed was brewing.

She came at me with a jabbing knotty finger. 'You, you have motor, yes?'

I must have appeared confused because she repeated it again but this time she accompanied it with the universal motion for twisting the throttle, complete with engine revving noises.

'Vroom, vroom! You have motor, yes? It is you?'

There was no point in denying it. Almost everyone in this room had seen my bike being loaded on to the train in Ankara, and anyone who had missed the spectacle had heard about it by now, via the Trans-Asia telegraph. There is no anonymity for the lone female British motorcyclist in Iran. I had a sudden cold fear that she was a spy for the Iranian Ministry of Foreign Affairs. Had she got wind of my bike-smuggling plan? Maybe my visa lady back home had been wrong and I was on some kind of 'no vehicle' list. I got a grip of my fevered imagination and 'fessed up.

'Er, yes, that's me, I have motor, yes.'

I awaited a steely grip on my wrist but instead she grabbed

hold of my face with her big fleshy hands. Then she landed an enthusiastic smack on my cheek as a huge smile erupted across her stern features.

'Very good! Very good!' she bellowed at eardrum-piercing volume, hugging me into the voluminous folds of her chador.

Now she was jumping up and down, whacking me on the back and squeezing my face again, hooting with laughter. 'Very good! Very good! Vroom, vroom!'

Her motorcycle actions became more animated until she was imitating the moves of a daredevil speedway racer, body swerving from side to side, hips swinging beneath yards of billowing black fabric. She spoke excitedly in Persian to her friend, who translated for her.

'She says she wishes you every blessing for your journey.'

The old lady took my face in her hands again and stared into my eyes with such feeling I was almost compelled to look away. She said something I couldn't understand and then smiled, repeating it, gripping my face even harder.

I looked to her friend for a translation. She nodded and smiled too.

'It is a saying we have in Iran,' she said. 'It means, "Go and wake up your luck."'

As a lone female foreigner, I was singled out for special treatment and found myself adopted by various groups of women, all of whom insisted I share a cabin with them. I was spoilt for choice for sleeping companions but ended up in the company of Arshia, an English-speaking Indian woman who deserted her Iranian husband and family to take care of me. The easy hospitality I had experienced with my Bahá'í companions seemed to extend to the entire population of this train. People would regularly check on me, give me a reassuring pat on the arm or just offer a friendly wave across the room, and it wasn't only the women. Any dealings I had with the male passengers were equally amenable and always accompanied by warm smiles and a respectful politeness. Everyone wanted to help me, to talk to me and, of course, feed me.

The Iranian train arrived three hours late, causing a surge of activity as the previously patient passengers bundled towards it in a flurry of black cloaks, patterned headscarves and a monumental amount of baggage, heaving and hefting vast holdalls and the ubiquitous bulging Chinese laundry bags up the steps while the ancient locomotive huffed and hissed with an un-Iranian impatience. Over the course of the night we creaked our way to the border, sleep eluding us as a bewildering amount of Turkish exit formalities dragged us from our beds on a regular basis. When dawn broke, we were summoned once more, bleary-eyed, on to the platform at the small border town of Razi, everyone hauling their vast amounts of luggage this time. It was a new day but something else had changed – every woman was now wearing a headscarf. This was the Iranian entry formalities and customs inspection. I felt a twinge of nervous excitement as I looked around me, watching the sun rise over the rugged mountains in the distance. I pulled my headscarf over my hair for the first time. This is it, I thought. I'm in Iran.

The first sight that confronted me on the ground was a life-size vinyl banner bearing an illustration of a woman wearing a head-to-toe chador. The accompanying text was in Persian and Turkish but I guessed what it said, and Arshia confirmed my deduction – under Iranian law all women must abide by the Islamic dress code, only hands and face can be uncovered. It was a peculiar moment, staring at that sign. Back home it had seemed like a dressing-up game, wrapping a scarf round my head in Snappy Snaps for my visa photo. Now the reality stared back at me; well, not quite – the artistic impression had replaced the woman's face with a blank white space, which only added to my discomfort. I had given a lot of thought to the business of visiting such an oppressive regime, but as a firm believer in 'When in Rome' I knew what I was signing up for. I had come to observe and see for myself. But it was all right for me, I didn't have to live here. Now here I was, confronted with the reality of life in the Islamic Republic. I looked around me at all the kind, spirited, open-hearted men and women I had met over the last few days and tried to connect them to this repressive religious diktat telling half of the population to hide their bodies and the other half that they are base, uncontrollable beings. And I couldn't for the life of me make the connection. It was my first true understanding of the chasm between the Iranian people and their government.

Bags were searched, passports were stamped and then – the moment I had been dreading – my bike was examined. The border guards and customs officers disappeared for hours with my documents. The anticipation was unbearable. I sat and stood and strode up and down the platform in the early morning sun, wondering if this was going to be the end of my journey. Finally, the men returned. My paperwork was stamped, sealed and delivered, and not one eyebrow raised about my plans to roam around their country on my motorcycle. The train set off for Tabriz, where I would disembark and my Iranian motorcycle adventure would begin for real. I settled back in my bunk, sinking into the most welcome sleep. It seemed my visa lady's hunch had been correct; I had got away with it.

But of course, it was never going to be that easy. Just as I was nodding off to the reassuring clickety-clack, there was a knock on the door of our cabin. Arshia and I hastily threw our head-scarves over our hair as a young policeman in a faded but neatly pressed uniform stepped inside.

'He says you must go to the restaurant car, with your passport,' Arshia translated, her expression nervous. I had the distinct impression that this time there would be no tea towels or Tupperware involved.

The Iranian rolling stock was antique compared to its Turkish equivalent, but you could tell that back in the day, the designers had splurged some big budget on the dining car. Unfortunately, decades of underfunded Trans-Asian service had taken its toll on the formerly plush decor, and its flouncy red satin curtains, ornate Persian carpet and pink velveteen upholstery were now threadbare and faded, affording it the shabby opulence of a backstreet opium den. Under normal circumstances I would have revelled in this fabulous milieu, but as I peeked through the beaded curtain in the doorway and caught sight of the group of policemen awaiting me, soft furnishings were the last thing on my mind.

A silver tea urn hissed away on the counter, steaming up the windows and creating an oppressive, airless fug in the carriage. Four uniformed police officers sat around a table with a tray of tiny tea glasses, a bowl of sugar cubes and a pile of passports. They were busy sipping and stirring and stamping but they all stopped and looked up when I entered the carriage.

'Sit down,' said the one who was obviously in charge, motioning to a seat in front of him. He extended an open hand.

'Your passport.'

His stern manner was intimidating but I couldn't help clock that he was quite dishy, in that despotic, Ahmadinejad way. Square jaw, thick dark hair, chiselled cheekbones; but when I met his gaze I felt a chill run through me. I'd never seen such mean eyes. This was bad boy appeal on a whole new level.

He took a long time looking at my passport, flicking through the pages, examining the various visas and stamps from around the world with great interest, no doubt wondering what I was up to, hopping between London and the likes of Rio, New York and Marrakech. He turned to the photo page and looked back and forth at me and the picture repeatedly, then made a detailed examination of my Iranian visa. He said something in Persian to his colleagues before putting my passport in the top pocket of his shirt. I didn't like this. Why wasn't it going in the pile with the other ones to be stamped? Once again, I feared I was going to be rumbled for my illicit motorcycle.

'You will be fingerprinted,' he said. Then added, as a cursory attempt at politeness, 'OK?'

Like I had any choice in the matter.

'Oh yes, fine!' I attempted a breezy tone of voice, *Like yeah, whatever, I'm always being fingerprinted by the Iranian police.* 'Can I go back to my cabin?'

After the sleep deprivation of the all-night immigration and customs procedures, I was desperate to lie down, even if just for an hour.

His eyes narrowed as he shook his head. 'No. You will stay here.'

This changed everything. He had my passport and I was forbidden from leaving his sight; he held all the cards. My lack of sleep combined with the general apprehension that comes with the first few hours in a strange country began to stir my imagination. After all, this is a nation where innocent tourists have been arrested for espionage. I recalled the recent reports that had made the news back home: a group of American hikers arrested for spying after accidentally straying across the border from neighbouring Iraq; the same for some Slovakian paragliders who had unknowingly flown over a sensitive military site; a British backpacker who had spent two months in Tehran's notorious Evin Prison for taking a photo. Why not me next? Could I be mistaken for a spy? It had all seemed rather far-fetched back in England, but now here I was, under the watch of the Iranian police, who had confiscated my passport and were about to take my fingerprints.

Suspicion of westerners was so ingrained in the Iranian authorities, having had it drummed into their collective psyche for the last thirty-five years, that I suppose I could hardly blame them. But how could I possibly expect common sense and logic to triumph over this level of fanatical dogma and paranoia? As I sat there in silence, I too became paranoid. Had someone tipped them off about my bike? Had the Turkish railway porters called ahead with the intel? I started concocting an escape plan. How would I get a message back home? A palpable, physical sense of panic coursed through me and I forced myself to breathe steadily.

Sitting motionless in the chair, I watched the other passengers in the dining car with envy. Their journeys continued as usual, they were drinking tea, eating breakfast with their friends and family, going home to their normal lives. I was suddenly aware of being exposed and alone. However friendly my fellow passengers had been, I couldn't expect them to stick their heads above the parapet on my behalf, not in a country where to be seen to be fraternising with a westerner could attract unwanted attention from the security services. No, I was definitely on my own here.

Many of the passengers were a generation or two older than me, men and women who would remember the pre-revolution era; they had probably supported the overthrow of the Shah at the time. Considering that over ninety-eight per cent of the population had voted for the creation of an Islamic Republic back in 1979, it was highly likely that most of these quiet, tea-drinking folk around me had ticked the YES box in that fateful referendum. I wondered if they regretted that decision now. Much of the revulsion and anger the Iranian people had felt towards the Shah's reign was fuelled by the brutal tactics of his secret police force, SAVAK – comparable to East Germany's Stasi – who routinely tortured and executed his opponents. Political dissidents, trade unionists and communists were targeted and demonstrators protesting against the Shah's lavish lifestyle were killed in the streets. But what had really changed with the revolution? Khomeini had whipped up a storm with all the rhetoric of a people's revolution, but as soon as power was seized and the Islamic Republic created, he quickly set about creating his very own brutal security services – the all-powerful Revolutionary Guards, and beneath them, the shadowy Basij, who were regarded as thuggish mercenaries doing the bidding of the ayatollahs. For the people of Iran, a new era of fear and intimidation had replaced the previous one, just with new uniforms, no neckties and more facial hair.

Glancing sideways at the police chief, I guessed he was a bit younger than me; probably in his mid thirties, which meant he would not remember his country's turbulent remodelling. He was the pure product of the Islamic State; indoctrinated in school by carefully vetted teachers, at the mosque by fervent clerics and at home via state-controlled television and radio. A loyal soldier of Islam, but I wondered how typical he really was; by all accounts, the Iranian people had been falling out of love with the Islamic Republic pretty much since it began. Or maybe my treatment was simply the unwelcome result of the wider British–Iranian relationship, the downside of bearing that passport, once so well regarded around the world. In the queue for the train I had seen a couple of other Europeans but hadn't had a chance to speak to them. They looked Nordic – tall and blonde with oversized backpacks and expensive outdoor clothing – and I had heard them talking to each other in what I guessed to be Norwegian or Danish. Now they were nowhere to be seen and I thought enviously of them tucked up in their bunks somewhere on the train, sleeping the peaceful sleep of travellers fortunate enough to hail from a country that hadn't spent the last century meddling in Iran's affairs.

I felt suddenly, terribly weary, crushed by the weight of a history that felt so remote yet wielded so much influence over this little business between me and the police chief, a guy of my own age, who, I supposed, would say that he was just doing his job. After half an hour of sitting patiently nothing had happened. My fear turned to boredom, which turned to frustration. I wanted to know my fate, to get it over with. 'Excuse me, when are you going to take my fingerprints?' I asked the police chief in my most polite voice.

This was clearly the wrong move. He turned to me, his face clouded with anger. I was tolerable if I sat there and shut up, but asking questions was a no-no. He muttered something under his breath to his colleague, who answered me.

'Not here on the train. We stop at the next town and we will go to police station.'

My stomach churned. They were taking me off the train to a police station? Where was the police station? Would the train wait for me? What about my bike, currently strapped into the goods wagon? I wanted more information. I needed to feel I had some sort of handle on what was happening, some kind of control over my destiny, but I knew that without my passport I was utterly helpless. *This is how it happens*, I thought, *this is how foreigners get locked up in Iran*. The naysayers had been right all along! The suspicion of the police chief was tangible. His unsmiling eyes focussed on me.

'How much do people earn in the UK?' he asked.

This seemed a strange turn in the conversation, but I came up with a rough figure. He translated my answer to his colleagues, who all made sucking-in breath noises and gestures to suggest this was a large amount of money.

'But things cost more there,' I pointed out. I didn't want them thinking I was rolling in it.

He pointed at my boots, a pair of scuffed leather Fryes.

'How much are these boots, to buy new?'

'Well, they would be about two hundred pounds but—'

I was about to say that I got them second-hand on Ebay for eighty quid but I didn't get a chance. I was interrupted by more translating and indrawn breaths from the policemen. This was not going well.

'How much is a house?'

'How much is a new car, a BMW?'

'Er, well . . . '

'What about a television? Flat-screen?'

'How much is an iPad?'

'Um . . .'

I tried to keep up, but never having bought a house, a new car, a television or an iPad, I was completely out of my depth. I got the impression that there was a 'right' answer I was supposed to give, but I couldn't work out from his inscrutable expression what it was supposed to be. Times were tough in Iran right now, or at least for a large part of the population. The UN sanctions that had been in place for seven years, following the nuclear enrichment row, had hit the economy hard and the trickle-down effect was affecting all Iranians in a myriad of ways. Inflation was escalating, certain medicines were hard to come by, and businesses that had depended on international import and export, facilitated by the global banking system, were killed dead.

The officer's eyes continued to burn into me, the interrogation was relentless and I could understand how he had come to rise through the ranks. Although he was undeniably good-looking, he had a strange tic that added to his menacing demeanour. When he spoke his head rolled around, his eyes widened and he bared his teeth, which were sharp and white. The whole effect was extremely disconcerting. I imagined finding myself alone in a prison cell with him – although, at least if he ended up as my captor there was always the possibility of Stockholm syndrome to look forward to.

My unsavoury thought process was interrupted by the screeching of train brakes, and I was marched out of the dining car by all four officers and led over the railway sidings to a bleak building a few hundred yards away. In a suitably intimidating, windowless inter-view room an inkpad and paper form was laid out in front of me. Fingerprints weren't enough, it seemed. Whole palm and knuckle prints were also required. I was rolling my hands around and splodging red ink all over the place like a sixth-form experimental art project. Then it was time to fill in all the usual personal details: name, date of birth and the one that always seems to crop up in oppressive patriarchal regimes – name and profession of father. As I transcribed the same old information, I imagined all the various Third World bureaucrats whose forms I have filled in over the years tracking down my dad to his semi in Swindon. I felt a rising hysteria at the image of a throng of Congolese, Colombians, Algerians, Angolans and now Iranians plodding up my dad's garden path, and feared I was going to be overcome with giggles. The lack of sleep and underlying terror that I was about to be arrested for espionage were taking their toll on my mental state.

'Now this one,' said the police chief, presenting a form headed with the Interpol logo. *Really?* I wanted to say. *You're adding me to the Interpol database? I've only come here for a holiday.* But of course I kept quiet and dutifully filled in the blanks while my tormentor stood over me.

I was directed to a bathroom to wash my ink-stained hands. A sign on the wall informed me that the water was suitable for 'derinking'. Out in the corridor the police officers were waiting for me.

'Now we go back to the train.'

Their expressions and voices remained stern and I still didn't know if I was free. Was this about my illegal form of transport, or was it simply my British passport? There were no explanations forthcoming. I followed them back over the tracks, feeling guilty about holding up the train, but we were already six hours late and nobody seemed to care, so I decided my fretting was simply another indication of my British neurosis about punctuality, efficiency and queuing. When was I going to lighten up and get into the Iranian mode?

Back in the dining car the police chief took my passport out of his pocket and made a big performance of handing it back to me, as if he was doing me a huge favour by not having me arrested and banged up in Evin Prison. Maybe he was.

'Am I free to go?' I asked.

He nodded slowly and his cruel eyes gave a final roll in their sockets. 'For now,' he said, baring his shiny teeth. But he wasn't smiling.

I collapsed into my bunk with a mixture of relief and exhaustion but I was too wired to sleep and an hour later the train pulled into Tabriz station. There was much commotion as every passenger disembarked, either because this was their final destination or to watch my bike being unloaded from the goods wagon and to wish me well on my journey. The crowd of well-wishers was a sight to see; phone numbers, email addresses, sweets and fruit were thrust into my hand, and from Arshia, a prayer.

'It works,' she promised me, 'I said it when we were at the border, I prayed they wouldn't search my bag, and they didn't!'

Is there any remover of difficulties, save God?
Say praise be God. He is God.
All are his servants and all abide by his bidding.

'It is a prayer against difficulties,' she said, giving me a hug.

I said goodbye to the elderly Bahá'í lady and her gentle son. The strong lady in the chador squeezed my face again and revved her imaginary throttle, and the Ali G lookalike computer programmer helped me pack my bike while his family insisted I call if I needed any help, promising assistance all the way to Shiraz, should I need it. Then the conductor was blowing the whistle and shouting and everybody bundled back on to the train. I stood on the platform, waving to every carriage, sad to see my troupe of friendly faces disappear from view.

I was suddenly aware of being surrounded by emptiness and silence, and for a moment I was frozen with indecision and the sheer enormity of what lay ahead of me. Shiraz was a long way down the road. But there was nothing to do but get on with it; I had to take that first step, that first revolution of my wheels, of this ride. This was always the hardest part. I pushed my bike out of the station into the street and paused for a moment before swinging my leg over the saddle. The sun was high in the sky and the thin mountain air was laced with a tang of diesel fumes. I fired up the engine and, beneath a vast banner of the Supreme Leader, set off alone, into the Islamic Republic of Iran.

3

Islamic Republic, Yes or No?

TABRIZ STATION WAS located some way from the city centre, so I made my way downtown, riding gingerly into this new world. Khomeini and Khamenei were everywhere; on giant billboards at the roadside, as vast lurid murals on concrete apartment blocks and, less impressively, on sagging vinyl banners outside schools and mosques. With their almost identical appearance and surnames they reminded me of an Islamic Thomson and Thompson, the hapless detectives of the Tintin books. But that, I feared, was where the similarity ended.

Khomeini was by far the most sinister of the pair, with his stern, furrowed brow and cold stare. Although dead for over two decades, he still represents everything the outside world finds terrifying about Iran. Architect of the Islamic Revolution, creator of Iran as we know it today, he was heralded as the saviour of the people in 1979 when he came out of exile to supposedly liberate the Iranians from the lavish excesses and cruel inequality of life under the US-backed Shah. Discontent had been smouldering for decades and the people of Iran were ripe for revolution. They took to the streets in their masses, chanting 'Death to America!', denouncing the Shah and everything his reign stood for. The Shah, with the help of his secret service, SAVAK, responded with violence, firing at protestors. Meanwhile, Khomeini, in exile in Paris, was busy broadcasting his revolutionary message via the BBC Persian Service and the nation was tuning in and turning on – his fervent rhetoric was music to their ears. On 1 February 1979 Khomeini returned to Tehran to a hero's welcome and a referendum was held at the end of March. The question on the ballot paper could not have been simpler: Islamic Republic – Yes or No? A glorious future was promised and the disillusioned masses signed up for it in their millions.

Thirty-five years on and things haven't quite worked out as hoped. Even in my short journey on the train, talking to the Iranians returning home and then being frogmarched around by the police, it was clear that one form of brutality and inequity had merely replaced another. As soon as Khomeini gained power he began his own reign of terror, starting with the merciless and public executions of the Shah's top men and eventually extending to the political parties and organisations that had supported his campaign. Although now regarded as an Islamic revolution, the campaign had in fact been a group effort, bringing together disparate strands of Iranian society from the middle-class intelligentsia to the Communist Party and the trade unions, all united by the same goal – ridding Iran of the Shah. But once he had his feet under the table, Khomeini had no interest in keeping his new gang together; he had seen what trouble they could be and, rather than risk them turning on him, he made sure they never got a chance. Khomeini and his loyal clerics won and their power has never waned.

Seeking total control of his citizens, strict dress codes for women were enforced, newspapers, nightclubs and cinemas were closed down overnight, and anything remotely suggestive of western decadence – dancing, drinking and pop music – was banned. This was in complete contradiction to statements he had made to the European press just months earlier, in which he had claimed there would be no oppression under his regime, that women would be as free as men, and even that he had no desire to govern this new Islamic Republic. The moneyed elite, including most of Iran's once thriving music industry, left in their droves, fleeing to Europe and the United States. The faithful remained, but over the years the murmur 'This wasn't what we signed up for' grew from a low grumble to the sweeping pro-democracy 'Green Movement' protests of 2009 led by a youth population who hadn't even been born at the time of the revolution. Yet each year on the anniversary of Khomeini's death, officially titled in typically melodramatic style, 'The Heart-Rending Departure of the Great Leader of the Islamic Republic of Iran', millions make the trek to his shrine on the outskirts of Tehran, although whether they go out of genuine devotion or coercion is another matter. The nation enters several days of official mourning, or, as one of my train travelling companions summarised it with an arch raise of the eyebrows, 'Yes, we all pretend to cry for a week.'

Ali Khamenei, Iran's leader at the time of writing, appointed after Khomeini's death in 1989, wields the same power as his predecessor, but possesses a slightly more benevolent expression in his promo photo. I wondered if this was something of a conscious PR move by the Iranian government, realising that the hardline stance was falling out of favour amongst the people. Khomeini's stare sends a chill through your bones while Khamenei's official portrait features a tiny hint of a smile peeking out of the big white beard, lending him a cuddly Father Christmas look. You could almost imagine him bouncing the kids on his knee at Debenhams. Almost.

As I rode into downtown Tabriz, gazing around at my new world, I realised I still had very little sense of what Iran would look like from a day-to-day travelling point of view. This northwest corner of Iran, the province of Azerbaijan, was mountainous but hot and dry, its faraway hills barren and brown. In contrast, the city was a hub of feverish human activity and a constant source of novelty as I weaved through its streets, head spinning at every turn. Of course, I had seen pictures of the great mosques, intricately tiled with gleaming gold domes, and the famous sites of Isfahan and Persepolis, but it was also the everyday and the mundane that intrigued me. The housing, the street signs, the petrol stations. Where people shopped and ate and got their cars fixed. My ignorance about the quotidian aspects of Iranian life was unsettling in one sense but in another way it was refreshing not to have textbook images or holiday brochure promo material to raise expectations – and the inevitable disappointment when it didn't materialise. It made me realise, even in our world of information overload, how little of daily Iranian life is known outside its borders, and how rare it is to be able to arrive in a country with the sensation of an utterly blank canvas waiting to be filled.

The area around the station seemed unusually quiet, but Tabriz had seen plenty of action over the years; Iranians even claimed it to be the location of the Garden of Eden. As the former capital city, due to its strategic position as Iran's closest major city to Europe, it had always been an important trading post. In 1721 one of the world's worst and deadliest earthquakes had wreaked havoc, but it had survived and been rebuilt. As the largest city in north-western Iran and an important halt on the Silk Road, it has always been a natural stopping point for travellers heading to and from Turkey, a place to gather your breath and thoughts after crossing the border, or to say your farewells to Iran if heading west. It felt like a good spot in which to pause and realign one's mindset for whatever hemisphere lay ahead. I also found something strangely reassuring about this sense of perpetual toing and froing; I was just another weary eastbound traveller on this well-trodden overland route, and maybe Freya Stark had cooled her heels here, or possibly, even Marco Polo himself had stood on this very spot, gazed up at those mountains and wondered, like me, what was going to happen next.

As the indecipherable signs, shop names and adverts flashed past me in a mind-bending jumble of lurid Persian squiggles, I was overcome with a rush of excitement followed by dread of the unknown. The foreignness of the car registration plates and the road signs was impossibly exotic and thrilling but I couldn't understand a damn thing going on around me. How was I going to find my way? Order food and fuel? Change money? Ask directions?

I was used to travelling in countries where I couldn't speak the language, but being faced with a completely unfamiliar alphabet took the challenge to a whole new level.

Although giddy from lack of sleep and food, I was eager to see my new world. After checking into a downtown backstreet hotel, where I was met with bemused politeness by the male staff, I dumped my bike gear and headed out on foot. I was itching to be out there, to be amongst it, to see, smell and feel Iran happening all around me. In my headscarf and shapeless manteau – a thigh-length dress coat required by law for women in Iran – I felt self-conscious and more exposed than I had on my bike. The motorcycle draws attention but it also provides protection, status and, most crucially, autonomy. On a 'male' form of transport you become an honorary man. But as a pedestrian, I was most definitely a foreign woman alone.

Out in the streets of the city centre, Tabriz was buzzing. With a quick 'Hello boys' to the two towering ayatollahs staring down at me from a huge billboard outside the hotel, I followed tidy concrete paths through a small manicured park, past fountains and formal flower beds of geraniums and petunias. Iranian flags lined my route, fluttering green, red and white in the breeze, and as Khomeini and Khamenei appeared again at the exit, I wondered how long it would take for me to get used to these two men seemingly monitoring my every move. I had travelled in many other countries where leaders ensured they loomed large in daily life, but I had never witnessed a cult of personality employed on this scale. I found the ayatollahs' constant presence intimidating and sinister, but I guessed that soon they would meld into the background and merely become part of the everyday fabric of life in Iran. This, of course, was the desired effect and, in its way, an even more chilling thought.

With no clear direction, I wandered with wide-eyed aimlessness along lively streets, each with their own identity – one selling work wear, army surplus and clunky Soviet-looking tools, the next all shoe shops and stationers. Heading into what looked like the busier part of town, I dodged the chaotic gridlock at every junction, hopping over kerbside drainage channels, allowing the audio onslaught of horns and shouts and babbling car radios to wash over me until I ducked for cover under an ancient archway. As if passing into a parallel universe, I found myself in a maze of winding cobbled walkways, worn and uneven underfoot from centuries of trade. I had stumbled upon Tabriz's world-famous bazaar, the largest in the world. High above, an elaborate, vaulted brick ceiling created a majestic, temple-like feel, and the late afternoon sun streamed through its windows like great white lasers, adding to the celestial sensation. But away from the beams of light were dark corners and secret nooks where one could easily imagine the ancient traders of the Silk Road cutting deals on saffron and silver. These days the silk of the Orient had been replaced by plastic and around me wiry young men rushed by, pushing carts piled high with bulging cardboard boxes stamped with the ubiquitous words, MADE IN CHINA. Here, in this ancient trading post, the old and the new worlds came together: traditional Persian handicrafts and exotic shisha pipes sat alongside knock-off Louis Vuitton handbags and bootleg Pokémon DVDs.

As I sidestepped the activity around me, it was thrilling to think that this very bazaar had once stood at the centre of the Silk Road or, to be more accurate, the Silk Routes, as it was never one formalised highway but a network of tracks with a maze of southern and northern routes that were used according to the weather and the time of year. It was always an East–West exchange, linking Europe to China via Turkey, Iran, Afghanistan and, crucially, Central Asia, where the grassy plains provided grazing for horses and camels. The list of goods that made their way to and from China reads like poetry, conjuring up a tableau of exotica that cannot help but stir wanderlust in even the weariest traveller: saffron, myrrh, sandalwood, pistachios, frankincense, silver, jade . . . The Chinese brought not only their silk but also porcelain and perfumes, gems and spices – all of this carried in a caravan of camels or on horses. And it wasn't just merchants plying their trade; the Silk Road served as a cross-cultural thoroughfare that saw pilgrims, monks and nomads of all ideologies and religions moving harmoniously along the 5,000-mile route. It was not to last. When the Europeans discovered sea routes to China, the once thriving Silk Road lost its lustre. But Tabriz's bazaar adapted and lived on, and Iran always remained at the heart of it, neither East nor West.

Here, in this bustle of contemporary commerce, there was much that had changed but also many reminders of that golden age. Saffron, the most prized spice in all of Iran, was still for sale – tiny bags at huge prices. Other spices, herbs and berries, all unrecognisable to my eyes, were displayed in jewel-coloured pyramids or piled up in heavy jute sacks, while gold, silver and gems each had their own dedicated zones. But despite the advent of truly global trade, it was plain to see just how isolated Iran was as a result of the long-standing international sanctions. There were no European goods on sale here and certainly nothing from America, or at least nothing genuine. The only American logos in sight were cheap copies of fashionable brands on T-shirts, trainers and baseball caps or, more charmingly, home-made versions of the worst America has to offer, including a fast-food joint I had spotted in the street outside featuring a hand-painted KFC logo that could, in a generous moment, almost be described as folk art. But these bootleg brands and hokey attempts to cash in on them only served to prove a point: that Iran's global isolation hadn't turned the Iranian people against the products of 'The Great Satan' – it had just made them more alluring.

The sheer size and maze-like nature of the bazaar was overwhelming. I was already disorientated. My map showed its area to be around seven square kilometres, with over twenty interconnected halls. Considering how much ground it covered and how significant it was to the city, its entrances were easy to miss; small, inconspicuous alleys and doorways nestled in the busy streets outside.

But once inside, it was easy to lose your bearings and even your sense of time, stumbling out, dazed and confused, into another part of the city. The locals were flitting about confidently and I realised that, unlike the great bazaars of Istanbul or the souks of Marrakech, this one was not geared to tourists but was truly the one-stop shop where Tabrizis dropped in for their daily needs, from soap to tea to socks and underwear, the latter including some racy little numbers that were displayed with surprising prominence by the male stall-holders, and examined, discussed and purchased by female customers of all ages, with neither party appearing fazed by the intimate nature of the transaction.

My wandering took me into a separate section, the Amir Bazaar, where only gold and jewellery were sold. The entire alley glowed a warm yellow from the sheer volume and quality of the merchandise, with trinkets bearing price tags that stretched to tens of thousands of pounds. I was intrigued by the spectacle, and the suggestion of great wealth in a country that was supposedly on its economic knees. The jewellery shops were hushed, with just a few wealthy Chinese and Russians browsing. This was the realm of the international elite, the super-wealthy of the East, clearly a world from which Iran was by no means isolated. The well-dressed owners of the jewellery stores dismissed me with polite but disdainful smiles, well used to spotting time-wasters, and I moved on through more alleys, passing stalls selling great mounds of decorative sweets and piles of loose tea where a shabbier breed of *bazaari* counted out their totals with abacuses. A final twist in the maze led me towards the Mozafarieh, the carpet bazaar.

Here was the heart of the action. The outside world melted away and for the first time since arriving in Iran I felt myself relax, no longer worrying about the minutiae of my journey, finally able to pause and marvel at the good fortune that had brought me to such an extraordinary place. The scenes around me could have been from a hundred or a thousand years ago. Small groups of men sat on the ground carefully repairing the intricate patterns of ancient rugs, fortified with an endless supply of sweet tea. Their merchandise adorned every floor, wall and chair and, in the ancient narrow alleys, carpets were being shuttled in every direction – on shoulders and handcarts, on bicycles, on the back of motorcycles. As I surveyed this exotic milieu I realised there was not a single sign in English anywhere, not one letter of the Roman alphabet and not a word being spoken that I could understand. But everywhere I went, I was welcomed with radiant smiles. As I soaked up the timeless hubbub of industry and commerce going on around me and revelled in the sounds and smells of such a foreign and faraway place, for a moment I felt as though I had been transported into a fairy tale on a flying carpet.

While many of the rugs in the swankier shops were going for big money, no doubt destined for Russian oligarchs and Chinese businessmen, there was a refreshing everyman approach to the carpets in general which I found endearing. Back home a Persian rug is something to be revered, a hallowed *objet d'art*. But here in Iran they are made to be used. Not only are they to be found on every floor in every establishment, they also appear in all sorts of unglamorous locations – an upholstery quick-fix for a ripped motorcycle saddle, slung across the bench seat of a delivery truck cab, folded up to pad out a street vendor's plastic chair. Truly part of the fabric of Iranian life.

It was dark by the time I emerged from the bazaar and the streets were alight with neon signs, bare strip bulbs and glowing shop windows. Families promenaded the pavement while groups of men sat together in shop doorways and young women gathered at juice bars or window-shopped the clothing stores. I was aware of people staring at me but I felt a peculiar combination of being exposed yet safe. There was no sense that my personal safety was under threat; the stares held no malicious intent or lasciviousness; it was more that I was an alien who had been beamed down from another planet and my otherworldliness was provoking curiosity among the earthlings. There were no other women walking alone, and certainly no foreigners anywhere. Despite my attempt to dress in the appropriate clothing, I had certainly not mastered the effortless chic of the Iranian women, who somehow managed to make the hijab and manteau look like something from a Parisian catwalk. Even with all the restrictions of the Islamic clothing rules, they still dressed to impress, interpreting the regulations with remarkable creativity. On the other hand, glimpses of my reflection in the shop windows suggested an ungainly, over-swaddled fraudster. I hurried on.

A busy main street offered a waft of smoky meat and other, less familiar cooking smells and a reminder that I hadn't eaten all day. My eyes alighted on the traveller's friend – the laminated picture menu. Thank heavens! Positioned at the top of a flight of stairs descending into what appeared to be an underground car park, it didn't look too inviting, but I was too hungry to care. Down in the basement, the cavernous concrete bunker contained a few plastic tables and chairs, the floor was covered in elaborate but grubby, threadbare Persian rugs, and the bare walls were decorated with curling prints of Iranian scenery in saturated seventies Kodachrome. A man in a chef's hat and an apron stood at a stainless steel serving counter and next to him, behind an ancient wooden desk, was a small, elderly gentleman in a neat brown suit with an old-fashioned receipt book and a cash box, a calculator his only concession to modern conveniences. Feeling thoroughly alone and foreign, I tried to convince myself that I was having an authentic Iranian eating experience. The two men stared at me. They spoke no English so I pointed at the salad picture with a hopeful smile and a poorly pronounced 'please' and 'thank you'. Ten minutes later a kebab turned up on an unfeasibly large pile of rice. I made a mental note to learn the Persian word for 'vegetarian'. It looked like I was going to need it.

At that moment, a clatter of footsteps, laughter and voices erupted down the stairs. A family of four, a middle-aged couple with two grown-up daughters, greeted the man in the brown suit and then, spotting me staring at my unwanted kebab, called me over to join them, as if I was an old family friend they had been hoping to bump into. I was struck, not only by their hospitality and kindness, but by the ease of it. There was no muttering between them as to whether it was appropriate, or checking that they were in agreement about the plan. No awkwardness in the invitation. It was simply an obvious fact that as a guest in their country, I would be joining them for dinner. No discussion required.

'Persian food, the greatest in the world. You must try it all!' said the father, rattling off a list to the man in the brown suit, who scribbled in his pad as fast as he could to keep up.

'*Ash-e jow, mast-o-khiar, ghormeh sabzi* . . .'

Piles of flatbread appeared with a raw onion on the side. Bowls of green stew. Yoghurt dips with tiny red berries and herbs. More rice. Kebabs all round, served with blackened grilled tomatoes. Mammoth amounts of rice covered in melting butter. And, surprisingly, cans of real Coke, something I assumed would have been banned, along with all other American products.

'Ah yes!' said the father with a knowing laugh as I expressed my surprise, 'Made under licence in Iran. Always a way to get around everything here. And Iranian cola, Zamzam, very bad. Not good taste at all.'

The two daughters wrinkled their noses in agreement. He pointed at their phones on the table.

'Apple products very popular in Iran. Everyone has an iPhone. They come through Dubai; everything comes through Dubai. There are many places where you can have them set up with VPN, then you have Facebook, Twitter, Whatsapp, Viber . . .'

'The more they are told they can't have something, the more people want it,' added his wife, and I thought of the bootleg products at the bazaar.

'The new iPhone 5 is coming out soon!' said the younger daughter with unconcealed excitement. The father was warming to his subject. Patriotism shone in his eyes.

'You can get everything in Iran, everything!' he waved his arms expansively. 'And you want something done? Yes? You can get anything done in Iran. Anything! So many rules but . . .' He shrugged as if he didn't have a care in the world. 'You get anything you want here! There is always a way.'

His indomitable spirit was uplifting, and unexpected. He wasn't going to let a despotic regime and a bunch of international sanctions get in the way of life, no way! Ironically, it reminded me of all the best elements of the United States, that go-get-'em, can-do positivity that is such a heartening aspect of American culture. It wasn't a comparison I was expecting to make in Iran, but I was already becoming used to being confounded and surprised at every turn.

'How can you get hold all of these things? How can people do business outside of Iran if nobody can send or receive money?' I asked him. I was already coming up against such problems, mainly that it was impossible to use credit cards or cashpoints in Iran, so I had set off from home with the entire funds for my trip in bundles of US dollars, currently stashed about my person and my bike.

He was nodding, listening, agreeing. 'Yes, this is true, it is more complicated to deal with Europe now, with the latest sanctions, but businessmen are still businessmen. If there is money to be made, people will find ways around these problems. Iran trades with Turkey and UAE, so the business comes through there, the paperwork is changed, this is easy.'

'Changed? You mean forged?'

He swatted away this minor point with another expansive wave.

'What about the payments?' I asked. 'You can't even use a Visa card here.'

'Cash. A lot of cash is moved, bags of money. But everyone knows what is happening – the government are behind all this; they need to trade. They will make a business in Europe, then they close down a few weeks later. Then another one sets up with a different name. This is happening all the time.'

He shrugged as if this was all easy, straightforward stuff, no big deal.

'There is always a way around the problem. Iranian people have become very clever at this. We have had a long time to practise.'

He threw back his head and laughed as if he had the world in the palm of his hand.

Finding myself in the company of such an expansive dining companion, I decided to mine him for information pertinent to a greenhorn in Iran. Firstly, a topic that had been much on my mind, the use of the names Persia and Iran, and if they could be used interchangeably. I asked him if each word had certain connotations that I needed to understand. This instigated a lively debate between him and his family, a babble of Persian and hand gestures that left me none the wiser.

'You must understand, we are all Iranians,' his wife said, silencing her husband and turning her attention to me. 'Persians were the first people of this land, Pars, it was called then, or Fars, and it is their language, Farsi, that has become the main language. Although in English you call the language "Persian", here we call it Farsi. But Iran has many different people, not just Persians – there are Turkmen, Kurds, nomadic tribes; you know we have Jews here too?'

Her husband piped up again. 'Many people in the West do not understand this, that Jews live without persecution in Iran.' He gave a loud laugh and thumped the table. 'A few years ago, Netanyahu said to the Jews here, come back to Israel, come back to your true homeland, and they said "No! Why would we want to live there? We are Iranian, we like it here, thank you very much!" Yes, we are all Iranian.'

He gave a slow, contented nod and offered a warm, open smile. He was gracious, refined and openly proud of his country but without any hint of jingoism or flag-waving nationalism. His quiet, understated pride seemed to run through his bones, as though he was innately aware of belonging to an important, ancient culture that went back millennia and would continue long after we were all dust. This current brutal state that called itself the Islamic Republic, was, you felt in his eyes, a mere blip in the great story of his beautiful land. He seemed serene, able to rise above it all – wars would rage, revolutions would wax and wane, kings, invaders, politicians would all come and go, but the essence of being Iranian, the sheer noble spirit of it all, was bigger than everything and would remain a constant.

I said I'd noticed that in Britain and America the word *Persian* is generally used for the 'nice' things: Persian carpets, Persian food and restaurants, poetry and art, that kind of thing. But when it comes to talking about politics, and say, the nuclear programme or human rights, anything that the western media considers intimidating or distasteful, then it's 'Iran' and 'Iranian'.

He seemed to find this amusing and gave another of his knowing laughs. 'Your country does not understand ours,' he said bluntly but without malice. 'Both words are used here. We would say we are Iranians. Our country is Iran but it was Reza Shah who changed the name, he wanted to modernise Persia, this was part of his plan, although the name had been used before that, a long, long time ago.'

'It comes from the word *Aryan*, the Iranians are Aryan people,' added his daughter. 'But here in Tabriz, in the north-west, most people are Azari, Turkic people, we have our own dialect and you will see people with red hair and pale skin.'

'I see . . .'

'Now please, please, do not worry about any of this,' said her father, butting in with an expressive wave and a twinkle in his eye. 'We are all Iranians. There is just one important thing for you to know on your journey, the most important thing of all . . .'

I prepared myself for this crucial insight. His expression turned solemn but the twinkle remained.

'Whatever you do, you must never call an Iranian an Arab!'

The whole family burst into laughter.

His daughter, Shohreh, was in her early twenties with a kindly, studious expression behind her glasses and a warm smile.

'I am so happy to meet you!' she said, 'I am an English teacher and I never have the opportunity to practise my English with a real English person. You know the truth, I have never met someone from England ever before today! Can I ask you some questions about your beautiful language?'

'Yes, of course,' I said, happy to provide assistance and feeling a pleasurable, if entirely unwarranted, glow of pride.

'Thank you. So,' she continued, taking my hand with an imploring smile, 'can you help me with gradable and non-gradable adjectives . . . I think it is relating to the comparative or super-lative forms, is this correct?'

'Er . . .'

I feared that my 1980s state schooling had not prepared me adequately for this situation. I was clearly going to have to raise my game if I was going to hang out with Iranians.

The family went on to talk about their pilgrimages to Mecca and how difficult it was to travel with an Iranian passport, even to Saudi Arabia for the Hajj.

'Everyone thinks we are terrorists!' exclaimed Shohreh. 'They fingerprint us when we arrive!'

'I know the feeling,' I said, and told them about my experience with the police on the train.

'I know a man, an immigration officer,' said the father. 'He told me that some time ago the British, they decided to take the fingerprints of all Iranians who visit the UK. So now, this is why Iran does the same to you.'

So, that is what it was all about, I thought. The tit-for-tat continues, even at this micro level. My new friends were all shaking their heads with the weariness of those who live in a climate of mistrust and intimidation. Just part of everyday life in Iran. I had related the fingerprinting story lightly, hedging my conversation topics as I was still unsure which subjects were appropriate. This family, although not hardliners, were definitely more conformist than the outspoken Bahá'ís that I had met on the Trans-Asia Express.

Then Shohreh intervened with a more pressing subject.

'So, what do you think about hijab? How does it feel to cover your hair? Is it strange for you?'

They all turned to me, inquisitive looks in their eyes. This was the topic of the times, a source of division among not just the Iranian people and their religious leaders but between Iranian women themselves. Hijab was enforced by law in Iran, but how you wore your headscarf, I was quickly discovering, was a political statement.

A lot of the younger women and the more obviously fashionable pushed their hijab to the limit, wearing it hanging off the back of the head or teetering on the top of a high bun, with plenty of hair on show at the front. The older women, and the religious and politically conservative, wore the chador, the long black cloak that covers the entire head and body – the name literally translates as 'tent'. Somewhere in the middle were my dining companions, who wore their scarves tied neatly under the chin, a sign of moderate conservatism and religious beliefs.

'So, does it feel weird to you, wearing the scarf?' Shohreh's sister pursued the line of questioning now.

I wasn't sure if there was a 'correct' answer. Should I say what I truly thought? My initial response was that the damn thing kept getting in the way and already contained a smudge of engine oil and evidence of this evening's dinner. I made a surreptitious dab at a yoghurt stain with a dampened napkin. But that was just the start of it. Was this really the time and the place for some feminist rabble rousing? I tested the water.

'Well, of course, it's a strange sensation for me . . .'

They smiled and nodded encouragingly.

'You know the expression, "When in Rome, do as the Romans do?"' I said to Shohreh and she nodded, translating it into Persian for the others. I omitted the obvious next sentence, *But it doesn't mean I agree with it*.

'A lot of the younger women in Iran are against compulsory hijab,' said Shohreh, picking up on my unspoken words, 'but the older women would feel uncomfortable without it – like for you being without clothes in public.'

'Reza Shah, who became leader of Iran in the 1920s, the father of the last Shah, he made it illegal to wear the chador, and the veil,' added their father. 'Many people look up to him now, because he wanted to modernise Iran. Make it more like a western country. He gave women more rights, he built many roads and railways and hospitals. But not everyone wanted to wear western dress. My mother, she did not want to leave the house without her hair covered, it was like an embarrassment for her. But the Shah's men, they would shoot people who opposed it.'

'And look, now it is the other way,' said his wife, shaking her head, as if exasperated with it all. She had my sympathy. The idea of these few powerful men deciding what millions of women should do with their hair just seemed ridiculous. So unimportant but yet so significant.

'I guess it would be best if it was a choice,' I said, and it seemed we all agreed on that.

I offered a crumpled handful of Iranian rials, still unsure how their millions converted into pounds, hoping it was enough to cover my share of the meal, but I didn't even get a chance to find out.

'But you are our guest! You do not pay!' they all cried.

We entered into the usual rounds of mock argument that I associate with British politeness, and bantered good-naturedly until my host stopped the conversation with an announcement.

'There is something very important you must know. This is *ta'arof*. Do you know of *ta'arof*?' I shook my head, not recognising the word. 'In Iran we have, this, how would you call it? It is a tradition, a custom, for politeness, it is like a great art and is always the same way. This is called *ta'arof*. Maybe if you take a taxi, you say to the taxi driver, "How much?" and he might say, "No, no charge, it is my great honour to drive you today" and you must say "No, I must pay you" and he says again "No."'

'Or he may say "*Ghorboonet beram*." This means "I will sacrifice myself for you",' added his wife.

I thought a sacrifice seemed a bit excessive, but I liked the general gist of it, and enjoyed the elaborate nature of the Iranian use of language. It wasn't only Khomeini and Ahmadinejad who employed dramatic proclamations; it was a national trait and so terribly un-British in its appeal.

'So it is like refusing out of politeness?' I said.

'Yes, but in the end he must accept.'

'Right. Because otherwise the taxi driver won't make any money?'

'Yes, this is correct. But *ta'arof* is not only for money, it is the same for food, or to open a door and let someone walk through before you.'

His wife joined in: 'If you are a guest at someone's house maybe they will offer you sweets and you say no, they offer again, you say no again, they offer once more, then the third time you take the sweets. It is always three times.'

'OK, I see. We do something similar in England but not so formal, I suppose. We don't have a name for it.'

'It is very good that you understand this. *Ta'arof* is very important in Iran. We do not *ta'arof* with our very close friends or our family, but it is always with guests or even at work with our colleagues or our boss.'

'I see. So,' I said, trying to navigate this slippery concept, 'I have tried to pay for my dinner tonight more than three times but still you insist on paying, so what do I do now?'

'Ah, but this is different, because you are our guest, a foreigner in our country. Of course you do not pay!'

They all looked aghast again. I was confused.

'Wait, are we doing *ta'arof* again, or what's going on?'

Now they were all laughing so hard the waiter came over and a spirited exchange broke out between him and my host, who was handing over handfuls of notes. They seemed to be entering into another round of *ta'arof* but eventually the bill was paid and my rials lived to see another day. Everyone seemed happy and I remained slightly confused but the *ta'arof* started up again when they insisted on giving me a lift back to the hotel and making plans to meet me the following day to take me around town.

I protested, part in the spirit of the tradition but also aware that I had many miles ahead and the familiar white-line fever of the first few days of a road trip was gnawing at me; I wanted to get moving. I told them about Habib's note and that my ultimate destination, Shiraz, was still a long way away, thousands of miles if I took all the detours and side trips I planned – to the Caspian Sea, into the deserts and the Alborz and Zagros Mountains, to Tehran where I had arranged to stay with friends of friends from London, and further south to Yadz and Isfahan. I insisted that I really didn't want to trouble them.

'But we must show you Tabriz!' they insisted.

'It will be good for me to practise my English,' insisted Shohreh.

Was this *ta'arof*? Did they really want to down tools to entertain me, a total stranger, or were they just being polite hosts, the product of a culture that prizes hospitality? I tried to *ta'arof* back with them but resistance was futile. If there was one thing I had learned on my first day in Iran, it was that you never quite know what's going to happen next. I reminded myself of another thing I had learned from my years on the road: itineraries are futile; the fun stuff happens when you give them up and go with the flow.

Back in my hotel room, as I settled into bed for my first night in Iran, staring up at the arrow on the ceiling that pointed to Mecca, I felt overwhelmed in the best possible way. I was all alone in a strange land but when I stared out of the window at the sprawling city and the moon over the mountains, I thought about my train-travelling companions, all back in their homes now, settling in for the night; and I thought of my dining companions this evening with their easy conversation and good cheer; and I felt waves of goodwill, like radio transmissions, being beamed in my direction from all over Iran. I tried not to think of the evil-eyed policeman and his suspicious colleagues, and of how many more of their type awaited me on the road. Instead I pulled up the bed cover, warmed from the outside by Persian polyester, and from the inside by something altogether less artificial.

4

Following Freya

AFTER A COUPLE of days finding my feet in Tabriz, I awoke on the morning of departure with the twitchy anticipation so familiar at the start of a long journey. My most immediate concern, regarding navigation, was calmed by the fact that there was a bilingual road sign for Tehran at the junction outside the hotel. I could see it from my window and I had come to view it as a kind of talisman. Easy, just follow the signs. There was a time in Iran's not too distant past when no English translation would have sullied any road sign, so I was grateful for these small concessions to outsiders.

In the underground car park I swapped hijab for helmet and, as I started the bike, felt the rush that exists somewhere between excitement and fear. Out in the street, the excitement quota quickly evaporated and I was left with nothing but terror as I tackled the rush-hour traffic and one-way systems of Tabriz and discovered that my dependable bilingual road sign was an anomaly. I never saw another one again all day. I kept riding in the suggested direction, at first hopefully, then with all hope abandoned, as I became entangled in a multi-lane melee of beat-up yellow cabs, fume-blasting buses and the ubiquitous *savaari* – shared taxis that operate as something between the two and whose trade works on the basis of making emergency stops in the middle of the road every few minutes to pick up a fare.

I had to admit it, I was stuck. I needed help. My first solution was to flag down a cab to lead me out of town to the start of the

Tehran highway, but I couldn't make the driver understand my request and we parted amicably if both more confused than before. Eventually I pulled into a petrol station, to fuel up for the long ride ahead but also hoping that someone would be able to point me in the right direction. The place was full of men filling up their cars and trucks. Only men. All of them, it appeared, extremely discomfited by my sudden appearance in their world of gender-specific roles. They stared and stared and stared. I had spent the last couple of days being escorted around town with Shohreh and her family, and in their company I had been an acceptable if unusual phenomenon, but it was their presence that had given me validation. Now I had to hold my own, as a foreign woman alone on a motorcycle. As I met their stares, it occurred to me that most of these men had probably never seen a woman riding a motorbike, ever.

'*Benzin?*' I said pointing at the tank, smiling weakly at a guy in petrol company overalls who was standing with the pump in his hand, gaping at me, unabashed. I had never felt so exposed and awkward. The men kept staring, standing at a wary distance in silence.

I attempted to ask directions to the Tehran highway but my pronunciation was poor enough to perplex them even further. After a while someone grasped the problem.

'Aah, *Teh*-ran!'

OK, emphasis on first syllable. This was important.

The frozen statues became animated. What man can resist being asked directions? There was much arm-waving and circular motions that I guessed indicated a roundabout, and lots of pointing and rapid Persian. I grasped a vague idea of what I should be doing and replicated their motions for approval – straight ahead, right at the roundabout? The men had abandoned their vehicles now and were gathering around while still maintaining a polite gap between us. When it transpired I had understood the directions correctly, their faces opened up into smiles and laughter and I rode away to the sound of their clapping and cheering. Maybe it was all going to be fine after all. But still, the freak-show sensation was not a pleasant one.

Tehran was a ride of about 400 miles from Tabriz, but before I plunged into the chaos of the capital I was keen to explore the northern shores of Iran, along the Caspian Sea, and then make my way to Tehran across the Alborz Mountains. This narrow but formidable range runs between the coastal strip and Iran's central plateau, stretching all the way from the borders of Armenia and Azerbaijan in the north-west to Turkmenistan and Afghanistan in the east, and had long held a fascination for me, inspired by *The Valleys of the Assassins*, Freya Stark's travelogue of her adventures in this region in the 1930s.

A refreshingly sparsely trafficked highway transported me out of Iran's north-western provinces, passing through barren, mountainous country. It was good to be moving again, back on the bike and easing into the familiar rhythms of life on the road. My jumping off point for the coast and the mountains was Qazvin, a bright, busy town where I was able to hole up in a slightly shabby 1970s hotel on the main street and roam with unusual anonymity, the residents seemingly distracted by a non-stop frenzy of commerce and socialising. Neon flashed outside my window, restaurants pumped out smoky meat smells accompanied by tinkly muzak versions of forbidden western easy-listening hits, and multistorey shopping centres stayed open later than I could stay awake. Women cloaked in black chadors window-shopped at boutiques offering surprisingly risqué clothing, pointing out lacy mini-dresses and tight, low-cut tops to their friends. Across the street, men, women and children alike clustered outside high-end electronics stores to admire displays of giant Samsung flat-screen televisions and, of course, the new iPhone 5, a contender for Iran's hot topic of the moment, only narrowly beaten by President Rouhani's historic UN talks, which were taking place in New York and gracing all the front pages on the news-stands.

While the inhabitants of Qazvin salivated over Apple products, I spent the evening in more analogue pursuits, poring over my maps and route-planning the next part of my journey. In the morning I was heading north out of town, taking the smaller roads that would lead me into the Alborz Mountains, following, quite literally, in the footsteps of Freya Stark. In 1930 she had walked from Qazvin along the same route I was to take now, charting the route and terrain as she travelled. Her journey had been a daring expedition to discover the ruined fortress of Alamut Castle, the former headquarters of the ancient Ismaili sect, better known as the Assassins, who had broken away from mainstream Islam and dominated this region under a reign of terror in the eleventh century. Legend had it that this cult had acquired their name from their ruthless leader's tactic of getting his followers stoned before encouraging them to murder top political and religious leaders with trippy, weed-induced promises of a paradise full of nubile young maidens in exotic gardens. These bloodthirsty stoners lapped it up and soon became known as the Hashish-iyun, named after their drug of choice, and giving root to the English word, *assassin*.

The Alborz Mountains were less intimidating to the traveller these days, but they still held plenty of thrills and a certain amount of foreboding. Their valleys were cavernous and isolated, their peaks and passes high and snow-covered with only small villages dotted here and there. Once over the other side I would descend to the shores of the Caspian Sea, which sounded impossibly romantic, although this image was based on no more than a childhood spent reading C. S. Lewis books. I had very little idea of what to expect from the Caspian, but I am always drawn to water of any kind, and the idea of an Iranian *corniche* was exotic and exciting. As Robert Louis Stevenson famously put it, I was travelling hopefully, which he also claimed was better than arriving. I would only find out if he was right once I set eyes on the sea itself.

I had already learned that, if possible, loading and prepping the bike was best done somewhere quiet and out of sight, before embarking on the tedious dressing-up game known only to the visiting female motorcyclist in Iran. Islamic clothing laws require not only women's hair to be covered but also the supposedly irresistible curves of hips, bums and thighs, meaning I had to wear my manteau along with my regular bike gear. Combining the practicalities of motorcycle clothing with the impracticalities of Muslim modesty was turning out to be a challenge and my look resembled the end result of a game of picture consequences – a confused mishmash made up of my vintage Belstaff jacket over a shapeless denim dress, itself worn over a pair of faded jeans tucked into my tan leather Frye boots. In my jacket pocket I kept my headscarf, a white chiffon affair that when swapped with my helmet only added to the bizarre get-up, resulting in something that could loosely be described as Steve McQueen meets Benazir Bhutto in Laurel Canyon circa 1972. It wasn't my finest sartorial hour, but hopefully it would keep the 'morality police' at bay.

My exit from Qazvin aroused the usual flurry of excitement and enthusiasm from fellow road users. Horns blasted in greeting, rather than the fury one automatically assumes as a Londoner. A blur of waving hands and encouraging thumbs appeared from every car window and at junctions I found myself constantly and regrettably turning down offers of hospitality.

'Madam! Do you need any help in Iran?' called one gentleman from his car.

'Very good! Very good!' shouted a woman from a passenger seat, leaning across her husband to beep the horn repeatedly, while he grinned like a madman and swerved all over the road.

'Please, drink tea,' insisted an elderly man at a hardware store on the outskirts of town, where I stopped to buy some oil. The tray, sugar cubes and tiny glasses appeared from nowhere.

It was hard to get going in Iran, with so much bonhomie and *ta'arof*, and I forced myself to resist my compulsive white-line fever. But it wasn't always easy to be in the present moment, and as I exchanged pleasantries with the owner of the hardware shop my attention was wandering ahead of me, to the mountains, to the changing autumnal weather that was turning more ominous with every minute, and to the usual concerns of the itinerant motorcyclist; where will I sleep tonight, where will I find fuel, what will I eat? I pushed these irritating thoughts out of my mind and brought myself back to the now, trying to remember to let the trip happen to me, rather than attempting to control every detail. 'One can only really travel if one lets oneself go and takes what every place brings without trying to turn it into a private pattern of one's own.' Freya Stark had penned these words of wisdom so many decades ago, and I wondered if she had struggled with the same conundrum on this very road.

These days, the route north out of Qazvin into the Alamut Valley was tarmac, starting out as a wide boulevard lined with blocky concrete houses, small shops and wide open drainage channels running with water straight off the mountains. Before long the outskirts of the town ebbed away and although the road remained in good condition, the scenery quickly turned harsh and rugged; not that different, I imagined, from the sight that had greeted Freya Stark as she headed this way.

As the road climbed away from civilisation there were still a few signs of modern life, including, thankfully, a petrol station and opposite, a home-made motocross track where local boys had carved out some jumps and whoops in the hard, shingly earth. This evidence of fun and frivolity was cheering and I was almost tempted to make a lap, but I pressed on up the valley, following a pretty meandering river where the inhabitants of Qazvin were washing their cars at the water's edge.

Winding my way up the mountain, the temperature dropped as snowy peaks appeared on the horizon and the whole range opened up before me in all its bleak beauty. A vast landscape of jagged black pinnacles stretched away in every direction; a

menacing choppy sea of rock, riven with deep valleys and dotted
with the occasional patch of green pasture, while dazzling caps
of snow disappeared into the clouds. I was the only person on
the road except for two young men on a tiny motorbike, its engine
straining under their weight. They would pass me with a wave
and disappear around a bend before I would pass them a few
minutes later, returning the greeting, as each of us stopped at
various points to take in the views. They weren't dressed for a
long journey, just wearing jeans, light jackets and trainers, and
I wondered where they were going until it occurred to me that
maybe they were simply out for a ride, for the fun of it. Eventually,
after several miles of overtaking one another, we both came to a
halt at a particularly spectacular vista of the valley below. Although
they spoke no English we somehow managed to celebrate the
simple joy of motorcycling along such a fabulous road, and equally
to commiserate over the universal experience of being cold on a
bike. There was no need for words; all three of us understood
exactly why we were there and why any pain was outweighed
by the pleasure. As we prepared to set off again one of the men
removed his scarf and handed it to me, urging me to take it despite
my protestations. We went through the comical pantomime of
insisting and refusing that I now recognised as *ta'arof*, and although
I played by the rules and he kept his scarf, just the gesture itself
provided me with a warm glow.

At the Chala Pass, more than 8,000 feet above sea level, the
road began its descent into the Shahrud Valley, the Great River
of the Kings. I was heading east along the valley towards the
village of Gazor Khan, or Ghazerkhan or indeed Qazir Khan, or
however the heck each western cartographer over the years had
interpreted the Persian pronunciation. With some application, it
was usually easy to connect the different spellings to the same
location, but sometimes they varied so wildly that I became
confused as to whether they were different places or not. As I
travelled along the valley road, looking out for road signs, I realised

that there was no point in worrying about it anyway; this issue of English spellings was purely academic; all the signs were in Persian now. I would have to rely solely on my maps, which proved especially contradictory and confusing out here in the sticks. A momentary panic washed over me as I imagined getting lost in these wild, isolated mountains, stranded and alone in the Valley of the Assassins – what a place to go AWOL! I had not seen another vehicle or human being for hours and there appeared to be tracks and roads leading off all over the place, some signed, some not. For the first time in my life, I wondered if I should have brought a GPS, but my innate dislike of gadgets and my wariness of depending on technology was too ingrained. Besides, it was too late to change my mind now; this was a strictly lo-fi expedition – paper, compass and asking the locals.

My thoughts turned once again to Freya Stark, who had set off up this valley with a map even worse than mine that named only a few villages and a couple of mountains. She had travelled with two local men as guides and carried an altimeter, notebook and pen in an attempt to correctly chart every route, river and village, and heights of the passes as she went. She soon discovered that in an unmapped world every feature has a variety of names, depending on who is being asked, and I wondered if this was where some of the vagueness of the British-made maps of Iran had arisen. Her method was to consult everyone she met, but this scatter-gun approach produced bewildering results including six different suggestions for one hill, some entirely fabricated names made up on the spot by over-obliging locals, and a mass of confusion about whether Alamut was a village, a castle or a river – or all three. Persisting in her mission with admirable determination, and despite her guides misleading her on more than one occasion, she achieved the results she desired. Her guerrilla map-making skills were eventually employed by the Royal Geographical Society and British Intelligence, giving her the hard-won approval of the establishment that she both desired and resisted.

Employing the simple tactic of keeping the river on my right, I continued east until I was rewarded with the sight of a small settlement that was so quiet it seemed abandoned. This little village had been bestowed with a proper concrete roundabout that seemed both unnecessary and at odds with the wild untamed surroundings. Even more peculiar, the centre of the roundabout featured a vast and poorly executed plaster sculpture of an eagle in flight, a clumsy affair that combined brash American imperialism with the clunky Soviet look of state-sponsored art. Iran liked to pride itself on being 'neither East nor West', but I was pretty certain that this overblown garden ornament was not quite what Khomeini had had in mind when he coined his famous statement.

Parked under the eagle's outstretched wing and wondering what kind of unholy alliance of local authority funding and dictator-chic designer had come up with this monstrosity, I spied the first human I had seen in hours. Relieved to see anyone, even this doddering elderly man in his shabby two-piece suit, I waved him down and attempted to wheedle some directions out of him, if only just to establish the name of this strange town.

We didn't get very far. He understood no English and I couldn't make out a word he was saying, even when we were both clearly attempting to say place names. I pointed at the map, he pointed somewhere else. He gabbled in Persian, I gabbled in English with a Persian accent. I tried all the names of the nearby towns with varying pronunciations but to no avail. Eventually I gave up on directions and tried to at the very least establish where I was right now. What is the name of this place? I waved my arms expansively, looked around in an exaggerated fashion and cocked my head on one side, in a charades-style attempt to demonstrate I was asking the simple question: 'Where the heck am I?' The old man threw his arms up in the air in exasperation and banged his fist against the leg of the eagle with an outpouring of what was obviously disgust. At first I was taken aback, thinking I had upset him in some way, but when he started laughing I realised he thought my gesticulations were a reference to the ghastly eagle. I nodded encouragingly and in response he rolled his eyes, made a spitting motion towards the sculpture and bid me farewell, ambling off and shaking his head. I was none the wiser regarding my location but I felt we had bonded on some aesthetic level.

After a while I heard the rare sound of an engine rumbling in the distance and saw a pickup approaching the roundabout from the opposite direction. It was one of the ubiquitous blue Zamyad trucks that I had already come to know and fear as Iran's greatest road menace. Driven by every tradesman in the country, these invariably dinged and dented motors had caused me several near death experiences over the last few days. But on this occasion I was overcome with relief to see one hurtling towards me. The driver appeared to understand my pronunciation of Gazor Khan, nodding, pointing and grinning enthusiastically while I waved my map in front of him. Pressing a plastic-wrapped fairy cake into my hand, he sent me off on the correct route, away from the menacing eagle, into a steep-sided valley lined with poplar trees and grassy meadows. The road became rough and muddy with a few small rivers tumbling down from the mountainside, creating splash fords that chilled my feet but added to the sensation that I was venturing into remote, wild lands.

In Freya Stark's day the ruins of the castle at Gazor Khan had attracted the grand total of roughly one visit a year, including none other than the British ambassador and his wife in the late 1920s. Thus it was considered a great tourist attraction in the region and had been advertised as such to Miss Stark by the villagers who were keen to show her around. Riding through the beautiful but lonely valley eighty years later, it didn't appear that its visitor count had increased much, but still, the inhabitants tried hard to make you feel welcome. As I turned off the main route and began the ascent up the steep track to the village, I paused at a bridge crossing a deep canyon to read a hand-painted sign. It featured an English translation as well as the original Persian script.

IT ISAGREAT PLEASURE TO WE-
LCOME TO ALL DEAR TOURISTS
TO THEANCIENT VILLAGE OF GHAZERKHA
N

As someone who frequently runs out of space when writing birthday card messages, I felt a fondness for the friendly signwriter whose hospitality outweighed his typesetting skills. With a gladdened heart I continued into the village with plans to spend the night, but sadly the litter-strewn dirt streets and dilapidated houses were far from the quaint ancient settlement conjured up by my optimistic imagination. The village had suffered an earthquake in 2005 and I wondered if this was the fallout, still evident eight years later. Everything was mud coloured, from the roads to the buildings to the stray animals and the spattered cars, and I felt that if I stayed too long I too would end up subsumed by the creeping dirt. There didn't appear to be anywhere obvious to stay the night, no hotels or B & Bs, but I made a hopeful circuit of the steep streets, dodging loose chickens and piles of rubble, sensing the stares of a few local men as I passed. After coming all this way I felt duty bound to travel to the top of the hill to see the ruins of the famous castle, but they were distinctly underwhelming too; just a few low walls remained surrounded by piles of timber, scaffolding and plastic sheeting flapping in the wind. It occurred to me that in Britain, we are rather spoilt when it comes to castles, and sadly this scene was more Travis Perkins than Kenilworth. As some compensation, the view from the crag was stupendous, but the evening was closing in and I was aware that if I wanted to find somewhere to sleep, I needed to get moving.

Riding further into the mountain range with the great Alamut crag and its battered castle high above me, I felt like a tiny insignificant creature, beetling along the valley floor. There were a few small villages ahead marked on the map and I was travelling 'hopefully' once again, this time in anticipation of some kind of hotel or guest house appearing around a bend. But Robert Louis Stevenson's words rung in my ears; when it came to Alamut Castle, his observation had been spot on. What hope was there for a place to stay on this lonely road? As the sky darkened and the temperature dropped I became anxious about the night ahead. I had my camping equipment with me so I would never be truly stuck, but the idea of pitching camp out here was disconcerting. It wasn't the cold or the remoteness that was off-putting, but the idea of being discovered by a passing local or the village policeman, or worse, the resident mullah. I stood out like a beacon everywhere I went in Iran and especially so, out here in the backwoods, away from the more modern, cosmopolitan towns. I recalled the guarded stares of the Gazor Khan villagers and imagined the reality of camping in a nearby field – and then being ambushed in my pyjamas, trying to explain myself in the middle of the night to a disapproving cleric or the village militiaman.

Coming round a bend in a steeply walled canyon I found the road ahead suddenly illuminated as two cars appeared behind me. I was riding slowly in the darkening gloom and expected them to overtake as soon as the road straightened out, but they continued to follow me, sticking close together. This continued for some time and, although they weren't flashing me or driving too close, I couldn't help wondering why they didn't make any attempt to pass. My imagination began its usual over-activity. What could they want? Were they going to run me off the road? Rob me? Attack me? Or worse? Who were they? Had the police tracked me and my illegal form of transport down at last? Had the old man at the eagle roundabout called it in, reported a strange foreigner disrespecting the street art? Had my inclusion on the Interpol list triggered some kind of APB? Could these cars be the Revolutionary Guards? Or the Basij, renowned for meting out all sorts of terrible punishments to those who dared to flout the Islamic code?

The two cars continued to follow me for several miles before eventually overtaking, much to my relief. I caught a glimpse of shadowy faces in the back seats, craning their necks in my direction as they passed me on a tight bend, but I didn't want to make eye contact. I was just glad to see the back of them, whoever they were. The mountain road was dark and lonely but in some ways it was better to be out here on my own.

I rode on through the twisty canyon with a sense of being walled in by the steep rock on both sides and the descending gloom above, all my hopes for sanctuary pinned on the next village, wherever that might be. Then around a corner the two cars appeared again. This time they had pulled over at the side of the road, engines running and headlights still blazing, lighting the empty road ahead but making it impossible to see inside them. Why had they stopped? To wait for me? It was at moments like this that I was glad to have the autonomy of my motorcycle, knowing that I was able, if it came to the worst, to disappear off down a muddy track or up a rocky mountain trail where no saloon car could ever attempt to follow. My lightweight trail bike with its off-road tyres meant I could pretty much go anywhere, and I could certainly shake off any four-wheeled vehicle once we left the tarmac.

The evening was not working out as planned. I had hoped to be tucked up in the cosy village of Gazor Khan by now but instead I was still on the road, with night falling and no idea where I would be sleeping that night. I was tired, cold and now, with the appearance of these cars, a little unnerved. I decided to keep going, not giving the cars a second glance as I accelerated past them as fast as I dared, trying to make a confident 'Don't mess with me' swerve as I took the next corner a bit too fast for comfort. The road behind me remained dark for a few minutes, but sure enough, within a few hundred yards their headlights appeared again as they continued their tail. I was painfully aware of my bright-yellow GB plate with its alien Roman letters and numerals, acting like a beacon: *I'm a stranger round here!*

I could see this cat-and-mouse game going on all night, or at least until one of us ran out of petrol. And if it was me, then what? Everything seems more intimidating and sinister in the dark, and I tried to not let my paranoia overtake me, reminding myself that people were forever stopping and staring at me in Iran with no malice or ill intent; they were simply curious. I also told myself that drivers stop at the roadside for all sorts of mundane reasons; maybe one of them needed the loo, or they needed to check the map. It was hard to keep up a good speed on the dark, winding road, littered as it was with potholes and fallen rocks, but despite my decreasing pace, the cars remained behind me in what was obviously a steady but deliberate pursuit. Maybe it was the ghosts of the drug-fuelled Assassins and their victims forever haunting these ancient rocks and routes, but everything seemed menacing to me now, as darkness fell and the black of the mountains merged with the night sky.

Then, amidst all this dark, ghostly wilderness my headlight beamed on a big, neatly printed sign at the side of the road. The words couldn't have been more welcome: the Hotel Alborz, seventeen kilometres away. For a moment I wondered if I was hallucinating a modern traveller's version of the Assassins' promised paradise; forget the exotic flower gardens with their fair maidens, this was my fantasy – a comfy bed and a cup of tea. But no, this was no mirage, the sign was right there, real and solid in front of my weary eyes. Seventeen kilometres. Roughly ten miles. I did the now well-practised kilometres to miles conversion in my head and checked my trip meter, watching the numbers turn slowly with every revolution of the wheels. *Come on!* I willed us on into the night, fired up with the knowledge of a refuge ahead and hoping that I would shake off my chase vehicles when I pulled into the welcoming civility of the hotel car park.

The cars tailed me all the way. My trip meter rolled slowly through the digits but when the estimated seventeen kilometres arrived there was no hotel to be seen. The road remained as empty and inhospitable as ever; there were no lights ahead and it was hard to imagine any kind of building cropping up in a place like this. Eleven miles, twelve, fourteen. Still no sign of any human habitation. Still the cars tailed me. Then, on a straight stretch, I saw signs of life in the distance on the left-hand side of the road, lights ahead. A building of some kind. My heart leapt with joy and relief. This must be it. At last! But as I approached I could see it was just a lonely house with no sign or car park, nor any other welcoming features of a hostelry. The cars remained behind, still close. The road darkened again. All I could do was keep moving on into the night, my body tense with apprehension. Five more miles and I was beginning to give up hope when I came around a bend to see a three-storey building built into the mountainside. It had lights and a carport at the front, and yes, thank heavens, a sign outside. The Hotel Alborz. At last! I didn't use my indicators, not wanting to reveal my intent. With a quick glance over my shoulder, I swung a sharp left across the road into the car park, only to hear the crunch of tyres on gravel behind me as my pursuers made the exact same manoeuvre.

The car doors flew open and eight people bundled out, loud voices, speaking fast, and now approaching me where I had stopped, still astride my bike, trying to assess the situation that was unfolding. Who were these mysterious night travellers? One of them was lumbering towards me, a big moustachioed figure with wild, messy hair, and I realised I was cornered. I offered a *Salaam* in a voice more confident than I felt. And then I saw the glint of metal in his right hand as he raised it in my direction.

5

Iran Underground

'Hey! You want some coffee?'

He offered the shiny steel espresso maker at me by way of greeting. I found myself laughing and babbling with hysterical relief. The wild-haired man smiled and, unusually, shook my hand, which I took as a coded message for *I do not subscribe to the beliefs of the Islamic Republic*.

'We have all been wondering about you. Where are you from? What are you doing here in Iran? My name is Jafar, welcome!'

The others gathered round, introducing themselves, asking questions. It soon transpired that my gang of murderous bandits was in fact a group of friends in their late twenties and early thirties, both men and women, from Tehran, who had come out to the mountains to escape the city for a few days – their destination, the Hotel Alborz. In the dim light of the carport I could see that they were a different breed from the Iranians I had met so far. Their clothes and hairstyles suggested an arty, bohemian flair, and beneath the women's regulation manteaus I could see evidence of skinny jeans and trainers.

The hotel owner appeared from the front door, an elegant older gentleman dressed in an immaculate light grey suit and open-necked shirt. He possessed an air of serenity and quiet intelligence that immediately put me at ease. Unfazed by this late and unusual guest, as if British women on motorcycles were always turning up in the middle of the night, a shed was found for my bike and I was informed that dinner would be served in half an hour. It was taken as read, of course, that I would be joining my gang of pursuers after dinner for the real action. Catching a glimpse of the *qalyān* water pipes and intriguing unlabelled bottles being unloaded from the cars, it appeared I had stumbled upon a party. Contrary to my stone-cold terror of the ride here, I now felt entirely at ease – excited even – about the night ahead, and as I stretched out my tensed-up limbs on the bed before dinner, staring up at the familiar arrow to Mecca, I admonished myself for my foolish paranoia.

I was used to the uncertainty of life on the road, of always having to judge every stranger I met and assess the safety of every social situation that came my way. I also knew that the unease and anxiety of the early part of a trip are part of the process that cannot be rushed. You have to go through it to hone your instincts; in the same way as your aching muscles ease out after the first couple of weeks, so does the mind. But I wondered if this process of acclimatisation would ever happen in Iran. The threats here seemed more real than in other countries I had visited. The idea that the security services really could, and would, lock you up was genuine – I had met people who had experienced just that: being arrested and interrogated for being in the wrong place at the wrong time, for snapping what seemed like an innocuous photo or talking to the wrong person. Simply by being here, alone and on a motorcycle, I was flouting the very bedrock of the Islamic Republic, confronting them with a real-life, free-wheeling female. Everything about my journey was a direct challenge to their laws and beliefs. So far, my dealings with the authorities had raised nothing more serious than some suspicious questioning and excessive fingerprinting. But, unlike in other countries where I had fallen foul of the police or military on occasion, in Iran I was constantly aware of being up against not only 'cultural differences' but a heavy-handed code of conduct enforced by a rigid regime. I feared my usual strategies of using reason, politeness or even hard cash would be futile if I ever had to wheedle my way out of a difficult situation.

Downstairs in the dining room, the charming proprietor and his wife were busy making me a fish supper. Sadly, his cooking skills didn't match his general bonhomie and I chewed my way through an unidentifiable blackened carcass with the usual mountain of rice and a can of the dreaded Zamzam cola. I was all alone in the room, so had plenty of opportunity to study the maps of the local area on the walls. They were Iranian-made so not of much practical use to me, but seeing the familiar land mass covered in Persian script made them seem all the more enticing, and I felt a thrill from seeing the shading of the mountains ahead and the curving line of the Caspian coast that awaited me. Amongst the maps were glossy images of flower-filled mountain meadows and nearby Mount Damāvand, the highest peak in the Middle East at 5,610 metres, a mountain so perfectly formed in its symmetry and snowy topping that it was almost cartoon-like in its perfection. I could see how Freya Stark had become so enraptured with this part of Iran and could only imagine how other-worldly and mysterious it must have seemed eighty years ago.

As if reading my mind, the hotel manager entered the room and beckoned me over to a glass display cabinet in the corner. Carefully he unlocked the case and reached in to present me with an English copy of Freya Stark's *Valleys of the Assassins*. He was beaming with pride as he opened it to the page of her hand-drawn map and pointed to his home village of Garamund, just a few miles up the road from where we stood.

'You know of Freya Stark?' he asked.

'Yes, she was a great explorer.'

'English lady. Like you! She came here in 1930.'

I nodded.

'You are Freya Stark, but on motor!' he declared, smiling as he carefully laid the book back in its rightful place and locked the glass door of the cabinet. It seemed an excessive amount of reverence for an eight-quid paperback, but this book, like its author, had travelled a long way to get here and was considered deserving of as much respect. His tiny village and these mountains were immortalised in exploration history.

My fellow guests had eaten earlier and were getting straight on with the business of getting the party started in the upstairs lounge, unpacking tea-making equipment, *qalyān* pipes and tobacco, and what looked like contraband alcohol. Glasses and cups chinked, hot water bubbled on a stove and headscarves were already discarded, strewn around the sofas and floor cushions. They called me in to join them and I felt immediately comfortable in their company. Sitting around in jeans and T-shirts, the couples together on the sofa, arms around each other's shoulders, a drink in hand, it was a scene that was so normal to me but that I now realised had been missing from the tableau of everyday Iran. You simply did not see this kind of activity in public places. When I commented on this, one of the guys shook his head in weary exasperation.

'It's been getting better lately. They don't hassle people so much now but it used to be a lot worse. I was arrested a few years ago for holding my girlfriend's hand; we were just walking down the street. I spent a few nights in jail.'

His friend nodded, adding, 'Most people have a story like that . . .'

'But still, we could not be like this in a café or tea house,' said his girlfriend, surveying the scene with a sweep of her hand. 'So many stupid rules! You know they have rules for everything, even men's hairstyles, no long hair, no spiked hair, women's make-up, no bright lipstick and no nail varnish on your toes, no open-toed shoes, *pah* . . .' She waved her hands in disgust. 'Even the mannequins in shop windows must wear hijab!'

The others joined in, each outdoing the other with increasingly outrageous examples of the demands of the 'morality police': 'My friend was arrested outside the bazaar for wearing a yellow T-shirt!'; 'My brother was stopped for wearing a necklace!'; 'They made my girlfriend's sister take off her make-up in the street and then arrested her for being too tall!'

'Are you making this up?' I asked, incredulous.

They shook their heads. They were laughing but it was the laughter of resigned despair.

As we settled down on the sofas and the *qalyān* was passed around, we talked about our meeting and were soon laughing real laughter at our misconceptions, on both sides.

'I thought you were following me' I said as I juggled a glass of tea and a lungful of sweet, apple-flavoured smoke. 'I was starting to get scared!'

'Well, I suppose we were following you,' said Jafar. 'We wondered where you had come from, what you were doing. We kept looking at your bike, trying to work it out, if you were a woman, who you were.'

'I guess I was trying to work you out too. I thought you might be *basiji*.'

Now they roared with laughter. They were about as far removed from an Islamist militia as could be imagined.

'This is the problem with our nations, this is the fault of our governments,' Jafar said, suddenly serious. 'They have made us all distrustful; you come to Iran and think you will be arrested and locked up, and we are looking at you, wondering what is this person doing here, what are they up to? We are more likely to think you are a spy than a tourist!'

I explained why I had come, about the closing of their embassy in London, and about Habib's note. They nodded sympathetically.

'Yes, I remember the embassy protest in Tehran,' Jafar said. 'But that is just a small group of idiots! Unfortunately, this is all you see on the television around the world, so everybody thinks this is Iran, full of crazy people.'

'Most people at home thought I was crazy coming here.'

'I work abroad,' he continued. 'I am a music teacher so I know how Iran is perceived throughout the world. It is sad, and wrong.'

'It is good that you are here,' said one of the women, Shirin, turning to me. 'Now you can go back and tell people the truth.'

'It's funny you should say that,' I said, recalling Habib's almost identical words in his note. I told them what he had said about Shiraz, and that I was heading there.

'Ah yes,' they all agreed, 'Shiraz is a wonderful city, the city of poetry, you know the Iranian poet, Hafez? And the Shirazi people, ah yes, everyone loves the Shirazis!'

'But I am sorry,' said Shirin, smiling, 'you will find there are many men called Habib in Iran!'

I had never expected to actually find Habib – that would be akin to travelling to England in the hope of finding someone called Dave – but the thought that he was out there somewhere was always at the back of my mind. 'I'm just glad to be here, and to have met you all tonight,' I said, 'even if you did scare the hell out of me!'

We all raised a glass to each other and our home-grown brand of international relations. I was happy that Habib's hopes seemed to be coming true. When the tea was finished, the mysterious unmarked bottles were uncorked.

'Now let's get the party started,' said Jafar. 'This is *araq*, like home-made vodka but made from raisins, and this is home-made wine. The Armenians make it – they are allowed to drink alcohol in Iran, you know?'

'So, everyone should have an Armenian friend?' I said.

'Ha! You would make a good Iranian!' said Jafar, laughing and nodding.

The *araq* was lethal moonshine, almost undrinkable, and the wine dark and sickly, both as unpalatable as homebrew the world over, but in Iran you take your booze where you can find it. The strange brew flowed along with more tea, laughter and conversation, translated mainly by Jafar for some of the others who were not so fluent in English. He explained to me that they were a group of old friends who were involved in music, the arts and film. Back in Iran for a short holiday from his teaching job abroad, he had rounded them up for the weekend, the plan being to get away from Tehran and head to the mountains. There was definitely a sense of illicit escape about their trip, and out here, away from the city, it was easier to elude the Gashte Ershad, the dreaded 'morality police'.

A couple of other guests wandered in and out of the room on occasion, sometimes staying for a glass of tea and a little conversation. They seemed unperturbed by the un-Islamic activities going on around them, and I noticed the women did not rush to cover their hair as they entered. One of them, an elderly man from Tehran, spoke fluent English and German and explained that before the revolution he had been a chemical engineer for Mercedes, travelling the world, setting up plants and systems.

'And then—' he trailed off and smiled sadly.

I nodded expectantly, but he stood up, clearing away his empty tea glass, 'Well, you know, everything changed then—'

This was the narrative I was beginning to hear again and again. 'Before the revolution' was the opening line of so many life stories in Iran, always with a weary shake of the head or a sorrowful gaze into the distance.

'Oh, they all thought it was a good idea at the time,' he said. 'They thought life would be better: no more Shah, no more SAVAK torturing people! It is hard to imagine now, how angry the people were back then. But I never believed it, not with this donkey, Khomeini, in charge! I would have left but it was not possible for me.'

As he turned and left the room he gave a resigned shrug. 'I never wanted this— this Islamic Republic!'

'Is this how most people feel about the revolution nowadays?' I asked Jafar.

He pondered for a moment but his friend butted in, angry.

'These old guys, they say this now, but they forget, they wanted it, they wanted the revolution.' He jerked his thumb after the man. 'He would have voted for Khomeini, everybody did. This is the generation that have made it like this for us. Now they are all sorry and say it was a mistake. But it is too late now!'

'Yes, this is true,' Jafar was nodding thoughtfully. 'But now I would say it is like this: maybe five per cent of the population still support the revolution and the regime – these are the hardline religious; often they are poor, working people. They will be the ones you see on BBC and CNN, burning the flags and shouting "Death to America" and all of that crazy stuff. Then another five per cent, they are actively against the regime, they are protesting, demonstrating, getting arrested . . .'

'Are they part of the Green Movement protests that happened a few years ago?'

'Yes, they would have been involved with that protest, but you know, thousands of those people are in prison or have disappeared. So, the remaining population – say, ninety per cent – they are unhappy with the situation but they will not do anything, or say anything.'

'Because they are scared of what would happen to them?'

'Yes, they are scared but it not just that. Life in Iran is bad in many ways, but in some ways, for many people, it is quite comfortable, just comfortable enough for them to not want to, how would you say, "rock the boat"?'

'Yes. You mean they have too much to lose? It is easier to just carry on as it is?'

'Yes, the middle classes will probably have a job, a house, good food, and if they know the right people they will have satellite television and' – he motioned to the bottle of wine – 'they will know where to get alcohol, and the authorities will ignore this most of the time. The women will probably be well educated, maybe have a good job and can send their children to a private school . . .'

'So everyday life is just about bearable?'

'Exactly, and this is not by accident. Sometimes when there is unrest the government will make a show of relaxing certain rules, maybe about clothing, or they will stop arresting people for small crimes, like having satellite television, or they will stop raiding house parties, and then people feel like things are getting better.'

'But you mean it's just for show?'

'Exactly. And of course, if people have children, they do not want to make a protest and then be arrested, questioned, tortured, locked up. This is the reality if you take a stand against the government in Iran.' He looked me in the eye. 'Would you take that risk?'

It was a difficult question. I liked to think I was the kind of person who would make a stand, but it was easy for me to say, coming from a democratic country with its unarmed policemen and the reassuring notion of habeas corpus enshrined in law. Taking a stand in Iran was a life or death decision.

As the bootleg liquor flowed, the conversation turned to more comfortable territory, to shared tales of Tehran's movie industry, a state-sponsored Iranian success story on the world stage of international film festivals and red carpets. But as with every aspect of Iranian society, there was another story, a covert subplot running beneath the surface.

'There is a lot of government money in Iranian film. They make good movies sometimes, but it is mostly bland dramas about rich couples and their domestic lives, with a bit of intrigue and scandal, an affair or something but nothing that will upset the mullahs, nothing too risqué, nothing to anger the censors, and there's always a good moral code at the end, of course. But of course nothing political, nothing about real life in Iran. So what happens is that these film-makers take their skills and training, paid for by the government, and use them to make their own films, underground films, music videos for bands, hip-hop artists, documentaries that tell the truth.'

'Criticising the regime?'

'Yes, exactly!'

'But how do they get shown? I guess it's too risky to put them on YouTube and the internet is so slow here that I don't suppose you can send them by email.'

'The internet is only slow for the public, for regular people,' said one of the others, 'the speed is there if they need it, but it does not serve the government to have their citizens able to upload and download and share files.'

'So how do you see these films? Where do they get shown?'

Jafar pulled something out of his pocket and held out his palm. 'Like this,' he said, showing me a USB flash drive. 'We share memory sticks. We have them with us all the time, handing them out to our friends, and then they copy them and pass them on in the same way.'

'The old-fashioned way, word of mouth.'

'There is always a way,' Jafar said.

This, I was beginning to understand, was the unofficial motto of Iran.

We polished off the wine, a couple of the guys smoked a joint out on the balcony and then something that sounded like 'paan-toe-mim' was suggested. After some attempts at translation, I realised that we were about to embark upon a game of charades. Our cultural differences came to the fore now as we struggled to find much common ground for our mimes, largely due to a 'no Hollywood films' ruling by Jafar, which was less about his political objections to the Great Satan and more to do with his aesthetic values as a cineaste. I chose books that I considered well-known classics, but judging by the confused looks, they had clearly never troubled the Iranian syllabus; the girls chose recent MTV hits beamed in by their illegal satellite dishes but that had failed to register on my radar. Nevertheless a slightly inebriated Anglo-Iranian game of charades can only be a source of high comedy, and we hammed up our acts like a bunch of am-dram queens and still failed to guess correctly, or even get close. It didn't really matter; the joy was in the sheer silliness of it, and I eventually rolled into bed, leaving them to party on into the night. As I drew the curtains in my bedroom, thunder crashed over the mountains and lightning illuminated the horizon that I would be heading towards the next day. The jagged outline of the Alborz Mountains looked wild and intimidating.

At breakfast the next morning Jafar was putting his shiny coffee-maker to work and I sat with Shirin and her friends, looking out at the morning mist cloaking the peaks. The teenage daughter of the hotel proprietor sat with us, silent but listening to our conversation with an expression of avid fascination. Because we were now in the restaurant, technically a public space even though it was empty, our headscarves and manteaus were back, just glimpses of highlighted hair and dangly earrings peeking out from beneath our layers of fabric. But spirits were still high. The girls were warm and chatty with me, and unsurprisingly the conversation turned to hair. But in Iran hair talk is never just about hair.

I described how I had wrapped my headscarf for my visa photo and showed them the picture. They laughed until their mascara ran down their faces.

'Is this what you thought Iranian women look like? Ah! People in the West think we are all hidden under black chadors,' said Shirin, 'obeying our husbands; not allowed to drive or go to work. I think people confuse Iran with Saudi Arabia!'

They all laughed some more.

'Before the revolution Iran was very modern because of the Shah and his wife. Tehran was a cosmopolitan city, the women very stylish. This is a long time ago now but people do not forget this. In our hearts we still think we are like Paris!'

I admitted to them that I hadn't known what to expect and that the Iranian women I had met and seen appeared to be the very antithesis of the down-trodden oppressed female.

'Yes, there are many educated, professional women in Iran,' said Shirin. 'Almost all teachers are women, a lot of doctors too, and lawyers. More women go to university than men.'

'But it's not just about that, it's something deeper than education or profession.' I tried to explain my thoughts, nascent as they still were. 'They also have this, I don't know how to describe it . . . this spirit. Iranian women seem very bold and confident, but not aggressive. Everyone is very kind, very warm with it.

Even the older, more religious women in their chadors, they have been so kind and welcoming to me.' Shirin was translating to her friends, who were all nodding in vigorous agreement. Shirin looked thoughtful.

'For women in Iran the laws are bad, yes; it is a difficult life in many ways. But difficult times, they make you stronger, that is why we are like this. So we must not let our situation break us. We must keep laughing, and keep trying, following our dreams, our hearts. Iranian women are very lively, funny, we laugh a lot, you know?'

I had felt this energy in just the few people I had met here already, men and women of all ages, this irrepressible appetite for life and connection, to take part and engage. I wanted to bottle it and distribute it back home.

'And you know, the Iranian people,' she continued, 'we are not conservative, not serious people. I know this is what the world thinks of us – traditional, religious, backward, angry people. But this is not how it is. We are always laughing, having fun, making jokes!'

I didn't want to admit that I had probably been guilty of such assumptions just a few weeks before. The fabled mind-broadening power of travel is usually a gradual affair, something that creeps up on you the more you put yourself out in the world, but in Iran it was a sledgehammer effect. I found myself rethinking, recalibrating just about everything every minute of the day. It was like being whacked in the face with my own prejudices and misconceptions at every turn; but it wasn't an unpleasant experience, it was thrilling.

Then the daughter of the hotel proprietor spoke for the first time. Her voice was timid but her eyes excitable. 'You know,' she said, looking out of the window at my bike parked in the yard, packed and ready to go, 'I have never ridden on a motorcycle, not even on the back.'

'Well,' I said, 'we can do something about that right now!'

A minute later we were in the saddle, her arms around my waist as we bumped over a few potholes and accelerated away up the mountain road, no helmets, just hijabs flying in the wind and both of us whooping our way around the bend. I think Freya Stark would have approved.

Back at the hotel we took photos of us all together before going our separate ways. The proprietor was studying my map as I packed my bike.

'Which route are you taking from here?'

I showed him, tracing the snaking dotted line with my finger from Garamund into the mountains to Pichebon and the Salambar Pass, almost 3,500 metres above sea level, from where I would descend to the Caspian, but he shook his head when my finger reached the pass.

'No, you won't get through here. The pass is blocked with snow.'

I looked at the mountains around me – they were tipped with white but I had assumed the roads and major tracks would be open. This was the only main route across the Alborz from here.

'Have you been up there recently? Won't it have melted?'

He shook his head. 'No, we had big snowfall just a few days ago. It was clear before but this snow was unexpected. I heard about it from a truck driver. He couldn't get through.'

'Well, maybe I'll go and see, I might be able to get through on my bike.'

He shook his head again, firmly. 'No, the snow is very deep. There is no way through right now.'

Having read of its lonely beauty in Freya Stark's book, I had my heart set on this route, winding its way through the high peaks and canyons, past meadows and waterfalls. It was going to be rough in parts, and if my map was correct, the tarmac would stop in a few miles and become a dirt track at its highest section. At the pass I wanted to see the ancient *caravanserai*, a station for the camel trains that used to cross these mountains, carrying goods to and from the Caspian coast. Although the hotelier's warning was well meaning and, I knew in the back of my mind, possibly well founded, I couldn't simply take his word for it and just turn back the way I had come without trying. I had a dirt bike and I was going to use it.

'Well, I'll go up there and give it a go. It might be OK.'

He tried to dissuade me, shaking his head with a knowing smile, as if dealing with an impetuous child.

'The snow might have melted,' I said hopefully.

'No, the truck drivers all turned around. Nobody has been through this week.'

He gave a helpless shrug of his shoulders when he realised I was sticking to my guns.

I wondered if I was making a big mistake but I reasoned that if I had listened to every warning about 'the road ahead' that I had ever received in my life, I would never have got anywhere – I wouldn't even be in Iran now! I was all for seeking out intel from the locals, but often I found it came tainted with old ingrained folklore and ancient prejudices about the neighbouring country or people. Sometimes it was merely idle hearsay about places that, when pressed, they would admit they had never seen themselves. I considered the hotelier too worldly to engage in that kind of casual jingoism, but the other problem I encountered when asking for local advice was a well-meaning but unhelpful sense of chivalry. As Freya Stark herself had put it: 'To be treated with consideration is, in the case of female travellers, too often synonymous with being prevented from doing what one wants.'

Over the years I had formed an unofficial policy of ignoring unsolicited warnings and advice, but I was always aware that my policy might catch up with me one day. Maybe today was the day. There was only one way to find out. The hotelier waved me off with a knowing look as I pulled away, the gravel crunching and spraying from beneath my tyres. I waved back as I took the bend, up and away into the mountains.

6

Snow, Sea and the Shah

THE ROUTE CLIMBED tirelessly, first passing through some
small villages with their own mini-mosques, always decorated
with elaborately patterned blue and yellow tiles and topped with
a shimmering dome. Even if a little tattered and tarnished, they
provided a welcome burst of colour amidst the mushroom grey
of an overcast sky and the mishmash of concrete and mud that
made up the settlements. People stared as I passed but always
waved and smiled if we made eye contact. As I continued to
ascend, any signs of human life ebbed away and I was climbing
high into the upper reaches of the Alborz, through steep-walled
canyons, dodging potentially lethal boulders that littered the road
while trying to snatch a glimpse of the river churning over rock
far below. The tarmac surface of the road, already in a state of
disrepair, came to an abrupt end for no apparent reason and from
there on I was slithering my way along a trail of mud and rock,
the ground soaked from last night's storm and the snow-melt that
trickled down from the slopes.

This route would have been plied by the traders and their camels
a thousand years ago or more, and I sang the old jazz tune 'Caravan'
out loud, relishing the fact that there was nobody around to hear
me. It kept my spirits up and set the scene nicely; long lines of
slow-moving camels carrying food, goods for the bazaars and bags
of silver coins up and over these mountains to the Caspian Sea.
These trade routes, offshoots and extensions of the Silk Road,
had been trodden for centuries throughout the Middle East and

Central Asia, and over the years had eventually become formalised, named and finally tarred to become the modern road network of Iran. The *caravanserai*, the traditional inns formed of a walled courtyard with rooms for merchants and their beasts of burden, would have been dotted along at intervals of around sixteen miles, a typical day's travel for a camel, but they had almost all disappeared out in these remote parts. They would have made a welcome sight for a traveller and I was focussed on reaching one of the few remaining examples high up at the pass. If I made it that far.

Despite the difficult conditions, I was feeling hopeful about the journey ahead. The riding was slippery, requiring concentration, and snow clung to the mountainsides in drifts often several feet deep, but so far it was nothing too daunting. In fact, I was energised and exhilarated by my surroundings. Travelling alone in the mountains can be an unsettling, lonely experience, and as a lover of all things maritime, I find a sense of relief upon returning to sea level. It is always a reassuring moment, catching that first glimpse of the ocean with its promise of onward travel and new lands on faraway shores. But the Alborz were having an unusual effect on me: I felt alive in the moment, like an eagle soaring high above the world. The mist had cleared to reveal a pure blue sky and the air was so crisp and clear, the outline of the mountains so sharp and the snow so startlingly white that my world had taken on the texture of an over-saturated, Super 8 film. Everything was heightened, pushed to the max, including my own sense of vitality. Had some of the Iranian spirit rubbed off on me already?

As I pressed on, despite the snow getting deeper and the temperature dropping, I was warming up fast, mainly because the riding was becoming more physical and required me to stand up on the pegs to tackle the rough ground. This is where the bike came into its own; the suspension soaking up every rock and pothole, and the off-road tyres digging in, keeping me upright on the loose, slithery surface. I was at such high altitude now that I could see for miles all around me nothing but the endless mountain range stretching in every direction; I couldn't remember the last time I had been in such an isolated spot with no idea if I would reach my destination, but I remained strangely calm; the sheer scale and natural beauty was both humbling and pacifying. A few faded hand-painted signs appeared along the roadside, poking out of the snow, but I had no idea if they bore good or bad news for the mountain traveller. As I climbed higher the snow became deeper at the side of the road until I was riding through a tunnel of white, the track narrowed as the snow crept in until it dwindled to a thin grey line of slush, and then it was gone. The col opened up before me, buried under a vast white blanket, carpeting the pass ahead. The hotel owner had been right.

I surveyed the situation with a mixture of fear and excitement, two sides of that same old coin that battled endlessly. Which one would win this time? The thought that the track was under there somewhere and would emerge on the other side was too tempting to resist. I decided to plough on through the virgin snow, hoping it would be just a short stretch to the other side and that I would soon be heading down towards the Caspian Sea. By the time I had paddled my way, breathless, another half a mile or so, I realised I had bitten off more than I could chew. I could barely make progress through the deep drifts, which were almost knee high, and although glorying in the natural beauty, any sense of fun was tempered by my increasingly cold, soaking feet. The truth was that I didn't know what lay ahead, or how long it would take me to reach civilisation, or at the very least, somewhere to dry my socks, but when faced with the unknown, optimism is still an option; a plausible happy ending can be imagined. Turning around and retracing my steps was a known quantity, but a defeat, and therefore unappealing. I pushed on.

The physical nature of forcing a 120-kilogram motorcycle through a snowdrift meant that I was at least keeping my blood flowing and my heart pumping, which kept my toes from freezing solid, but my heart was banging in a whole different way when an hour later all I could see ahead was more white – smooth and endless in every direction. The only sign of life was an eagle dipping and swooping high above, but it soon disappeared into the white. I feared I had become disorientated and my thoughts raced with all the possible catastrophic endings that awaited me. When at last I spotted the faint shape of a structure in the distance, relief rushed through me, and with it a new surge of energy. As I pushed and shoved and heaved and panted towards this evidence of human agency, I realised that I was looking at the squat shape of the *caravanserai*, the most welcome shelter in what felt at that moment like the world's loneliest outpost.

I could almost have thrown a stone into its courtyard, but as I pushed and heaved some more I realised that the truth was, there was no way I was going to be able to reach the building. The snow ahead was so thick, so heavy and deep, that I simply did not possess the physical force required to shove my way through. I stared at the impossible scene ahead for what felt like an age, until the cold began to numb my feet and hands and I knew I had to start moving, somewhere. I had to admit defeat. It pained me beyond belief, but with a regretful glance at the *caravanserai*, I lugged my bike around 180 degrees and retraced my tyre tracks, cursing myself aloud for my foolish ways and stubbornness. Why hadn't I listened to the hotelier? Why did I think I knew better than him?

I have an almost pathological aversion to retracing my steps, but there was no way around it on this occasion. Slithering back down the mountain was a lot quicker than struggling up it at least, and I pressed on past Hotel Alborz with just a swift glance, wondering if I would be spotted making my predicted retreat. As I examined alternative routes to the coast I now had to accept that I would most definitely be riding in the dark, something I was fanatical about avoiding, especially on roads like these and especially with Iranian drivers thrown into the mix. I found myself back at the evil eagle roundabout, but after that I ended up confused by the usual map versus ground conundrum, and it was several hours later, with nightfall upon me, that the mountains gave way to lowland and something that passed for civilisation appeared ahead. I was so relieved that I didn't mind the thin clear air of the Alborz being replaced with diesel fumes, and when the small clusters of mud buildings that lined the outskirts turned into a street with shops, a petrol station and a rundown hotel, I couldn't have placed it on a map but I no longer cared.

It took me the whole of the next day to wend my way around and over the mountains on snow-free roads to the Caspian coast. Away from the main highways a theme was emerging – due to my useless maps, the lack of road signs and overstretching my ambitions, it seemed I was fated to end each day riding in the dark, vaguely lost in a blur of confusion, frustration and exhaustion. How bloody hard can it be to find the Caspian Sea? My sense of direction told me that if I kept going I would hit the main east–west highway running along the coast. I eventually came to a set of traffic lights and my tourist's heart jumped for joy as I spotted a road sign in English. It was for a town the name of which bore no resemblance to anything on my map, which only confused me more, but I was used to that by now. Never mind, there was hope! This was the Caspian corniche, where I was supposed to have been twenty-four hours earlier. I rode for several miles through sprawling towns that all merged into one another, until I spotted a row of bright lights and what looked like a large municipal building on a hill where there was clearly some kind of activity, with cars coming and going. Iran's nightlife is not always obvious, but shops stay open late so my instinct was to find people, and from there somewhere to hole up for the night. The Caspian coast was by all accounts littered with hotels from its golden era as a pre-revolution holiday resort, and I guessed I would find somewhere to stay easily enough. I was suddenly desperate to stop. The adrenalin that had spurred me on over the

Alborz had leached out of me, replaced with exhaustion so deep that it seeped into my bones. I feared I would fall into a crumpled heap as soon as I stepped off my bike.

Cresting a hill, the glittering lights that had been beckoning me appeared suddenly in the most dazzling display, illuminating a grand, white wedding cake of a building atop the hill. I could do nothing but stop and gasp at the sight before me. If this was a hotel, it was a mirage of the highest order, my own version of the drug-induced fantasy world of the *hashishiyuns*. Judging by its style – a blocky but imposing 1930s design approached by a wide, sweeping staircase – it dated from the era of Reza Shah, first king of the Pahlavi dynasty and father of the last shah. I guessed I had stumbled upon the family's Caspian holiday palace. This meant I was in the town of Ramsar, where the Iranian royal family used to come during the summers to escape the heat of Tehran and indulge in hunting and shooting in the nearby forests. I examined my maps, getting my bearings, and turned and stood with the palace behind me, trying to catch a glimpse of the Caspian Sea. It was too dark to see anything except the black sky and the faint silhouettes of palm trees, illuminated by streetlights, tall and still in the cool night air.

Turning towards the palace, I climbed unsteadily from the bike and forced my wobbly legs up the steps towards the entrance, where an oversized and ludicrously ornate chandelier glowed through the front window. There were a few people milling around but when I walked up to the door I found it locked and upon peering through the window I could see that this was not a building in regular use. The glass panes were smeary and a thick layer of dust had settled on the gold and velvet chairs inside the reception room. The interior had a tired air, threadbare and a bit grubby, like the fossilised boudoir of a long-dead but once glamorous great aunt. I surveyed the scene around me and on closer inspection saw that the exterior paint was peeling too and the grounds were a little overgrown. So here was the lavish world of

Reza Shah, the military man who had taken control of a 'backward' nation and whipped, cajoled and forced it into the modern age. I wondered how, in 1979, the palace had escaped the destruction of the revolutionaries, who had happily felled statues of both shahs, father and son, as well as attempted to erase the Pahlavi legacy by renaming landmarks and streets. Maybe they had intended to colonise his many palaces and residences for themselves; I figured even the most hardline of clerics would have fancied getting their hands on this place.

It was strange to see this token of the old era still obviously held in some regard by the current government. The relationship between Iran's religious establishment and its royal family had always been uncomfortable, dating back centuries, with the religious leaders acquiescing to the royals most of the time. But inevitably the brutality, excesses and the cosying up to western powers would prove too much to bear for devout Iranians, and the nation erupted in protests and riots. The 1979 revolution was of course the most famous and explosive example of this dissatisfaction, but it wasn't the first time the masses had shown their disdain for a corrupt shah. Back in 1906, a series of protests resulted in the creation of the first Persian constitution. A parliament was formed for the first time in Iran's history, but it did little to stop the royal dynasties carrying on their tradition of extravagance and inequality, although they did tone it down a touch from the heyday of the eighteenth century, when the royal establishment included an extensive harem of various wives, daughters and concubines, plus approximately four thousand slave girls. I had to concede that the highlife of Iran's twentieth-century royals looked relatively austere in comparison.

Intrigued to catch a glimpse of how the Pahlavis had lived, or at least holidayed, I descended a flight of steps, towards a chink of light through a half-closed door, and came upon a wholly different scene. Below stairs the basement of the palace had indeed been colonised by a new generation of Iranians. But these were no angry, flag-burning Islamic fundamentalists. It seemed I had stumbled upon the hippest hangout on the Caspian coast. Low lighting, arty prints and achingly cool music set the scene for Ramsar's beautiful people to lounge gracefully on sofas and cushions amidst a blur of *qalyān* smoke. It was a young mixed crowd and I was struck, not for the first time on this trip, by the natural good looks and effortless poise of the Iranians. As gazes were lifted towards me – all tight T-shirts and immoral spiky hair for the boys and long lustrous locks and thick make-up for the girls – I was aware of being very pale, grubby and hopelessly, haplessly British to my very core.

'Is the palace open to the public?' I asked a young guy who had come down the steps behind me.

'Not all of it, not anymore. It was a hotel for a long time but it's been closed for years, it's a museum now. Is this your first time in Iran?'

I nodded and he smiled, sweeping his arm to display the scene.

'This is how things used to be, before the Islamic Republic. This was the palace of the Shah. Almost as beautiful as your Buckingham Palace, yes?'

He gave an endearing grin. He was a child of the revolution, too young to remember those days, but I guessed he had picked up this theme from his disillusioned parents or by the osmosis of popular opinion. Thirty-five years of intimidating and dreary Islamic rule had created a rose-tinted view of the pre-revolutionary era. The arrests, the intimidation, the decadence of the elite, the horrors of SAVAK; it had all been forgotten, replaced by a revised, romantic version of the good old days. Among Iranians of a certain age and class, the swinging sixties and seventies are recalled with a poetic yearning nostalgia; an era of mini-skirts, freedom and hedonism. 'I haven't had a glass of wine since 1979,' one man had told me at a petrol station in Qazvin; 'I miss the 1970s,' he had added with a mournful, faraway look. Many people I spoke to turned misty-eyed at the mention of the last Shah, and in particular his glamorous wife, Farah Pahlavi, who signifies everything that is now outlawed for Iranian women. There are Facebook pages dedicated to them both, each boasting thousands of followers, and in the flea markets and antique shops of Tabriz I had seen banknotes, stamps and coins bearing the Shah's image selling for high prices. The man who in my lifetime had been ousted for being a spineless puppet of the USA, was fast on his way to becoming an Iranian icon.

'This part is still a hotel,' the young guy was saying, pointing in the direction of what looked like Ramsar's answer to the Arndale Centre, a 1970s concrete extension that would no doubt have set the original architect's teeth gnashing.

I strolled through the grounds and entered the lobby, guessing it would be out of my price range but curious to see what Persian Brutalism looked like. It certainly smelled like the 1970s, and the decor had survived long enough to have passed through tackiness and come out the other side with a certain vintage charm. It would have been built a few years before the revolution, with all the optimism of that mid-century era and no inkling of the dramatic events that were about to transform this country. But at the reception, as expected, the only thing that had moved with the times were the room rates, and so I wandered back to my bike, all of a sudden overwhelmed by exhaustion, hunger and wet feet. As I stood staring at my map, wondering what to do next and trying to talk myself out of an overpriced night of nylon sheets and an avocado bathroom suite, a car pulled up next to me and a young man stepped out, all eager grins, and from the passenger seat, his consort, another beautiful Iranian woman, waved with a shy smile.

'Welcome!' said the man. 'Where are you from?' He was examining my bike's licence plate. I told him how I had come from London and had just arrived in Ramsar after crossing the Alborz.

'Do you need somewhere to stay tonight?'

'Well, I . . .'

'Please, come! Don't stay here, this is very expensive. Come with us, we have an apartment just a few minutes away, with a spare room. We are going there now. We will eat and you can rest and take a shower. It will be no trouble!'

He placed his hand on his heart, and bowed his head slightly. 'My name's Hossein, my wife, Leila. Please come, it will be our honour.'

I paused only for a moment. Heck, they could be the Iranian version of Fred and Rose West for all I knew, but my old travel instincts were kicking in and I had a good feeling about them. I jumped on the bike and followed their car down the hill.

'We come here at weekends, we live in Tehran during the week,' Hossein explained as we entered an apartment complex, passing under a security barrier. It was obviously a high-end development but there was a half-empty, wind-blown feel about it, as if its residents had not fully settled in.

Unlike most of the Iranian women I had met so far, Leila was quiet and shy, leaving Hossein to do the talking while she prepared food in the kitchen. He explained how they had lived and worked in Canada for several years but had recently decided to return to Iran.

'Why did you want to come back?' I tried to not sound too surprised, but the idea of leaving a secure life in a progressive, liberal democracy for an uncertain economic future under an oppressive regime seemed to fly against common sense, or at least my version of it. 'We are all led to believe that everyone wants to escape to the West,' I added.

'Of course, and many do. It is hard to explain but, it is more . . . more, real here, the people, how they are with each other. In Canada it is cold − I do not mean just the weather,' he laughed. 'You can be very alone in Canada, even when you are with other people. Life in Iran, it is just−' He paused, trying to find the word. 'Just more, real. That is the only way I can describe it. Real.'

'So, even with all the restrictions on your lives, and the economic problems here, the sanctions, the inflation, you wanted to come back?'

'Yes, I know it sounds strange but in Iran I feel alive, even when I am out, walking around in the streets. In Canada I often felt alone, lonely, cut off, even with other people. It is as if they are not fully alive, there is no connection between people, or not the kind I am used to.'

'What were you doing there for work?'

'I am a software engineer.' He gave me his business card, printed in both English and Persian on heavy-quality stock, with a collection of letters after his name. It reeked of highly educated, high-ranking professionalism. 'I am what we call a "Farsi-fier". I translate programmes, Microsoft or Adobe, that kind of software, into Farsi. Now I have my own IT firm in Tehran.'

I was suitably impressed. Intelligent, successful, worldly, sophisticated, handsome, well off, nice car, holiday home, good-looking wife. Not bad, and certainly not the image of the average Iranian man that gets much airtime back home.

'But I also have another life,' he added with a smile. 'I am a part-time actor.'

The mystery of Hossein deepened.

'Yes, I have been in some short films and television adverts. If you watch television while you are in Iran, you may see me'– he offered a shy smile that revealed his film-star white teeth – 'advertising carpet cleaner.' He reached into a cupboard and from behind a large hardback book of Hafez's poetry, produced a bottle. 'You like whisky?'

I sensed this would be an evening of surprises.

As the conversation continued and the whisky flowed, I felt relaxed in his presence. He was happy to talk openly and easily on any subject, asking and answering questions with disarming honesty, to which I replied in kind. There was no topic that was off limits, but his conversation didn't feel intrusive and I relished the direct, non-judgemental exchange of thoughts and ideas. We looked each other in the eye when we spoke. There was no cynicism, no hedging around subjects or embarrassed laughter. This openness was something I had noticed with many of the Iranians I had met and I wondered if this was part of what Hossein meant about being 'real'. We were speaking in almost faultless English but it felt like a different language, compared to the awkward circuitous small talk employed among strangers in Britain. The great British conversation taboos of politics and religion were fair game in Iran, too. In fact, it seemed obligatory to discuss nothing else.

As if reading my mind, Hossein turned to me and said, 'Do you believe in God?'

I answered truthfully in the negative.

'Really?' He looked unusually surprised, almost unsure of how to process this concept. Although the idea of the 'secular Muslim' was common in Iran, it was definitely considered unusual to have no religion at all. Most people, it seemed, would describe themselves as Muslim, even if they had not stepped inside a mosque for years, never prayed, and despised their Islamic rulers.

'You do not think that there is some kind of higher power, even if you do not follow a religion?'

I shrugged and thought about my response. 'Well, I believe we humans are capable of much more than we probably realise. I suppose you could say that I believe in us as a great power.'

'But what do you think happens when we die?'

'Well, I guess that's it.'

'No afterlife? No heaven? No hell?'

I shook my head, almost feeling the need to apologise. He looked so surprised. But he was nodding and listening with a serious expression, consciously trying to appreciate my point of view. There was no sense of disapproval or judgement, just a genuine effort to understand.

'So do you believe there is an afterlife?' I asked him.

'Yes, I think so. I hope so. You know why I hope this?' He

paused and looked me in the eye, waiting. I shook my head. 'Because I want Khomeini to suffer. I want to believe he is suffering now, for what he did to the Iranian people, all the people he killed and tortured and drove away from their homes. All the lives he has ruined.'

He poured another round of whisky. I had to ask.

'But Hossein, if you are a Muslim, is it not forbidden to drink alcohol?'

He gave me a cheeky smile and shrugged his shoulders. 'Yes, I am a Muslim. I pray, I drink whisky. I do not see a problem!' He giggled like a naughty schoolboy and raised his glass.

Leila began a delivery of trays of food from the kitchen. Piles of watermelon, bowls of yoghurt, bread, rice, soups, stews and sauces. It kept on coming. I wondered about her life in Iran, and if she too had wanted to return from Canada, but she was shy and didn't speak much English. She seemed happy with Hossein, and he with her; they were clearly deeply attached and touched each other frequently, which was unusual in Iran. In a country where sexuality is almost invisible in public, these two had some serious electricity buzzing between them. As the whisky bottle emptied and the dining table came to resemble the wreckage of a great banquet, Hossein's conversation became more mystical, his language more opulent, as he continued to discuss religion, reincarnation, morals and spirituality.

'What do you think when you see someone begging for money in the street? Do you give them money?'

'Sometimes.'

'Sometimes I do, but other times I think, what will they spend it on? Why should I give them money that I have worked for, and then I feel like a bad person for thinking this.'

His expressive, open face looked tortured.

'That's probably a normal response,' I reassured him. 'Most people feel different things about it at different times, I suppose we can never fully understand anyone's situation.'

'Yes, I try not to judge people like this. But you know, sometimes it is hard. And when I see someone who is crippled or deformed, I think maybe this is punishment for their past life.'

'Do you really believe that?'

He looked at me. 'Yes. No . . . I don't know—' He stalled. 'I try to be kind. To help people, it is important to be kind.' He nodded silently as if thinking hard about his own words and intention. Then he broke into something that came out almost like a wail. 'That is why I am so hurt by our government, you know the terrible things they do to people, to my friends.'

'What do you mean?'

'They torture people. They lock them away. Why? Because maybe they write something online, or they speak out against the regime. A friend of mine, a man I worked with in Tehran. One day he never came to work. We didn't know why. We are calling him, going to his house. His wife, she doesn't know where he is gone either. Then two weeks later he comes back. No words. He will never say what happened but he is broken, he looks different, I hardly recognise him. He is like a wreck, like he is one hundred years older. He says he cannot tell me, but they took him.'

'Why?'

'I cannot say, I do not know. He will not speak of it.'

I sat in silence, unable to think of any kind of fitting response.

'But we all know this can happen. We all have friends this has happened to.' He looked so pained. 'It could happen to me, to you. Please be careful.'

It was the early hours of the morning. I had another long day's ride ahead and after my wet, cold crossing of the mountains, I was ready to hit the sack. But I had one more question.

'Hossein, if there are such risks here in Iran, if you feel you are always in danger, why did you stop me in the street and invite me, a total stranger, into your home? You and Leila have come here for a weekend away together. You could have just driven past me, or stopped to talk and then carried on.'

'No! I could not drive past you. Because I know what it is like to be alone in a foreign land. I saw you and I felt that you needed help.'

He placed his hand on his heart. 'A human being is a human being. We must take care of each other. It does not matter if you are Christian, or Muslim, or any religion, or nothing! We must help each other if we can. This is what I believe!'

Leila showed me to the spare room and as I closed my eyes, the conversations of the evening continued to churn in my head. Hossein epitomised all that was fascinating about this complicated, contradictory country; religious yet hedonistic, practical yet poetic, modern yet rooted in tradition, equally at ease taking his guidance from a prayer, a poem or an algorithm. I drifted off to the sound of him and Leila enjoying themselves in a time-honoured fashion, and was glad that I hadn't cramped their style too much.

7

Riding the Revolutionary Road

DAYLIGHT REVEALED THAT with regard to the Caspian coast, at least, Robert Louis Stevenson was on the money. The promise of sparkling waters and white sand that had spurred me on over the mountains manifested itself as a flat grey expanse lapping at a pebbled and garbage-strewn shore. Still, as I waved goodbye to Hossein and Leila and headed out along the coast road, it was thrilling to gaze across the water and think that on the other side of this great lake lay Kazakhstan, Turkmenistan, Russia and Azerbaijan. But no ferries ran from Iran these days, and the beaches were empty, save for a few lonely fishermen whose dilapidated shacks and boats demonstrated how Iran's caviar industry, once a booming export, had become a casualty of both uncontrolled fishing and international sanctions.

I clearly wasn't the only person who had been optimistic about the potential of the Caspian Sea. Resorts, villas and motel complexes lined the corniche for miles, many built in the experimental styles of the sixties and seventies, featuring futuristic detailing that merged Palm Springs modernism with Eastern Bloc utilitarianism. It was easy to see how the Caspian coast would have been the grooviest place to be before the revolution, but the last three decades had taken their toll and many of the apartment blocks and hotels were long abandoned, their empty car parks reclaimed by weeds and the once bold architecture now streaked and pitted, victims of the mid-century curse of concrete cancer. It was a sad state of affairs, reminding me not just of business ventures crushed and summer holidays ruined, but of how the joy had been sucked out of this nation, or at least been forced underground and behind closed doors. Pictures and footage from the past showed laughing families, couples and friends frolicking in the Caspian, ice creams in hand, and I wondered if I would ever in my lifetime see Iranians returning to these beaches in their bikinis and Speedos, as had been the norm before 1979. Iranians still decamped here during the summer months, but there was a forlorn desperation about the whole strip. Nowadays, if an Iranian woman wanted to swim, she had to enter the water fully clothed.

After an exploration of the coast, I was heading for Tehran, turning south from the Caspian and back over the mountains, taking a circuitous route over a few days that would see me skirt around Mount Damāvand, then touch the northern fringes of the salt desert, the Dasht-e Kavīr, before entering the capital. This time my crossing of the Alborz was on a brand new road with spectacular views, but there wasn't much opportunity to enjoy the scenery as my full quota of concentration was required for dodging and tackling fellow road users. It was a mystery to me how the Iranians, so warm and helpful in person, became lethal maniacs behind the wheel. Cars, trucks and buses tore past at terrific speeds, so close I wobbled in their slipstreams. Often drivers would be yelling words of encouragement out of their windows, giving me the thumbs up, or even filming me on their mobile phones as they simultaneously forced me into the ditch. I mentioned the phenomenon to a few people in passing when I stopped for tea and fuel, and was met with laughter and cheerful boasts that Iran had the highest rate of road deaths and injuries in the world. It seemed churlish to complain in the face of such national pride.

In Tehran I had a couple of contacts to look up, both British Iranians who had returned to settle in their homeland. My first port of call was a friend of a friend of a friend named Sina, who would apparently be able to help me extend my visa, which, when it had finally come through before I left the UK, had inexplicably been issued for just fourteen days. There had been no explanation for this and my visa fixer couldn't explain it but had assured me it could be extended at the Ministry for Foreign Affairs once I was in Tehran. Iranian born, Sina had moved to England as a teenager and had returned to Iran a few years ago to help run the family business, a well-known patisserie that was considered something of a Tehran institution, having been in business since the 1950s. We had spoken on the phone a few times and I had felt immediately reassured by his incredibly precise directions to his house in north-west Tehran, where he lived with his wife and daughter. You can tell a lot about a person by how they give directions, and Sina was one of the best. And when it came to navigation, I needed all the help I could get. City plans were scant on my maps and some even featured pre-revolutionary road names; there was no way you would find a Kennedy or a Roosevelt gracing an Iranian street corner these days.

After the revolution most of the major roads in the cities, especially in Tehran, had been renamed with the appropriate amount of anti-western fervour, changing the likes of Eisenhower Avenue to Azadi Avenue (meaning 'freedom' in Persian) and Shah Reza Square to Enqelab Square (the Persian word for 'revolution'). My map recce also showed up a liking for using street names to show allegiance to Iran's friends and allies, such as the ubiquitous Felestin – Palestine – which cropped up in many Iranian cities. There were more pointed allegiances too; the street that housed the British Embassy, Winston Churchill Street, had been renamed in typically cheeky Iranian fashion as Bobby Sands Street (it was transliterated as 'Babisands'), in tribute to the IRA hunger striker. In 1981 the embassy had been forced to move their official entrance to a side street so as to avoid the embarrassment of having Sands' name on their headed notepaper. Martyrs from the Iran–Iraq War, important ayatollahs and cultural figures such as the poet and author, Ferdowsi, made up most of the street names, but as I had found with Freya Stark's maps, the English spellings of these had never been formalised, so each map-maker seemed to have invented their own phonetic version. Each of my maps had its own virtues, so in the end I did some elaborate origami of the best three, enhanced them with my own hand sketches and directions, and carefully arranged everything in my map case so I could consult them simultaneously while navigating the traffic. My brain ached before I had even set off.

Navigation headaches aside, this was a good time to be on the road in Iran. My journey coincided with a momentous occasion: the Iranian president, Rouhani, was in New York to address the UN and for talks on Iran's nuclear programme, which, if they came to fruition, would mean a lifting of sanctions and Iran's re-entry on to the world stage. The potential was enormous and the future exciting. At my first petrol station stop, the pump attendant revealed himself as a psychology student at the local university and was so excited about having a real-life English person to practise speaking with that I ended up staying for half an hour after filling up my tank.

'I think our countries will become friends,' the psychologist-in-training concluded, after sharing his thoughts on global politics and Iran's societal and economic problems in immaculate English. He pointed at a newspaper that lay folded on a plastic chair.

I unfolded it to reveal a clumsy composite picture of Rouhani standing next to Obama, both of them smiling. Although they hadn't met in person they had spoken by telephone, the first time an Iranian leader had communicated with his American counter-part for thirty-five years. Unlike Britain, which had been upsetting the Iranians for a couple of centuries, Iran's unhappy relationship with the US was relatively recent. Until 1953, when the CIA masterminded Operation Ajax, the coup that ousted Iran's nation-alist prime minister, Mosaddegh, the Iranians had considered America a friendly nation, even supportive in their future plans to break away from imperialism. Britain was the main enemy at that time, with its uncompromising stance on the Anglo-Iranian Oil Company and refusal to allow Iran to nationalise the industry. The Brits had been angling to get rid of Mosaddegh and his uppity ways for years, but America, under President Truman, had always refused to get involved. But when the Eisenhower administration took office at the height of the Cold War, fearing that Iran would fall to the Soviets, the White House found a sudden enthusiasm for a coup. For most Iranians, who at that time felt positively towards the US, the revelation that the CIA had orchestrated the removal of their most popular prime minister was seen as a terrible betrayal. Any hope of democracy that the Iranians had ever had was snuffed out with Mosaddegh's removal – and to discover it had all been organised by their 'friends', the Americans, was a shocking blow. It took another twenty-five years for this shock and anger to foment, simmer and finally explode into the Islamic Revolution, when the USA was frozen out for good.

It had just been a quick phone call between Rouhani and Obama, but it was considered big enough news to warrant the Iranian picture editors knocking up hastily Photoshopped images of the two leaders standing side by side, positioning them as tentative new best friends. They had even made their goodbyes using each other's respective colloquialisms. 'Have a nice day!' Rouhani had said, to which Obama had responded with a cheery '*Khoda hafez!*' This is going to upset a few people, I thought, but my gas-pumping psychologist was enraptured by the idea. He held the newspaper up, triumphant.

'Yes, yes, our countries are going to be friends, at last!'

I didn't bother pointing out the minor detail that Obama wasn't my president. It didn't seem important. American, British, whatever. Great Satan, Little Satan, we had all been merged into one by the Islamic Republic's propaganda machine. No different from how Persians and Arabs are all one and the same in many western minds, I supposed.

'Our last president, Ahmadinejad, he was very bad for Iran, he turned the world against us even more. But now we have Rouhani, he is better. I think he will communicate with your country. Iran needs to communicate more with the whole world, we must share more together.' He smiled at me, his face glowing with optimism. 'Do you agree?'

I nodded emphatically.

'Yes, this is good for our future,' he said, smiling and patting the newspaper approvingly.

Two older men who were filling up their cars looked over our shoulders, pointed at the picture and laughed between themselves. Maybe they had seen too many smiling politicians, and much worse besides. But I liked the hope in the young student's face and his positive words sent me on my way with a good feeling about the journey ahead.

'I am so glad you came here today,' he said as we exchanged our farewells.

Now the roads were becoming busier, little towns merged into one another, bustling with industry and commerce, and here the bike came into its own, easily nipping through the small-town chaos and beating fume-laden traffic jams. But even amongst the frenetic hustle, still I made for a curious spectacle, with clusters of onlookers gathering around me and the bike when I stopped, their reactions ranging from wary curiosity to unabashed excitement.

Whenever conversation ensued, it was the UN meeting that was the talk of the town, of every café, every truck stop, of the whole country. Right now, on the streets, there was a tangible sense that Iran could be re-entering the world again, and I didn't meet a single person who didn't welcome it, although some were more sceptical than others. 'Rouhani has no real power, he is just the puppet of the Supreme Leader' was a grumble that came up occasionally. But most people were genuinely excited about the possibilities of Iran's future. Everyone wanted to know my opinion on this momentous occasion, as if I was somehow directly involved, and perhaps more tellingly, as if they were directly involved; there was a belief their lives could be changed by this thawing of relations. Away from the cynical, disengaged landscape of contemporary British politics, I was reminded of an era, admittedly that I could only just recall in my lifetime, when the average person felt a direct connection to the actions of their leaders.

Not everyone was so optimistic, though, and it wasn't just the Islamic hardliners who were sceptical about this new dawn of international relations. That night I stopped at a hotel in a small town and was immediately pounced upon by a teenage girl whose sweet plump face and wire-rimmed spectacles belied the sharp mind and fearlessness of a rabble-rouser. She was on her way home to Tehran with her family after a trip to visit relatives in Turkey and happily settled alongside me for the evening after dinner. Like all the Iranians I had met, she was keen to discuss topics that two British strangers would skirt around politely. It was as though she had been saving it all up for this moment, and the frustration came pouring out of her.

'When I leave school I am going to train to become a doctor,' she told me, 'then I can leave Iran. I will go to America. I have an aunt living in Colorado. I cannot stay in Iran, the way they treat women. Why must we wear the stupid headscarf, why can they tell us what to wear? They control every small detail of our lives, we cannot even listen to the music we want, they try to control the internet, television, everything . . .' She looked away for a minute, out of the window at the darkening streets, and then turned back to me, fire in her eyes. 'This is not living. I do not call this living.'

I had to agree with her. It was no life for anyone, especially an intelligent, sparky teenage girl. I felt a fond admiration for her. She was angry but she wasn't bitter. Despite her fury at the oppressive minutiae of her day-to-day existence she was full of life and hope and humour, and I knew that she would become a powerful, positive force some day. But, if things stayed the way they were, not in her home country. She struck me as an asset to any society, although I doubted the Iranian mullahs would agree – vocal women are not generally appreciated in a theocracy. Anyway, if she had her way they would lose her, and all her brightness and energy to the evil USA, but maybe they preferred it that way.

'What about Rouhani?' I asked her. 'Do you think he will make a difference?' I mentioned the excited nature of the conversation I had had with the psychology student at the petrol station, but my new friend was unconvinced.

'Hah!' she spat, the contempt flashing in her eyes. 'He can't do anything, it is the Supreme Leader who controls everything in Iran. Khamenei has all the control.'

'But what is the role of the President, if the Supreme Leader makes all the decisions? What does Rouhani actually do?'

She shook her head. 'Not very much. He will have talks with other world leaders, he can make decisions about economic policies, this type of thing, but,' she shrugged, 'that is all. Rouhani cannot change anything for us, for the people of Iran. The really big important things, they are decided by Khamenei. He controls the Army, the Revolutionary Guards, he can decide if we go to war, he can decide what the newspapers and television tell us, who is in prison, who is executed. He and his clerics, they rule everything.' She gave a tired laugh that made her sound older than her fourteen years and said, 'This is why he is called "Supreme Leader"!'

Her words were chilling. They sounded Orwellian, almost fantastical, but this was her reality, her everyday life.

'So, you feel your only future is to leave Iran?'

She slumped her chin into her hands and looked up at me through cow-eyed lashes.

'Yes, but I do not really want to. I love Iran, my family is here, my friends. It is my home. But what life is this? It makes me crazy!' She grinned and polished her glasses, which made her look very un-crazy and rather sweet. 'We tried in 2009. Did you hear about our Green Revolution in the UK?'

'You mean the protests when Ahmadinejad was re-elected? Yes, of course. It was reported all over the world.'

I remembered it well. It was a story that nobody thought they would ever hear coming out of Iran, and the western news lapped it up. The youth of Iran, rising up against the ayatollah! This great swell of Iran's young generation, the product of Khomeini's revolutionary breeding programme of the early eighties, had turned against the regime that had created them. Could it really happen? Could the Islamic Republic be overthrown? Could our old adversary become a modern democracy? The answer was, sadly, no. The Iranian authorities reacted violently and swiftly, sending in the Revolutionary Guards and the Basij to kill protestors and crush the movement, making its leaders take part in show trials, forcing confessions from them, locking them up and ensuring they didn't try anything like it again. But for a short moment there had been a glimmer of hope and the world saw a new image of Iran; a youthful, mobilised, internet-savvy nation using covert access to social media to spread their message, a million wrists bearing the green bands that came to symbolise the movement, young men and women chanting 'Where is our vote?' and 'Death to no one!', echoing the famous 'Death to America!' mantra of the 1979 revolution that is still heard among the hardliners at Friday prayers.

'Yes, the election was a fraud,' my schoolgirl revolutionary continued. 'This was the biggest protest in Iran since 1979, since the Islamic Revolution. It started because of the election but it became a big movement, the Green Movement, for democracy, human rights. It is a peaceful movement, only non-violent protests, you know, like Gandhi.' She came over all dreamy for a moment. 'He is my hero!'

'Wait a minute,' I said, doing some rough calculations. 'How old were you in 2009?'

She gave me a cheeky smile. 'Eleven years old. I protested with my parents.'

'So what happened?'

'People were killed, shot in the street, you know they used snipers? I saw them, people bleeding in the street. Then afterwards it was terrible, so many people were arrested, questioned, tortured, sent to Evin Prison, hundreds of people. Sometimes they come out, sometimes they disappear. Many people, they have never been heard of again. Young people, young women and men, their families do not know what happened to them.' She shook her head. 'But oh! You should have seen it, such a beautiful sight, millions of us. We filled Azadi Street, all the way from Azadi Tower to Enqelab Square. You do not know Tehran yet but you will see, this is a very long road!'

'I remember seeing the pictures.'

'And do you know what these words mean, Azadi and Enqelab?'

I nodded, remembering my maps, past and present.

'This is, how do you say . . . ironic, yes?'

'So do you think it will happen again? Could there be another revolution?'

For the first time in our conversation she looked defeated. She slumped down in her seat, shaking her head. 'I hope. All the time I hope. But no, I do not think so now. The protests, they lasted for many months. But people became scared and tired of fighting. There are still some who believe it can happen. The Green Movement is still alive but our leader, Mousavi, he is under house arrest and the people, they have much to lose. They are scared for their lives and their families.'

'By the way, my name is Aheng,' she said, offering her hand. 'It is a Kurdish name, I am Kurdish. Aheng means "harmony".'

'Your parents must be very proud of you.'

Her family had retired to their room with a casual wave, seemingly relaxed about leaving their teenage daughter in the company of a foreign stranger.

'Oh yes, my parents are very progressive. They like to encourage me to do what I wish with my life. If I want to be a doctor and go to America, they will support me. But of course they will miss me too. And I will miss them.'

'Are your friends like you? Involved in politics? Campaigning?'

'I guess so, most of them.'

I told her that back home she would be considered unusual, that most people of her age had little interest in politics.

'That is because in Britain you are free,' she said simply. 'It is impossible for us not to be interested, do you see? To not care, that is a luxury only for the free.'

When she got up to go to her room she offered me a surreptitious view inside her shoulder bag. 'Look,' she said with a giggle that was more naughty schoolgirl than subversive revolutionary. 'I smuggled in fashion magazines from Turkey!'

The following day I was on the road as dawn broke. My surroundings changed fast as I descended the mountains and headed towards the desert, with Mount Damāvand dominating the scenery for miles around. Its influence was apparent in the small towns that sat in its foothills, with their climbing outfitters, hiking tour companies, and even statues of mountaineers, celebrating Iran's long and illustrious history in this field. As my route took me closer to the capital, the roads became faster, more congested and polluted. But the upside was an increased sense of anonymity. I was beginning to realise that I could never be truly anonymous in Iran; as a woman riding a UK-registered motorcycle I was a constant source of interest, bemusement or excitement, depending on who had spotted me and my unusual form of transport, but as is the case anywhere in the world, the nearer I got to the metropolis, the easier it was to slip by unnoticed. This rule was, however, negated any time I took a break, at petrol stations, truck stops and toll booths, where, just like in the small towns, I would be stared at and questioned, but often fed and watered with genuine concern for my well-being. The interest was almost always friendly but it was hard not to feel self-conscious, as so many pairs of eyes invariably turned in my direction.

This incessant attention meant that hotel rooms became my only harbours of sanctuary, as well as the one place I could find freedom from my restrictive clothing. Half a day's ride from Tehran, I stopped early, with the plan of tackling the capital the following day. Releasing my hair from its confinements, I collapsed on the bed, revelling in the visual assault that can only be found in cheap Iranian hotel furnishings. On this occasion, a gold nylon bedcover that when pulled back revealed a faux fur zebra print blanket and beyond that a Barbie-pink sheet. None of it was too fresh but still, it livened up the otherwise drab little quarters.

Flumping back on the shiny gold satin, I turned on the television. The hotel manager at the check-in desk had told me with great pride that his establishment was the only one in town with an English-speaking cable channel. I didn't catch the name of it but I was pretty certain it wouldn't be the BBC, which is denounced, and therefore banned by the Iranian government, along with CNN and most other western news sources. I messed around with the bewildering selection of remote controls, twiddled some knobs on the ancient set, but couldn't get anything on the screen except a black-and-white strobe-fest of horizontal lines with a soundtrack that sounded like the call to prayer put through a revolving Leslie speaker.

After ten minutes of faffing I was no closer to the reruns of *Lovejoy* and the *Miss Marple* marathon that were forming my homesick-induced television fantasy, but the bit was firmly between my teeth now. I would conquer this Iranian television, dammit! So I nipped down the two flights of stairs to the lobby and asked the manager how to make it work.

'I will come and show you,' he said and followed me up to the room.

There was nowhere to sit except for the bed, but when I perched myself on the edge he sat next to me, very close. His thighs were touching mine. He picked up the remote controls and smiled at me, leaning in, his brown eyes and white teeth just inches from mine. It was at this moment I had a sudden and horrible realisation. I had forgotten to put on my headscarf. I felt a wave of shame and horror wash over me. It had completely slipped my mind, caught up as I had been with trying to get the television to work. Without thinking, I had merrily popped out of the room, down the stairs, and, with red hair flowing, had essentially invited a strange man up to my room. 'Ooh, Mr Manager, my television doesn't work, please can you help me?' It had all the hallmarks of the opening scenes of a bad porn film. I tried to calm my imagination; maybe I was overreacting, maybe it wasn't as bad as I thought. The problem was that I still had no real sense of the social nuances between men and women in this country. I truly had no clue as to how inappropriate my behaviour could be considered. Was I worrying about nothing, or was it wildly provocative? Then an altogether different wave of shame hit me. Ashamed at how quickly I had subscribed to the idea that to be seen without the hijab deserved this reaction. Now I felt annoyed with myself about that. But what to do right now?

I could see my headscarf lying on the floor next to my motor-cycle helmet in the corner of the room. But to get to it I would have to squeeze past my over-attentive hotel manager, who was still sitting on the bed, idly fiddling with the remote controls. This little manoeuvre would essentially involve me shoving the supposedly irresistible curves of my bottom in his face, unless he had the good grace to stand up and let me pass, which didn't seem likely. Gold and fur bedspreads, headscarf tossed aside, my arse, your face; there was nothing about this scene that suggested it was going to end well.

Suddenly a loud, abrupt crackle burst out from the television. The horizontal lines morphed into some shaky footage, and noisy chants of 'Death to Britain! Down with Britain!' came blasting out of the speaker accompanied by the image of a group of men burning the Union Jack. A voice-over in accented English followed: 'In 2011 protestors gathered at the British Embassy in Tehran to protest over Britain's hostile policies against the Iranian government. They called for the British ambassador to be expelled and for Iran to cut all diplomatic ties with Britain.'

'Death to Britain! Death to Britain!' the chanting continued, filling the tiny room. Could this situation get any more awkward? I wondered. The manager grinned, slightly uncomfortably, to give him credit. What was I meant to do now? Say 'Er, yes, well, sorry about the sanctions, stealing all your oil, deposing your favourite prime minister and all that, but can you stop rubbing your thigh against mine now please.'

'Television all good!' he said.

I assumed he meant its function rather than its content, but I couldn't be sure. He was still sitting there.

'Er, yes, great, thank you.'

Still sitting.

'Um, just got to get something from my bike,' I heard myself saying as I attempted a vault across the bed to avoid the embarrassing squeeze-past. My foot got tangled up in the frilly edging of the gold bedspread and I landed awkwardly on the floor. Whatever allure I may have once held was definitely eliminated. I made a lunge for my headscarf and bundled it around my hair as I ran down the stairs to the underground car park.

I dilly-dallied with my bike until I felt enough time had passed to make it clear that I definitely wasn't planning on returning for some sanction-busting hanky-panky. On my way back to my room, I cringed as I passed through the reception, feeling the manager's eyes following me.

'Everything fine, madam?' he asked coolly from behind the desk.

'Ah, yes, fine, fine, thank you. Just, er, needed to get this.' I waved my Iran road map ostentatiously to show the purpose of my visit to my bike.

'Got to plan my route for tomorrow, going to Tehran, lots of roads, very confusing . . .' I was talking too much. As I continued up the stairs he started laughing and called after me, 'Death to Britain, ha-ha-ha!' The Iranians certainly weren't lacking in a sense of humour.

The television was still blasting away. It turned out I had stumbled upon a programme all about Britain's negative influence and destructive relationship with Iran. And the scriptwriter had not been sitting on any fences. The station airing this enlightening show was PressTV, a controversial English-language news channel funded by the Iranian government that had broadcast from London until recently, when some decidedly suspect reporting had seen it banned from operating out of the UK. It now beamed its propaganda from Tehran but still featured several British presenters, including politicians Ken Livingstone and George Galloway, whom I imagined welcomed the opportunity to give the finger to the British government, even if that meant taking the ayatollah's shilling. PressTV's official manifesto was to provide English-language news from an Iranian/Islamic perspective, but controversies surrounding accusations of anti-Semitism, the airing of forced confessions and giving airtime to extreme right-wing commentators had not helped its cause in the global media and had seen its licence revoked in Europe and the channel removed from certain satellites.

I watched the show with an interest verging on morbid fascination, following Iran's official version of our countries' stormy history over the last two hundred years. Although the timeline was factually accurate, and one couldn't condone Britain's interference and skulduggery, the tone and language of the narration was so bitter and aggressive I felt almost personally under attack, irrational as I knew that to be. I was surprised to find myself taken aback at the unadulterated vicious manner and opinions of the commentary. I suppose I had been raised on the more restrained tones of the BBC, which arguably had its own agendas, but at least promoted them with a little more subtlety. Forthcoming shows were trailered in the breaks, each one focussing on a current international news story or a documentary about an historical event, always serious in style and with professional production standards, but no matter what the specifics of the programme, the theme was always the same: the West in disarray. Race riots in Sweden, British student protests, the rise of the far right in central Europe, chronic shoplifters in France. The voice-overs were grave and loaded: 'Once again, American police brutality make the headlines . . .' There were news items on Saudi meddling in the Middle East and plenty of not-so-subtle highlighting of the misdeeds of Sunni Muslims in the region, and occasionally a rent-a-cleric talking head would pop up from some shabby studio: 'The arrogant powers cannot control what happens in Iran!'

Here was the rhetoric of the revolution, still going strong after thirty-five years. But who really cared about all this now, I wondered? Who watched this stuff? Not the people milling around the boutiques and electronics stores in the bustling towns. Not Aheng or the petrol-pumping psychology student. Not Hossein, despite his loyal passion for his country. Not the young guys manning the motorway toll booths who donated me their lunch, not the persecuted Bahá'í or the truck drivers giving me thumbs-up out of their windows, nor the chador-clad women who stopped me in the street and welcomed me with curious, open faces and eager questions. From the little of Iran I had seen so far, Press-TV's message seemed outdated and irrelevant, the background noise of a tedious old man ranting on about the olden days. Unfortunately, the 'old man' was running the country and could have you tortured and killed if he so desired.

Next morning at breakfast I had the good fortune to be able to get some of the answers to my questions when I was approached by Raha, a glamorous, confident woman who was staying at the hotel on a business trip. It was unusual to see women alone, but I had noticed that it was more common the closer I got to Tehran. Raha certainly didn't operate like someone living under oppression, with her tailored suit, Macbook and designer sunglasses.

'I saw you arrive yesterday, I wanted to speak to you,' she said, inviting me to join her at her table, 'but I had to go for a meeting over dinner. I saw you and I was very interested in you! I wondered where you were from.'

I told her about my journey and asked her what she did for work.

'I am from Tehran. I studied luxury brand management in America, but I came back after university, so now I am working with showrooms, galleries, boutiques.'

As our conversation unfolded, I mentioned the programme I had watched the night before.

'Oh, PressTV!' She rolled her eyes. 'Yes, it is the English mouthpiece of the government. Nobody watches that rubbish! We all watch Manoto. It is broadcast from London, but it is against the regime.'

'It's a satellite channel?'

'Yes.'

'I thought that satellite TV was illegal in Iran, but it seems to be everywhere, quite openly,' I said.

She gave a cool shrug of her shoulders. 'Yes, technically it is illegal. The same as alcohol and many other things, but you can get all these things easily. You can call someone and order vodka or whisky and they deliver it to your home. You just have to know who to call.'

'So there are illegal satellite TV installers in Iran?'

'Yes, of course. And most of them work for the government!' She laughed at the irony. 'It is the same with the alcohol smuggling. It is profitable to control the supply of illegal goods, so why would the government let the criminals take that trade?' she said with the authority of a business consultant. 'The Revolutionary Guards make a lot of money from smuggling alcohol.'

She shrugged her shoulders again. 'Everyone knows this. Sometimes the police will make a show of arresting people. They used to come to people's houses and take their satellite dishes and look for alcohol, but they do not do this so much now.'

'But in Sharia law, isn't it wrong to drink alcohol?' I wasn't sure where Sharia law stood on watching satellite television, but the Islamic views on boozing were clear. 'And most people in Iran are Muslim, so they support Sharia law, presumably?'

'Well, yes, we are Muslims, but Iranians love to party!' she laughed and added in a serious tone, 'I love vodka; Stoli is my favourite but it is hard to get here.'

'I see.' I said.

But I didn't. The hypocrisy of the authorities was not surprising, but the whole story was confusing. Who really believed in what? Did anyone believe in anything? I recalled the similar conversation with Hossein. The contradictions of Iran were still churning in my head and I was waiting for them to settle into something clear and ordered, something from which I could create theories and see patterns that made sense to me. I feared I would be waiting a long time.

I asked her if she wanted to return to America or work somewhere else abroad, as so many educated Iranians seemed to. But she looked unsure.

'I thought I would. I didn't want to come back but you know, it feels different here now. Things are changing in Iran. Tehran is a fun place to be right now, and of course it's always good to be close to Dubai in my line of work. And' – she gave me a conspiratorial look – 'that's where all the best parties are, obviously.'

I sensed that Raha and I attended very different parties.

At that moment we were interrupted by the familiar voice of the hotel manager, who was striding towards our table with a pot of tea in his hand.

'Ha-ha-ha! Death to Britain!' he declared, almost doubling up with laughter as he splashed the tea into our cups.

Raha gave me a quizzical look.

'It's just our little joke,' I said as he wandered off, still laughing to himself.

Raha was talking about television again.

'If you watch the news stories about the UK and America on the Iranian channels, you will see they change what people say to suit their message. The subtitles in Persian are not always the same as what the people being interviewed are saying. You can only notice if you speak English well.'

'What do you mean?'

'Well, when your royal baby was born recently, yes?'

'Prince George?' I had never thought of him as my royal baby, but I suppose technically, I was contributing to his upkeep.

'Yes, Prince George. The Iranian television channel showed interviews of British people in the street, in London, asking what they thought about the new prince. The subtitles on the screen were saying bad things as if the people didn't like the British royal family. But I could see the people were saying something different to the words on the screen. I could hear them saying they were happy about the new baby.'

I was astounded and burst out laughing. It seemed such an underhand yet silly thing to do. But propaganda takes all forms and I supposed insidious, subtle messages like this were as powerful in some ways as the upfront, hardline documentary I had watched last night.

'I am able to see it, to hear it, because I know English, because of attending university in America,' she said. 'But if you are an uneducated person, who speaks only Persian, you will not be able to hear the truth. You understand?'

I understood only too well.

8

Tehran: Politics, Pollution and Parties

To arrive in Tehran on a motorcycle is like being pressganged into playing a relentless video game. Constantly forcing you onwards and upwards, level upon level. You must keep moving, keep up the pace, never stop. If you drop your guard, just for a second, you're done. It's a commitment; once you're in, you're in and if you're lucky, you'll be spat out at your destination, trembling and disorientated, and fundamentally altered on some molecular level. Many don't make it, as is apparent by the roadside displays of mangled car wrecks, mounted like billboard ads in an attempt to temper the Iranian driver. It hasn't worked.

Like a wild animal preparing for attack, teeth bared, all senses on overdrive, I charged into the Tehran-bound traffic. Every muscle in my body tensed, switched to fight or flight mode, until I realised my mistake – it was fight *and* flight that was required here. At top speed, one eye on my maps, the other pretty much everywhere else, I weaved, ducked, dodged and yelled my way into this most unholy of capital cities. Twelve million people in their horn-blasting, fume-spewing bangers, all playing the same fast violent game. It's hard not to take it personally, but once I had altered my western road user's mindset and understood that none of Tehran's drivers were actually *trying* to kill me, it made it slightly easier. I simply had to learn to ride like an Iranian. This meant the only rule I needed to understand is that there are no rules; red traffic lights are advisory rather than obligatory, four lanes marked on the road actually means seven in reality, and no vehicle should ever be further than one inch away from another. Breathing deeply as another maniacal taxi driver hurtled towards me, I trawled my past travels for motivation and reassurance. Remember Kinshasa? Guatemala City . . . C'mon, you can do this! Istanbul, just a few weeks earlier, had seemed like hell on earth but now felt like a dawdle through Toytown. None of them compared to this insanity.

But today Allah was on my side. I pulled up outside Sina's house breathless, shaking, grimy with sweat, dust and diesel fumes, but triumphant and euphoric. When Sina opened the door, with his warm smile and familiar accent, the sound of home, I made an instinctive but fundamental error. I gave him a hug. There was just a moment's hesitation as he hugged me back, but I sensed him looking over my shoulder. We were on the street, his neighbours were coming and going from their houses, they could see us. I had broken not just a social code but the law of the land. Men and women who are not married or related are forbidden from touching each other in public; they will never greet each other with a hug or even a handshake. My arrival at Sina's house would raise eyebrows and it was entirely possible that having me stay could attract unwanted attention from the authorities. I had known of other western travellers who had used couch-surfing websites to find accommodation in Iran, only to discover that their hosts had later been interrogated and warned by the police.

It was easy to forget, amongst all the bustle and noise and the easy-going hospitality of the Iranians, that a large chunk of the population are paid to keep an eye on the rest. These guardians are easy to spot when they take the form of uniformed police, but the Gashte Ershad, Iran's infamous 'morality police', go about their business in plain clothes, scouring the streets for un-Islamic behaviour. Their unmarked vans, the bane of liberal Tehranis, cruise the streets with a team of wardens including a chador-cloaked female assistant whose job it is to bundle young women into the back of the van, take them to a holding facility, remove their make-up and lecture them on the evils of 'bad hijab'. They are then forced to write an apology before being returned to their parents, invariably angry and resentful and no doubt keen to reapply their lipstick and nail varnish as soon as possible. In recent months, President Rouhani had made public requests to the Gashte Erhad to ease off on the harassment of young Iranian women, but as Aheng would have been quick to point out, his words had little power, and the 'morality police' continued their rounds, taking their orders from the Supreme Leader and his clerics.

Luckily, no one had seen my faux pas, and Sina took it in his stride, ushering me graciously into the garden of his villa-style home where his wife, Avid, rushed out to greet me. They were the picture of relaxed Iranian hospitality, proffering cool drinks and a tray of snacks as soon as I crossed the threshold, with Sina offering me any assistance I could wish for. It was a relief to be insulated in this safe haven with its leafy garden, down a quiet side street, knowing that the madness continued to rage outside. I had to savour it while it lasted; sadly Sina and Avid were due to leave town a couple of days later, so I couldn't allow myself to get too comfortable. But I would not be leaving Tehran right away as I had another friend of a friend to look up.

'He lives in an area called Vanak,' I said to Sina, reading out his address.

'Very nice,' he nodded approvingly. 'That's a posh neighbourhood, not far from here. Who is he?'

I explained I didn't know him either, only that his name was Omid. It was another loose connection through a British-Iranian acquaintance of mine in London. Omid was an old business colleague of his from years back who had made a similar life journey to Sina, returning to his homeland after spending time in the UK and America as a restaurateur. My friend had told him about my journey and he had insisted I come to stay with him and his family while in Tehran.

'He's quite a character,' my friend had said with a grin. 'He'll show you a good time.' So far my only contact with Omid had been by phone from Tabriz, just to let him know I had arrived in Iran, and even in that short conversation I had found his enthusiasm and humour infectious. His chirpy cockney accent, from a youth spent in south London, put me instantly at ease and he chatted and laughed easily. I was looking forward to meeting him.

The following day, before Sina left town, he helped me with my truncated visa as promised. It had felt like a gamble to set off with such uncertainty but now I was here, I was relieved to find that Sina knew where to go and what to do. My first day in Tehran was spent in a windowless basement, filling in forms, having my offending wisps of hair tucked under my headscarf for my ID photos, and finally, waiting for hours alongside clusters of thin, silent, weary men. They wore shabby loose-fitting cotton trousers and construction boots, and sat with their heads bowed to their knees, resigned to the bureaucracy.

'They are Afghans,' Sina explained. 'Migrant workers, getting visas to work in Iran, for building sites, and cleaning, street sweeping, all the dirty work.'

I was granted thirty days to roam freely in Iran, no questions asked about my form of transport, and the next day I was moving on once again, but only a few miles this time. It was just a short hop along the Chamran Highway from Sina's home in Shahrak-e Gharb to Omid's in Vanak, but even that small burst of Tehran driving was enough to send me into sweats and palpitations. When I arrived at Omid's house I was ready to lock myself in for the duration.

As soon as I pressed the buzzer I could hear him approaching, an excitable London accent calling my name from behind the locked gate. I felt immediately cheered.

'Lois! You made it!' He exuded enthusiasm. Commandeering my bike, he pushed it into the courtyard and as the gate shut behind us, I stepped into a secret pleasure zone. Helmet, headscarf and manteau were cast aside and illegal pastimes reigned. BBC

World chattered away on the television and behind a corner bar, in a nod to Omid's former life in London as well as a defiant 'up yours' to the Iranian authorities, a row of optics lined the wall. Omid's wife, Tala, a warm-hearted, supermodelesque Iranian beauty and their delightful eight-year-old daughter, Sorena, welcomed me like an old family friend and I felt all the tension of the past few weeks melt away. In their company Tehran became a source of excitement and fascination, rather than the over-whelming monstrosity it had seemed just minutes earlier. After the obligatory tea and sweets, with energy levels high, we hit the streets of the city in their car, heading for a late evening meal in the northern suburbs. Before we set off, Sorena stood beside me in front of the mirror by the door, frowning at my reflection.

'No, no. This is all wrong,' she said, tugging at my headscarf. 'Let me show you.'

She removed it and draped it artfully and loosely over the top of my head, flipping one end back over my shoulder, adding a much needed fashionable edge to my weirdo white Muslim convert look.

'Yes, that's better,' she said nodding in approval, with the authority of a professional stylist, then she looked up at me, eyebrows frowning. 'Do you like it, wearing the scarf?'

'Well, no . . .'

'I hate it. It is stupid. And I hate him!' She opened a school exercise book that was lying on a side table, showing a full-page portrait of Ayatollah Khomeini on the inside cover. Picking up a pencil, she drew fangs on his mouth and wrote *Na-na-na-na-na. BAD MAN* next to his head, giggling uncontrollably. I loved her immediately.

Omid, with a foot and a passport in both Iran and England, proved to be an illuminating and insightful companion, able to view his home country with typical Iranian passion and patriotism but also the detached, sardonic eye of a true Brit. One thing quickly became clear; the disdain for the regime was a family affair. This was made obvious as we set off into the streets of north Tehran and a robed mullah crossed the road in front of us, head down, scurrying along with a pile of books under his arm. Omid blasted the horn and banged on the window.

'That means FUCK YOU!' he shouted, roaring with laughter, adding, 'And he knows it!' as the beleaguered cleric gave a jumpy glance in our direction and hurried on, scowling under his white turban as he dodged the traffic. The Iranian drivers showed no mercy, not even for a man of the cloth.

As we cruised the heaving streets, Tehran began to take shape, transforming itself from a howling mess of concrete and metal into a city with a distinct form, character and even charm. Orientation was easy, with the snow-topped mountains domi-nating the northern skyline and, in the west of the city, the Milad Tower rising up out of the low-level chaos. A relatively recent addition to the skyline, the 435-metre-high structure is a telecoms tower, cultural and convention centre and revolving restaurant, mainly used as a highly sanitised social hub for Tehran's well-behaved citizens and visiting tourists – the public face of state-sanctioned leisure in modern Iran. These two beacons kept me orientated and once I had become acquainted with Tehran's central artery, Valiasr Street, an eleven-mile tree-lined boulevard that runs north–south along the entire length of the city, I was beginning to get my bearings.

Over the next few days, as we drove and tramped the streets of Tehran, it became obvious that this was a divided city – one divided not just physically, by Valiasr Street, but on its other axis by something less tangible. The north of Tehran is home to the wealthy and westernised. Bountiful restaurants, glitzy shopping centres, blacked-out SUVs and elegant, bejewelled women fill its streets. Homes are villa-style behind high walls or anonymous apartment complexes, and the ski slopes of the mountains are in easy reach. In the south of the city, beyond the railway station and the bazaar with its hustling money-changers and swaggering *bazaaris*, are rundown dirty streets where the poor and, by default, the pious reside. Here, the women are hunched under black chadors and bearded men sit in groups outside scruffy little grocery shops, grizzled and suspicious of outsiders. The homes in the south of the city are low-rise, built of breezeblocks or crumbling brick and whole families are transported around the dirty streets on whiny mopeds, while in the parks and squares drug addicts and prostitutes do their best to keep a low profile. But the defining features of Tehran, the brownish yellow smog and the anarchic traffic, know no physical or social boundaries; they cannot be escaped by the rich or the religious.

In the city centre these two worlds merge in a whirl of commerce and feverish industry among a mishmash of majestic old buildings and shabby concrete decay. I took a cab into the centre of town and listened to the driver's running commentary on all that ailed his beloved city, on the good old days when he could have a beer and a dance, and how he had escaped to America to study engineering but couldn't afford the university fees and was forced to return home after a year.

'Now, drive taxi in Tehran. No beer. No fun.'

He shrugged, resigned to his fate. After about twenty minutes, once his English vocabulary had been depleted, his analysis of Tehran's problems was distilled down to two descriptions as he pointed at buildings in turn as we passed by.

'Reza Shah!' he would shout triumphantly at anything remotely grand or old.

'Islamic Republic!' he spat at each shoddy concrete office block.

'Reza Shah! Islamic Republic! Reza Shah! Islamic Republic!'

It was strangely catchy and became my Tehran mantra, repeating tirelessly and soundlessly in my head for the rest of the day.

Just over a mile apart in the city centre the American and British embassies, two buildings that are decidedly 'Reza Shah!', stood uninhabited, each comprising an entire city block. The British Embassy had been shut since the 2011 spat that had spawned this journey of mine, but the American Embassy's closure dated back to the year that changed everything, 1979. A group of students, hopped up on revolutionary fervour and angry that the USA was harbouring the Shah, stormed the embassy and took fifty-two members of its staff hostage. It was the harbouring of the Shah that clinched it, one of the hostage takers later admitted. The Islamist radicals had long memories. They recalled that the last time the Shah had fled into exile, in 1953, just before the CIA coup of Mosaddegh, the USA had returned him to the throne, along with several million dollars to keep him in their pocket. Seeing history repeating itself, Khomeini's revolutionaries feared that the USA was about to return the Shah to power once again; the storming of the embassy was their response. It was the last straw in the volatile relationship between Iran and the Great Satan. Four hundred and forty-four days later, when the hostages were eventually released, it was obvious that diplomatic relations between the two countries could never resume. Sanctions were imposed and the big freeze began.

The embassy complex had certainly not been neglected by its hosts in the intervening years. I was surprised to see that the exterior was in good shape and in particular the colourful murals that adorned its long low walls. The Iranian government had been busy and imaginative; a skull-headed Statue of Liberty leered over the American flag, its red stripes morphing into barbed-wire as they extended over a map of Iran. A black-gloved hand bearing Israeli and American flag wristbands gripped the globe, and just in case you were in any doubt about the overarching message, freshly painted bold capital letters screamed DOWN WITH USA.

There was no denying that the artwork was well executed. Under the suspicious gaze of twitchy guards with their AK-47s, I studied the murals, wishing I could have been a fly on the wall at the brainstorming sessions that resulted in these images. Whoever the artists were, they certainly had their work cut out; these vast anti-US murals appeared across Tehran, usually featuring the Stars and Stripes, images of bombs, guns and other symbols of military oppression and the ubiquitous slogan *Down with USA*. But despite the fresh paint the message felt antiquated and tired. There was something passé about the whole thing, but charmingly retro too, as if the Islamic Republic had employed Wolfie Smith as their copywriter. *Nobody says 'Down With' anymore*, I wanted to tell the gun-toting guards, *it's just so seventies*.

Back in the northern suburbs, Omid and Tala plunged me into their social whirl. By night we dined, danced and partied with all the illicit accoutrements one could hope for. Jack Daniels and Smirnoff were easy to come by, gin and decent wine not so much.

'I do miss a good French red,' Omid told me, with a mournful smile, recalling his days as a London restaurateur.

Hash, heroin, ham, hip-hop and heavy metal were all equally illegal, and just as accessible, if you knew who to call.

'I can get you bacon if you want,' offered Omid with the sneaky wink of a playground drug dealer. I almost felt I was disappointing him by being a vegetarian.

Living day to day with Omid and his family, meeting their friends and colleagues, I became fully aware of, and immersed in, the low-level subversion involved in everyday life in Iran. Sanction-busting business deals are facilitated through Dubai or Turkey, the internet is accessed by VPNs – Virtual Private Networks that reroute your server to a different country in order to circumvent the state censorship. Low-cut tops and tight skirts are hidden beneath shapeless manteaus and blonde highlights beneath plain headscarves. Parties and gigs are strictly word of mouth in private homes, and special buses with curtained windows are chartered by night to take groups of young ravers out to the desert to secret locations.

'The authorities know exactly what goes on,' said Omid, echoing the words of Raha, the young businesswoman I had met in the hotel. 'They're in it up to their necks. They organise all the smuggling, the booze, the satellite TV, prostitution; it's a big racket run by the Revolutionary Guards. And everyone knows it.'

I was stirred and inspired by all this subversive defiance. No amount of revolutionary rhetoric blasting from the radio and television, or moralistic messages bearing down from billboards and murals around the city, seemed to make a dent. After thirty-five years the weary Tehranis had heard it all and it had become no more than tedious background noise. Human desires cannot be contained so easily, and it seemed that nothing would stop the inhabitants of this city squeezing the joy out of life, as if the repression and constant hectoring made them even more intent on living every moment. But Omid was growing weary of it all.

'We want to leave Iran,' he explained as we drove home one night, slightly drunkenly, from a birthday party in the northern suburbs. 'Get out before Sorena has to wear the veil at school – nine years old they make them wear it. It's bullshit.'

We shot through some red lights and found ourselves stationary, stuck in a lengthy traffic jam.

'And also, so she doesn't have to do this kind of thing . . .' He was pointing out of the window at the multiple lanes of traffic that had slowed to a virtual standstill. I noticed all the cars were brand new luxury SUVs and sports cars, many with blacked-out windows and tricked-out features. We crawled along, suddenly conspicuous in our little Peugeot saloon among the Porsches and Maseratis.

'What do you mean?'

'I wanted to show you this,' Omid said. 'This is Iran Zamin Boulevard, this is a Tehran phenomenon. This is how young rich kids in Tehran get laid.'

I looked at the scene around me and spied a few glamorous girls peeking out of their car windows behind giant designer sunglasses, despite the fact it was two o'clock in the morning.

'This is the pick-up strip,' said Omid. 'Groups of boys, groups of girls all come out in cars that Daddy bought for them, they drive up and down for hours, checking each other out, then they pass notes with their phone numbers. Half of their fathers will be working for the government,' he added.

It was a sight to behold. Some of the fancier cars had pulled over, holding up the traffic while their drivers lounged, peacock style, on the bonnets. Flashes of bling sparkled under the streetlights as girls craned out of their windows for a better look, eyeing up the goods on offer.

'Or sometimes they drive off somewhere and do it in the back of the car,' said Omid with a grin.

The whole futility of the Islamic Republic was embodied in this most blatant celebration of consumerism and carnal desire.

'Will you ever move back to London?' I asked him as we snaked our way through the hormone-fuelled congestion.

'Maybe, but it's too expensive there now. We'd like to live in Thailand. We go there a lot, we love it there. The people are so friendly.'

I said that I had been moved by the kindness and hospitality I had encountered here in Iran, but he was sceptical.

'Yes, people will be friendly to you because you are a foreigner, a visitor. That is part of our culture, to welcome strangers, but if you are an Iranian, it is different. We have to be careful with people we don't know. We cannot just make new friends with people we meet. In Tehran people have their own group of friends they can trust and they keep it like that. It's the same everywhere in Iran. You don't know who is involved in anything. There are informers all over, and you can't always tell by looking at them.'

'It seems like clothing is a kind of code here, how women wear their scarves or if the guys wear jeans and trainers?'

'Yes, you know that a woman in a black chador will be religious, an Islamist. We wouldn't mix with people like that, I hate to even see these idiots! You know, I've seen these women attacking young girls in public, actually fighting them in the street because of their clothes and hair. Crazy!' He shook his head. 'But you can't ever be too careful. One time I was in the police station, just to see a guy I know who worked there, and I saw their undercover agents being briefed. They looked like these kids . . .'

He motioned out of the window at a group of overly groomed young men strutting past in distinctly un-Islamic tight T-shirts bearing designer logos, skinny jeans and expensive Nikes. Their hair was gelled and spiked, gold chains glinted at their necks and wrists, you could almost smell the aftershave.

'The guys in the police station, they were young, dressed like that, wearing *I Love NY* T-shirts, you know? They were being sent out as a set-up. No, you can't trust anyone.'

He shook his head again and flung the car sharply to the left to avoid a motorcyclist who was careering towards us, simultaneously texting on his iPhone while smoking a cigarette.

'Look at that nutter! Classic!' He roared with laughter. 'Don't get me wrong, I love Iran in many ways, but not what it's become under these donkeys. But I don't like what England has become either. So many rules now in Europe, different kind of rules to here but so much restriction compared to when I was there in the eighties. It sounds crazy, I know, but in some ways we are more free here. It's more real here. Look!' He gestured around him at the heaving streets and the honking horns. 'This is real life, you feel alive here! When I visit England it is like people are walking around half dead the whole time! This is real!'

Real. It was the same word that Hossein had used to describe his reason for returning to Iran from Canada. I was beginning to understand what they meant. I could feel this 'realness' around me all the time in Iran, and it was energising. It felt like it was how humans were supposed to interact with each other; look each other in the eye and talk about the things that really mattered, really feel everything, and not worry about the little things. I suddenly had the chilling thought that maybe this *joie de vivre* was because of living under an oppressive regime, rather than in spite of it. But when I put this idea to Omid he disagreed.

'No, this is how it is to be Iranian. We were like this before
the revolution and we will always be this way. We love life.'

'I need to show you something' he said suddenly and swung
the car around. We began heading into the steep streets that snake
out of north Tehran and towards the foothills of the Alborz. After
a while he pulled over and pointed across the road.

'Look. Do you know what this is?'

I stared out of the car window, seeing nothing but high concrete
walls stretching down a dark, shabby street.

'Evin Prison,' he said. 'This is the other side of life in Iran. If
you're not careful.'

I studied the plain anonymous walls. You could walk past and
never know. In the dark of the night the scene took on an even
more sinister edge.

'Don't take photos,' said Omid. 'You know what happened to
that Canadian journalist? She took photos of the prison. Next
thing, she's dead. Tortured, raped, beaten to death.'

The prison had been built in the 1970s, under the reign of the
Shah, and run by SAVAK, to house a few hundred people,
including Khomeini himself at one time. Now its population is
in the thousands, and the reports from the few that have been
released are chilling. Rape, torture, beatings and even enforced
druggings are used to elicit confessions once prisoners are addicted
and left to go cold turkey. Iran's government does not recognise
the category of political prisoner, but by all accounts there is an
entire wing created solely for dissidents, the notorious Section
209, a top-secret detention area allegedly run by Iran's Ministry
of Intelligence. At any one time it contains hundreds of journal-
ists, bloggers and anti-regime activists, members of banned
political movements, lawyers and intellectuals; even students and
foreign tourists suspected of spying are considered fair game.
Anyone arrested for criticising the regime ends up in Section 209.
Many never see trial, some are never seen again.

Unsurprisingly, conditions at Evin are brutal, with prisoners crammed into tiny spaces, either in total darkness or under flick-ering strip lights twenty-four hours a day, unable to wash or even lie down. Illnesses such as hepatitis are rife and medical care basic at best. Food is poor and when prisoners are released they return to the world broken in all senses of the word: deafened and blinded from beatings, malnourished, sick and mentally and emotionally damaged by the psychological torture. I recalled Hossein's story of his work colleague who had disappeared for two weeks and returned a ruined, silenced man. I wondered if this is where he had spent that lost fortnight. A chill ran through me as I stared at the high walls. What freedoms I took for granted back home.

'I spent a night in there once,' said Omid.

'What for?'

'I was a teenager. A bunch of us were out driving around, messing about. The police picked us up and put us in a cell for a night. My dad got me out the next day. I was lucky. It's a different story these days. It's been packed since the 2009 protests, after the election. Thousands of people were arrested after that. Hundreds have just disappeared. People don't even know if their own kids are in there, if they're alive or dead. This is why we have to get out of this country.'

'They execute people here too,' he continued. 'They hang them. It used to be firing squads and even stoning, but these days it's always hangings. They used to do public hangings, I remember that when I was a child. I went to see one, once. Lots of people turned out to watch, but they don't do it in public anymore.'

'Will Rouhani try to change this? Surely he can't be seen to be bringing Iran in from the cold, doing trade deals, speaking at the UN, and still be allowing this to be happening?'

As I spoke I knew it was a naive question, and that I already knew the answer.

'Rouhani is just a sop,' said Omid. 'He's been put in place to keep the masses happy, to stop more protests like the ones in 2009.

He can't change anything, even if he wanted to. But the idiots have fallen for it, they think he's going to save Iran!'

I thought of my hopeful psychology student, working hard, studying, pumping gas, predicting a great new dawn for Iran under the new president. And of glamorous Raha and her brave new world of luxury brand management. Had they been duped?

We drove back through the dark streets. Behind the locked door Omid poured drinks and we sprawled in front of the television, flicking between channels, catching up on world news and casually browsing the internet. Normality and domesticity reigned once again but outside the machinations of deceit, intimidation and fear continued to churn. Behind the locked doors of Evin Prison, hundreds of men and women who had dared to speak the truth awaited trials that would never come and wondered if they would ever see their families again.

9

All Different, All Relative:
Iran's Forgotten Explorer

WHILE IN TEHRAN, I had some detective work to do.
Somewhere among the twelve million inhabitants of the
city was an elderly gentleman in his eighties that I was keen to
track down.

Issa Omidvar had been something of a celebrity in pre-
revolutionary Iran, appearing weekly on national television until
1979, when Khomeini's new regime crushed his career overnight.
Now he lives in relative obscurity; only a few Iranians of a certain
age still recall his exploits, but I was on a mission to introduce
him to a new generation of fans. Issa is one half of the Omidvar
brothers, Iran's only global explorers and self-styled anthropolo-
gists who spent a decade travelling the world by motorcycle and
filming their adventures. Between 1954 and 1964 they crossed
every continent, documenting endangered tribes in a style that
fused gonzoesque immersion with scholarly sensitivity. Nothing
was too outré, dangerous or extreme for the Omidvars, but their
gung-ho approach was tempered by what I was now beginning
to understand as a particularly Persian phenomenon; a unique
blend of humanity, humour and razor-sharp intellect.

I had become aware of Issa and his brother Abdullah a few
years earlier, while researching an article I was writing about early
overland expeditions. It was easy enough to find British, Americans
and Europeans who had pioneered long-distance overland travel

in the colonial era, but upon digging a little deeper I came upon a grainy black-and-white photograph on an obscure German website. It depicted two dashing young men wearing casual shirts and goggles, astride 1950s motorcycles. Further digging and some sketchy translation revealed them as the Omidvar brothers of Iran, who, according to the caption, had made a circumnavigation of the world on two British-made bikes. This discovery led me to a web page in Persian that looked as though it had been designed, and subsequently abandoned, in the early dawn of the internet, but beyond that, the trail went cold. Who were these mysterious Iranian adventurers? Were they still alive? How had their story been forgotten so quickly? Intrigued, I rounded up a Persian-speaking friend in London who called her aunt in Tehran, and we set about trying to find anyone in Iran who knew anything about the Omidvar brothers.

We discovered that Abdullah had been living in Chile since the 1960s but Issa was alive and well in Iran, serving as keeper of the Omidvar brothers' flame. After many phone calls and emails between London and Tehran, I could hardly believe it when an envelope bearing Iranian stamps arrived in my letterbox. It contained a home-burned DVD of the brothers' documentaries. The footage was almost unreal, a 1950s *Boys Own* comic come to life; the brothers deep in the Amazon transporting their bikes in a dug-out canoe, eating maggots and monkeys with a tribe of headshrinkers; in Alaska watching Eskimos catapult their children into the air to seek out animals to hunt, and taking part in African tribal rituals involving Abdullah in a trance-like state spearing his face with metal spikes. Wearing my other hat, as a founder of the Adventure Travel Film Festival, I emailed Issa to ask if we could show the film at our UK festival. He agreed. It was the first time their documentaries would be screened in the West.

Omid was too young to remember the Omidvars' weekly television show, but when I showed him the footage he became equally intrigued by their story. With a few phone calls he discovered that Issa now curated a mini-museum about his travels, based in north Tehran. Further investigation revealed that he attended his museum once a month and that with serendipitous fortune, his next visit was planned for two days' time, just before I was due to leave town.

The Omidvars' treasure trove was tucked away in a leafy corner of the grounds of the Sa'adabad Palace Complex, another of the Shah's former homes, comprised of eighteen suitably grand buildings scattered across more than 100 hectares of mountain parkland on the northern edge of Tehran. Here the excesses of the Pahlavi dynasty are available for all to see, frozen in time, as if it was only yesterday the Shah had hotfooted it to the States. It was through these gates that CIA agents had been smuggled, hidden under blankets in the back seats of cars, arriving in the dead of night to brief the Shah on the details of the plot to oust Mosaddegh, and in these sumptuous rooms that the details of the coup were hatched. While it was fascinating to examine the furnishings, paintings, collections of photographs, letters and personal effects, including the Shah's car and motorcycle collection, the most striking sight in the entire complex stood outside the palace: two giant, disembodied bronze legs, the remaining half of Reza Shah's statue, the head and torso having been felled during the revolution when protestors stormed the palace and sawed the figure in two. Now his legs stand Ozymandias style, vast and trunkless, at over eight feet tall, the top of his Cossack boots level with my armpit.

Omid and Tala, both true *bon vivants*, took the nostalgic view of the Shah's era, and as we toured the site they talked wistfully of the old days of freedom and fun. I could see that between the two regimes, the Pahlavis must now seem infinitely preferable to the reality of the Islamic Republic. If oppression is a dish that must be served with a side order, then let it be glamour and excess rather than religion and hypocrisy.

A steep, winding trail took us to the small outbuilding that contained the Omidvars' collection. Through the trees, outside the entrance, I caught a glimpse of the brothers' road-weary motorcycles that I recognised from the films, displayed alongside a 1960s Citroen 2CV they had used to traverse the Sahara, bleached and battered from the desert sand and sun. The front mudguards of the motorcycles still bore the message they had taken around the world, hand-painted in both Persian and English, *All different, all relative*, and on the rear, simply the word *Peace*. It seemed a world away from the stance of the Islamic Republic, and even from the bombastic pomp of the Shah's era, but in another sense it was an embodiment of the time when Iran was a world player. In many ways the Omidvars' timing had been perfect; with colonial rule discredited and unravelling, their non-European status and open-minded, gentle approach, 'neither East nor West', proved a great asset to their explorations, especially in their interactions with native tribes. Sadly, the Islamic Republic put paid to all that; a young Iranian wanting to follow in the Omidvars' footsteps these days would not get far. As everyone I met was keen to tell me, to travel with an Iranian passport nowadays means an onslaught of searches, suspicion and declined visas, but sixty years ago it was positively an advantage.

Entering the building was like stepping into the pages of a Tintin book. My first thought, as a fellow two-wheeled globetrotter and souvenir collector, was of all the admin that would have been involved in sending this stuff home – how the hell did one get a shrunken head through customs? The room was bursting with poison-tipped darts, blowpipes, tribal masks, spears, elephants' feet, animal-skin drums and, courtesy of the Amazonian Jivaro tribe, two tiny shrivelled human heads, blackened with age but clearly possessing the fair hair and European features of some unfortunate swashbuckler. Black-and-white photographs of the brothers in the most extreme and exotic situations covered the walls; a boa constrictor wrapped around Abdullah's neck, Issa filming African pygmies on his huge 16 mm clockwork Bolex, the two brothers digging their sinking car out of a Saharan sand

ALL DIFFERENT, ALL RELATIVE: IRAN'S FORGOTTEN EXPLORER

dune and taking part in ritualistic tribal ceremonies with dervishes and witch doctors. At the other extreme were images of the boys impeccably turned out in suits and ties, meeting foreign dignitaries, grinning excitedly with glamorous princesses and posing in front of the Eiffel Tower.

A door opened and from the small office a museum employee entered with Issa. Although tiny in stature, his beaming smile and energy filled the room. Beyond the white hair and elegant suit, you could still see the eager, curious boy who had dreamed of seeing the world. His assistant explained to him that I was the lady from London who had shown his films in England. He waved his arms in the air, and if we had been somewhere else in the world, I sensed he would have flung them around me in a welcoming embrace.

'No! Really? It is you! I cannot believe you are here in Tehran!'

I told him I had come to Iran on my bike and he fairly hopped up and down in excitement. As we walked through the museum, talking through his exhibits and memories, we chatted like all motorcycle travellers do, of our experiences on the road, the ups and downs of two-wheeled adventures, of getting cold, wet and lost, of punctures, breakdowns, and the kindness of strangers, and compared places we had both seen, many decades apart. His enthusiasm was infectious and even now, in his eighties, he fizzed with energy, insight and warmth, and a distinctly cheeky sense of humour.

'We left Iran, August 1954,' he said, pointing at a photo of him and Abdullah ready for the off, fresh-faced astride their mint-condition bikes, a group of friends and family holding the Quran over their heads. 'We left with just ninety dollars each! Can you believe this?'

'How did you survive?'

'We carried Persian artworks and photographs of Iran and everywhere we went, we made shows about Iran at universities and embassies, everywhere! This way, we met many important people too. Sherpa Tensing, Indira Gandhi, many heads of state. But most of all, for us, we were interested in the tribal people. Because we could see how the world was changing so quickly, that many of these tribes in Africa, the Amazon, even the Eskimos, their lives would not last for very long like this. We wanted to document this, to show the world and to understand.'

By way of illustration he paused at a photograph of Abdullah squatting down in a mud-hut village with a colossal reel-to-reel tape machine, surrounded by a circle of bemused, grass-skirted tribesmen.

'This is in the Amazon, the Yagua tribe. Sometimes it took many weeks, sometimes months for them to trust us, to allow us to film. In Africa, they thought our camera was a magic box! They did not trust it for a long time.'

'Do you think being Iranian was helpful in your travels?'

'Yes, sometimes, because in Africa there were many wars for independence at this time. This was early 1960s so everywhere we go, they do not like the French, or the British.' He grinned, apologetically. 'But in those days, Iran was not a bad word, not like now. Even the Arabs looked after us so well in Saudi Arabia. We met the Saudi king, and also the father of Osama Bin Laden.'

'What was he like?'

Issa gave a dismissive wave. 'Not an impressive man. Not educated, he had never left his own country. But still he had three private jets!

'We went to Mecca, of course, this is important pilgrimage for all Muslims, to do this once in our life. But you know to film in Mecca is forbidden? So my brother, Abdullah, he hides the camera under his robes and he says he has stomach surgery and this noise,' – Issa made a comedy impression of a whirring film camera – 'he says this is his mechanical stomach!' He doubled up with laughter at the memory.

'Lois, you will know this because you have travelled also, but people are very friendly everywhere. Even in America, Abdullah, he was hit by a car and the driver's son, he came to find us in the hospital and says we must stay with him until he recovered. This, I believe, is the essence of humanity. You understand?'

'Yes, of course. I have many stories of kindness like that too, from all over the world.'

'The only problems we have is the Jivaro tribe in Amazon, they became very drunk at a celebration, they make this alcohol from bananas and' – he mimicked a spitting motion – 'their own saliva! They wanted to shrink our heads, like this . . .' He pointed to the two shrivelled skulls. 'This one, it is an unlucky German man. We were lucky. We escape in the canoe but, peeow, peeow!' Issa made ducking motions to accompany his sound effects. 'They shoot poisoned darts at us. But we got away.' He tapped his skull. 'And with our heads still the same size!'

'No,' he continued once he had stopped laughing, 'the only problems with being Iranian, were in South Africa. Because of, you know, the apartheid system there. We have big problems because the white people in South Africa, they do not like Asians, but the black people, they think we are white men! It was very sad, really, to see this terrible system. It was very difficult for us. We were not welcome by any of them. This is not how mankind is meant to live. You know our motto, all different, all relative. I still believe this.' He nodded quietly for a moment before his usual smile returned.

'And you know what our name means, yes? Omidvar? *Omid* is the Persian word for "hope". Omidvar it means to be 'hopeful'. I think I could not have been blessed with a better name, no?

'But this,' he said, pointing to a photo of bare-breasted tribes-women, 'this was really the biggest problem for us after we come home. When Khomeini takes over, no more of this, not suitable for Islamic Republic!'

Issa gave a sardonic laugh and shook his head.

'I think of this problem in the Amazon, I say to Abdullah, Muslims in Iran will not like to see naked women, so I found some cloth and I give it to the tribeswomen. But they did not understand. They say, why wear this cloth, there is no reason to be ashamed. But they like the cloth so they kept it to decorate their homes instead!'

'So was it a problem to show this on Iranian television?' I asked.

'No, not during the time of the Shah, but after the revolution, suddenly, no more television show. We used to be on the national channel, every Friday evening, it is like your David Attenborough, yes? And we toured the country, showing our films at cinemas all over Iran. Then, bang! Psst! No more.' He shook his head and then gave me a saucy grin. 'Just breasts, nothing to be scared of!' He burst out laughing again.

'But even now, I make our book just this last year, and look,' – he opened the page to the offending photo – 'English edition OK, Spanish edition OK. But Iranian edition, no, this photo not allowed.'

'Did you ever consider living in another country after your travels, like your brother?'

'Afterwards, I spent time in India but I always came back to Iran. Abdullah, he married a Chilean woman, this is why he stayed there.'

'Do you miss him? Do you stay in touch?'

'Of course, and my son too. He lives in the UK, in Cardiff. He is a doctor there. He says to me, "Dad, why do you live in Iran?" And I say to him, well, I think this is the biggest adventure of all!'

Issa laughed until the elephants tusks shook in their glass case.

After my tour of the museum, I said to Issa that I'd like to buy the English version of his book and asked if he could dedicate it to my husband, also a great motorcycle traveller and film-maker.

Issa looked astounded. 'You have a husband?'

I nodded, wondering if I had broken some code or unwittingly overstepped a mark. I was still finding my way around Iranian social protocol and constantly feared making some accidental faux pas.

'But where is he, where is your husband?'

'At home, in London.'

He looked perplexed. 'Your husband is at your home in London, and he, he—' Issa struggled for the words. 'He lets you ride your motorcycle to Iran, all alone?'

Cautiously, I answered in the affirmative, still not sure where this was going.

Issa's face, always expressive, was agog. He banged a fist on the glass cabinet and waved his arms in the air. Then he brought his fist down again and shouted, 'I think that is *great!*'

He signed the book with a flourish and looked me in the eye, smiling. 'Lois-*jan*,' he said, using the Persian affectionate term meaning 'dear', 'I can tell you will be successful in your life. Iranian women, they are so oppressed. It is so very sad. Many of them, they come here to see me, and they tell me how they would love to do what I did, to travel the world, to ride a motorcycle, to be free. It makes me very sad but I am happy when I see you, and what you are doing. You are seeing the world on a motorcycle, the real world!'

One of these women had just arrived, bearing a bunch of roses for Issa. She was a regular visitor, by all accounts, who travelled over 300 miles from the city of Yadz to see Issa every time he made his monthly visit to the museum.

'Oh, I just love him so much,' she said, touching her heart with typical Iranian passion. 'He is my great hero and such an amazing man.'

She can't have been much older than me so wouldn't have remembered his television shows or been aware of his adventures at the time. But she was a true believer and loyal follower. Issa greeted her like an old friend, making a sweet fuss over the flowers.

His assistant made a few calls and rounded up the official photographer of the museum complex, telling her about my travels and how Issa's films had been shown at our festival in England.

The photographer, a young diligent woman in official uniform, took some time to adjust my headscarf, tucking any stray strands of hair out of sight before positioning Issa and me at a suitably modest distance apart from each other for the pictures. The results looked awkward and stiff, so different from the animated conversation and laughter we had shared over the last hour.

When the time came to say goodbye to Issa I had to quell my natural urge to give him a hug. We had bonded easily and warmly and I had felt an instant connection with him. Here was a man from a different era, continent and culture but, as I was well aware from my time on the road, the camaraderie of motorcycle travellers does not recognise such borders. However in the Islamic Republic there could be no hug, not even a friendly pat on the shoulder; we couldn't even shake hands. I sensed Issa felt the same but, unable to act upon our human instincts, we just stood facing each other, about three feet apart, and bid each other farewell. With his right hand to his heart he gently bowed his head, wishing me good luck on my travels in Iran and extending an invitation to visit him at his home in Tehran any time. I dearly hoped we would meet again somewhere.

Back at Omid and Tala's house, it was time to start thinking about moving on. My visa was ticking, Shiraz was still 600 miles away, and I had plenty of detours to make along the way. But it was going to be hard to wrench myself away from my adoptive Iranian family. Despite having made it this far alone, just a week of comfy sofas, home-cooked dinners and convivial companionship had softened me up. The world beyond Omid's gate seemed daunting again, Iran's mean streets more intimidating than enticing, and Omid was also starting to worry on my behalf, which only made it worse.

'Don't go out alone at night; keep your money hidden. I'll put some of your cash in a bank account and you can use the debit card, that way you don't have to worry about being robbed.'

Until then I hadn't worried about it at all. Now my mind was running wild.

Ayatollahs Khomeini and Khamenei, former and current Supreme Leaders of Iran, adorn everything; from buildings to banknotes and stamps to stadia.

My journey coincided with the first phone call between the American and Iranian presidents for over three decades. This historic moment dominated the news stands and was the hottest topic on the streets.

Who wants to be a millionaire? It's easy in Iran! With its bewildering amount of zeroes, the rial is in dire need of devaluation. This is the equivalent of about US $400.

In a country with few supermarkets, the bazaar is at the heart of Iranian life. All you need is here, from gleaming chandeliers to counterfeit western perfume brands. Hugo Boss and Davidoff Echo are some of the knock-off fragrances on offer in the bazaar of Tabriz.

High in the Alborz Mountains, attempting to reach the Caspian Sea. The pass was snowed in at 3,000 metres, forcing me to turn back and take an alternative route. I would not have got this far without my trail bike.

Official anti-US murals are found all over Tehran. This one adorns the wall of the former US embassy, stormed in 1979 during the Iran 'hostage crisis'. It has never reopened and is now maintained and patrolled by the Revolutionary Guards.

The legs of Reza Shah, standing outside his former palace in north Tehran; the upper body was sawn off by revolutionaries in 1979.

Meeting the great Iranian explorer Issa Omidvar. He and his brother travelled the world by motorcycle between 1954 and 1964, documenting the lives of tribal communities. Their films were featured on Iranian television during the 1960s and '70s.

Fin Gardens in Kashan.
Persian gardens are a triumph
of ingenuity and design, oases
of tranquillity that provide
much needed respite from
the chaos of the streets.

Isfahan is 'half
the world',
according to an
ancient Persian
proverb. Although
frequently quoted,
when you get
there, you truly
understand why.

Iranians will picnic
anywhere: truck
stops, roundabouts,
motorway verges,
central reservations
. . .As a guest in
their country, I was
invariably invited to
join the feast.

In the tribal areas of the Zagros Mountains the boys travel around on little motorcycles, whereas the older generation opt for a lower carbon footprint.

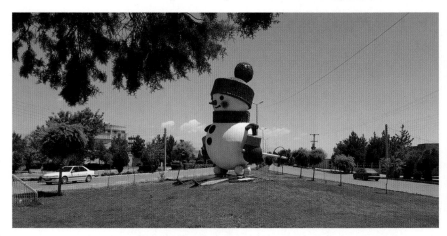

However small the town, it always features a vast, and often charmingly inappropriate, diorama of public art. Here, on the edge of a sun-baked desert, is a colossal snowman complete with skis and bobble hat, obviously.

Despite Iran's censoring of the internet, the police have no problem accessing Google Translate.

A complex of palaces built by the Persian king, Darius, Persepolis is a unique hybrid of Greek, Assyrian and Persian influences. Built around 515 BC it survived less than 300 years before it was sacked by Alexander the Great.

Famed British explorer Henry Morton Stanley left his mark at the ruins of Persepolis. Now a UNESCO World Heritage Site, graffiti is no longer encouraged.

Iran is a nation
of bibliophiles.
Bookshops and
stalls are plentiful,
and poetry is
celebrated by all.

Built as a royal court, and
later used as a prison, the late
eighteenth-century fortress
Arg-e Karim Khan dominates
the centre of Shiraz. One of its
turrets now leans considerably,
having subsided into the
underground bathhouse.

The bazaar of Shiraz is a
warren of alleys and arches,
all providing unofficial
motorcycle parking for the
city's thousands of bikes.

'You'll be all right once you get to Shiraz – the people there are the best, everyone loves the Shirazis – but be careful in Isfahan. The Isfahanis can't be trusted, they're a dodgy lot. Always on the make. And whatever you do, don't take photos of any military buildings or nuclear sites, or any government or official buildings. You don't want to end up in Evin Prison.'

He grinned to suggest this was a joke but we both knew it was entirely possible. All the fears I had successfully vanquished in the previous weeks were now roaring their way back into my consciousness.

'People are going to find it strange, a foreign woman alone on a motorbike,' Omid continued. 'You'll probably get stopped by the police a lot. They might want to question you, take you to the station, check your papers. Be careful who you talk to and what you say; don't tell people where you're going or where you're staying.'

The pull of the road battled with the fear of the unknown, as ever, but I knew the road would win. It always does. I just needed, as my American friends would have it, to grow a pair. If only I could, I thought, ironically; that's exactly what you need to get on in the Islamic Republic of Iran.

'I've been thinking,' said Omid later that evening. 'Before you leave, I think you should meet someone, a friend of mine, he could be quite helpful. He's one of the top guys in the secret police. I've arranged to meet up with him tomorrow afternoon.'

Omid obviously sensed my wariness about voluntarily meeting with a head honcho of the Revolutionary Guards.

'Don't worry, he's all right. He wants to get out of the job but they won't let him. He keeps trying to resign but he's in too deep. He's helped me out in the past, and I've helped him out with stuff. He's a useful guy to know. It would be good to have him on your side, he could pull a few strings if necessary, y'know, just in case anything goes wrong, or you get in any trouble.'

Omid was a master of making the system work in his favour.

He knew when to speak up and when to keep quiet. He knew who to call if you needed a car, the latest iPhone, a pack of bacon, a pound of opium, or the necessary piece of paperwork for whatever business deal was going down, so it wasn't a surprise that one of Iran's top policemen featured on his speed dial list. He understood the importance of keeping friends close, and your enemies closer. Simply, he knew how to survive in Iran.

The following afternoon Omid, Tala, Sorena and I convened at the appointed time. The venue was a traditional tea-house garden where we lounged, half outdoors, half indoors, in little wooden huts among overhanging trees, reclining amongst mounds of cushions, slipping off our shoes and stretching out our legs on soft Persian carpets. The sun was warm, the tea hot and strong, served in tiny glasses with sugar cubes and a bowl of fruit. Omid ordered a *qalyān* and some melon-flavoured tobacco, passing the pipe between us. A gentle breeze rustled the leaves of the trees and the afternoon sunlight streamed through the water vapour from the pipe while the sweet smell of the tobacco drifted around us. It was a scene of serenity, peace and good cheer. We drank tea, chatted and laughed, and Sorena coloured in pictures in a drawing book and taught me some Persian words, much to her amusement. Then our visitor arrived.

It wasn't anything specific, just a subtle shift in the mood. We were introduced and I was greeted with a curt nod. As is usually the case between men and women who are not known to each other, he sat away from me so Omid and he were together, with me, Tala and Sorena at a slight distance in the other corner. Omid made some valiant and cheerful attempts at group conversation, telling his friend about my journey, but I could feel the frosty air permeating our cosy little nest. He made brief acknowledgements of my presence, as little as he could without appearing obviously impolite, but eye contact was avoided after our initial introduction. During the conversation he never addressed me in person, and I noticed that whenever I took a toke on the *qalyān*, he made a point of looking away.

There was much debate in Iran at the time about women smoking *qalyān*. Although the tradition goes back centuries, and in small villages you will see elderly ladies smoking, there had been a recent call from government ministers for women to be banned from partaking in the habit. This was not directed at the villagers so much, but was more of an insidious attempt to clamp down on what was seen as licentious behaviour amongst young urbanites. A five-year ban on the practice had been lifted in 2012 and now it was one of the few activities that men and women could enjoy together in public, with the result that many tea houses had become zones of what the state considered to be blatant debauchery – boys and girls mingling together, talking, laughing and sharing a pipe. Only recently, the commander of Iran's police force, the boss of the man who was currently shooting me disapproving vibes, had criticised the new wave of contemporary tea houses and coffee shops, describing them as immoral and improper, encouraging corrupt behaviour, and demanded they be closed down. The owners of the tea houses and women's rights campaigners were both arguing fervently against the move, albeit with different motivations.

After a while the conversation slipped into Persian only, with the men talking in serious tones, about what, I could not tell but it was most definitely a closed shop. A few words were spoken to Tala, and shortly after, she quietly suggested, in her most gentle and kindly way, that we should probably head back home. I gathered up my belongings, slipped my shoes back on and realised that 'we' meant me and her only. Sorena stayed behind with her dad. I wasn't sure exactly what had gone down and I sensed that Tala was trying to avoid making me feel uncomfortable, so I didn't pursue the topic. But from the little she said, it was clear that it was considered inappropriate for the police chief to be seen in my company.

This incident only served to fan the flames of my trepidation about hitting the road alone again. There were so many social mores and subtle aspects of behaviour that seemed so normal to me but that could easily trip me up, and this brush with the authorities had not emboldened me, if anything it had made me more wary. If only everyone was like Issa Omidvar, but I feared it would be a while before the Islamic Republic adopted 'All different, all relative' as their official motto. I spent the evening studying my map, planning my route out of Tehran the following day, aware that there was so much more to navigate here than just the tangle of motorways.

10

I Fought the Law

I HAD BEEN in Tehran for over a week and it was time to hit the road once again. I was not yet halfway through my journey to Shiraz and although I had managed to extend my visa, the bulk of my miles were still ahead of me. Omid and Tala offered to escort me out of Tehran. Not wanting to put them to any trouble, I protested, part *ta'arof*, part English politeness, but was secretly relieved when they insisted. The route across town to the start of the main southbound road out of the city was complicated and although travelling in convoy would have me sitting in miles of traffic jams rather than ducking and weaving through the gaps, it would make the navigation simpler, easing me back into the routine. And I was reluctant to say goodbye to these dear friends who had taken such good care of me; I wanted to squeeze out every last minute of our time together.

The sun was baking the streets by mid morning, the density of traffic and pollution already at oppressive levels. Overheated and uncomfortable, wrapped up in my Islamic motorcycling get-up, I longed for the open road and the clean desert air that awaited me beyond Tehran. In any other country, it would have been a jeans and T-shirt day, but this was only an option for the men who whizzed past me on their mopeds, cigarettes and mobile phones in hand. Some of the older men sported suits or formal jackets on their motorbikes, looking incongruously smart amongst the chaos of their surroundings. Tehran had a relatively new and efficient Metro system as well as the battered public buses, antiquated and segregated, and an endless stream of *savaari* taxis that plied regular routes. But most Tehranis preferred to run the gauntlet in their own wheels, whether it was the ubiquitous Paykans, the Iranian version of the 1960s Hillman Hunter, or the latest SUVs, shipped in from Dubai with an eye-watering one hundred per cent customs duty. To tackle the Tehranis' love affair with the car, the authorities had introduced a system whereby only certain numbered plates could enter the city centre on certain days, but it made little difference – people just bought a second vehicle. As I plunged into this anarchy for the last time, eyes pinned on Omid's rear bumper in front, I felt a pang of sadness about leaving Tehran. I had become strangely fond of the city, with its layer upon layer of intrigue, double dealing and whispered stories. It was dirty, noisy and chaotic but it was also subversive, creative and truly alive, a testament to human ingenuity and the Iranian spirit.

The midday heat was rising off the tarmac as we negotiated Tehran's jungle of freeways. I noticed a few cars and small groups of people had pulled over on the grassy motorway junctions and verges, and assumed their cars had overheated, but then realised I was mistaken. I had seen similar scenes in the more rural areas in the north of the country, but I hadn't expected to see the same phenomenon here in the capital. Iranians had clearly not been schooled in the same motorway reverence that is drummed into us in the West, and these 'breakdowns' were in fact people having picnics – on the central reservations, roundabouts and hard shoulders. Sometimes it was just a couple of guys lounging on the grass smoking a *qalyān*, but as lunchtime approached whole families emerged, laying out rugs and tablecloths, brewing tea and breaking open the Tupperware. In my slightly anxious state it was reassuring to see these gentle scenes, the simple pleasures of life being enacted with such contentment amongst the seething madness of Tehran's streets. I recalled Freya Stark remarking on the 'charming trait' that everyone she met in Persia understood the pleasures of a picnic; it was something that connected deeply with the British psyche. As I surged in front of a dented Paykan that was trying to squeeze in between me and Omid, I thought of a line from one of Hafez's poems: 'Bring all the bottles of wine you own to this divine table – the earth we share'. The Islamic Revolution may have put paid to that idea being taken literally, but the sentiment lived on throughout Iran and this shared Anglo-Iranian love of picnicking gave me a much needed flush of optimism and a warm feeling about the rest of my trip. All different, all relative.

Then the car drove into me. It was a gentle but definite bump against my rear wheel. I glanced over my shoulder briefly but I was so focussed on keeping Omid in my sights that I didn't give it much thought. All part of the rough and tumble of Tehran traffic, where nobody gives anybody an inch. The four lanes were gridlocked, everyone bumper to bumper, horns honking, radios blasting out new music and old propaganda, the midday heat rising off the tarmac, shimmering between the cars, noxious gases and fumes lying heavy in the hot air. Street sellers dodging through the gaps, hawking chewing gum, flowers and fruit, pedestrians taking their chances with typical Tehrani fatalism. Then it happened again; the car behind rolled into the back of me, bumping against my back wheel and jolting me forward. And a third time. This time I felt some resistance as I tried to move forward and I realised that my number plate had become caught under the front bumper of the car. Now I felt slightly annoyed. I looked behind, unable to see the car's occupants clearly through the tinted windscreen, so I made waving and pointing motions. There was no response. I was entangled with their car and if I pulled away I would rip my licence plate off.

Flicking down my sidestand and dismounting from the bike, I went to the driver's window to explain my predicament, assuming they had been careless, probably distracted on the phone. The car was a big, solid Mercedes, and when the electric window made its steady descent it revealed four middle-aged men with neatly trimmed beards in open-necked shirts and suit jackets. They were laughing, the two in the back seat sprawled across the leather seats, condescension and arrogance oozing from every pore. I had spent enough time in Tehran now to have gained some sense of the subtleties and signifiers of people's appearance, and I knew immediately and instinctively that these men were not on my side.

Omid, who had been keeping an eye on me in his rear-view mirror, was out of his car and next to me right away.

'What's happened? Are you OK?'

The men were still laughing, heads cocked back, legs spread wide, confident and untouchable. Omid spoke to them in Persian as I released my bike and checked for any damage.

'They're saying that it was your fault,' said Omid, 'that you rolled your bike backwards into their car. Fucking bullshit,' he muttered as an aside.

It was the most pathetic school-yard defence, it wasn't even worth engaging in the debate. I could barely touch the ground with my tiptoes, so the idea that I could forcibly push my loaded bike backwards was just silly and we all knew it. The men were calling out of the window, words I didn't understand, but their tone was taunting. Omid was in there like a bulldog, snarling back at them. Then everything escalated. All the men were out of the car, crowding around him, posturing, threatening, everyone shouting, ten arms waving in the air, index fingers jabbing at chests. I didn't need to understand Persian. They were pointing at me, sneering, angry and dismissive.

Omid turned to me. 'I know who these guys are,' he said, 'they're security service.' He came closer, eyes flashing with fury, whispering. 'These fuckers, I know from the rings they're wearing, see those signet rings. Look, with the inscription from the Quran on them!'

I caught a glimpse of their hands, big lumps of gold, the Quranic lettering glinting in the midday sun. This was a new layer of detail to the dress code, one that I would be watching out for in future.

'I know these bastards!' Omid said under his breath. 'They're *basiji* commanders, they report to the Revolutionary Guards. These are Ahmadinejad's men!'

By now everyone was out of their cars to watch the spectacle. The street sellers had stopped their hawking, passers-by on the pavement had propped their bicycles up against the railing, forming an audience, and women were shouting messages of support for me from their cars. Even Tala, normally such a gentle, soothing presence, had steamed in. She was shouting at the men too. They turned on her now, harassing her about her headscarf not being worn correctly. This was the last straw for Omid, and I thought a fight was about to break out. Tala turned to me and gripped my arm, her beautiful face riven with anger and fear.

'Oh Lois! Do you see? Do you understand? This is why we have to leave this country, this is why we must get out of Iran! I hate this place, I hate these people!'

The crawling traffic had come to a standstill as we blocked the lane; some of the drivers had abandoned their cars, joining in, some just watching. The heat was merciless but I couldn't remove my helmet and risk exposing my hair, not in front of these men. I tried to remain calm, but my heart was racing, adrenalin coursing through my body. Omid was alternating between shouting at the men and translating their accusations.

'They're saying they're security . . . you damaged their car. They're saying . . . call the police if we want, or they will! They're going to call the police on you!'

I sat motionless on the bike, trying to still my heart and breath while Tala looked as though she was about to burst into tears.

Then Omid exploded. 'We'll fuck them up! Fucking Islamists!'

The traffic roared past on the other side of the freeway, horns blasting non-stop, shouting voices I couldn't understand all around me; fear and anger, a barrage of white noise.

'We'll fuck them up!' Omid's voice cut through the racket.

He turned back to the men and in a fast and furious stream of

Persian, I heard him mention the name of his friend who we had met yesterday, the top guy in the security services. The mood changed instantly, from shouty playground bullying to something more sinister and threatening, the men's eyes narrowing, teeth bared, nose to nose. Omid took his phone out of his pocket, ready to make the call. Suddenly they were trying to placate him, their voices now unctuous and wheedling.

Perturbed by this unexpected turn of events, the most aggressive of the men marched over to me and jabbed a finger in my face. He was attempting to speak English.

'You damage my car! You drive into me! Yes?'

He was trying to force a confession out of me. He used intimidation, then he tried cajoling, then back to the threats. Ah, so this is how it happens, this is how they do it. I remained silent. I stared at his face, looking into his eyes, feeling the full force of his loathing; his entire demeanour and tone emanated disgust, disgust at me and everything I represented. He despised me. It occurred to me that I felt exactly the same about him. If this trip was supposed to be an exercise in cultural understanding, of open-mindedness and trying to see the world from another's viewpoint, then right now I was failing. But I didn't care. Until now I had kept quiet, remained calm and purposely not engaged with the situation. But now I felt a shift inside me, a physical sensation of something rising up, boiling over. Ha! Mr Basiji, I didn't grow up in 1980s anarcho Bristol for nothing! My anti-establishment blood runs deep. An ingrained, lifelong mistrust of authority and hatred of bullies in uniform found its way to the surface right there on the baking streets of Tehran. I could not have stopped myself if I tried. And I didn't want to.

So I looked him in the eye and told him to fuck off.

No matter where you are in the world and what language you speak, everyone understands this instruction and sure enough he flinched and recoiled. For a moment he was lost for words; I watched the shock pass over his face, before it quickly turned to confusion, then fury. I wondered if a white western woman had ever spoken to him like this. I was enjoying myself now. The genie was out of the bottle.

'Fuck you! You're fucking lying and you know it.'

The others were staring now too, silenced.

'Fuck you! You drove into me on purpose, now why don't you just fuck off and leave me alone!'

His shock was replaced by anger, real fury now. The threats were in Persian and they were coming thick and fast.

Omid rushed to my side, trying to calm me down. There was a miniature crisis meeting between the men and Omid, heads together, shooting me glances as if I was some hysterical banshee that needed to be brought under control. I sensed they were telling Omid to take command of his unruly guest. They threw patronising glances my way, as if they had decided it was my time of the month.

'OK, OK. We all need to calm down,' Omid said quietly at my side. 'They're going to let it go, they're going to drop it. Let's just take it easy, let's get out of here.'

They couldn't back down that easily, so there was some more muttering and snarled, underhand threats, making out they'd done me a favour by letting me off my crime. I heard Omid mention the name of his friend again and eventually the men skulked back to their car, pride wounded but still seeping arrogance, tossing insults our way as they slammed the car doors. The crowd dissipated gradually, with some of the women showing their support with pats on the arm and knowing smiles and thumbs-ups from their cars. No doubt many of them had suffered this Gestapo-style intimidation themselves over the years; it was all part of life in the Islamic Republic. The traffic jam began its steady grind back to the normal Tehran speed and I fired up the bike and followed Omid and Tala down a side street. Omid bought us all cold cans of Zamzam and we stood on the pavement, simmering down, Omid repeating his pledge, 'I'm going to fuck them up.'

Half an hour later Omid and Tala deposited me at the start of Highway 7, the Persian Gulf Highway and the fastest route through the southern outskirts of Tehran towards Kashan, my next stop. Before we said our goodbyes, Omid checked his phone for messages.

'Ha! I sent their licence plate to my friend in the security services. He just sent me a message, he says he's tracked them down and they have made an official apology to you. Oh, and he's confiscated their car.'

He grinned. I felt bad for Omid. He had made such efforts to ease my passage through Iran, looking after my every need, trans-lating for me, ferrying me around Tehran, putting me in touch with his friends across the country, all way beyond the call of duty. But as ever, he saw the amusing side.

'Well, at least you can say you've had an authentic Iranian experience,' he said, laughing, as he and Tala bade me farewell at the toll booth.

We had made our clandestine hugs in the privacy of their home before we set off, so we waved each other goodbye with promises of future plans and meetings. There was a little lump in my throat as I watched their car turn around and disappear, swallowed up in the stream of Tehran-bound traffic.

I relived the incident over and over as I headed south. The riding was easy, a wide empty road with nothing much of note among the barren wasteland except scrappy industrial estates and unappealing truck stops. I was grateful for the opportunity to ride in a slightly mindless fashion, but I could not escape my unease. I feared that telling a member of Iran's security services to fuck off was not my wisest move, and as I moved into more remote country, my paranoia took hold. I was pretty certain I was the only British female on a UK-registered motorcycle in Iran at that moment. I wouldn't be hard to find with an APB to all checkpoints and patrols within a hundred miles of Tehran. The Basij commanders reported directly to the Revolutionary Guards, and they certainly had the authority and means to organise that; their power was far-reaching and, frankly, terrifying.

The very idea of a government-organised militia was alien and intimidating to me, coming from a society where the army and police force have clearly defined roles. In Iran the grassroots militia, the Basij and the more official Revolutionary Guards occupy a murky position somewhere between the two, and the latter do what it says on the tin – they guard the ideals of the regime, their full title being the Army of the Guardians of the Islamic Revolution. But in the years since the revolution, and following the Guards' involvement in the Iran–Iraq War of the 1980s, their numbers had swelled to over 125,000 troops across ground, air and sea, and under the last government, their powers had extended into social, economic and political areas of Iranian life.

This is what Omid had meant when he had shouted 'These are Ahmadinejad's men!' Under the former president's hardline rule, the Revolutionary Guards' powers had spread yet further into all aspects of Iranian society. They had their own media division, they owned and controlled universities, construction and engineering companies, they provided elite protection for top clerics and security at Iran's nuclear sites, trained troops in Lebanon and Syria and, of course, were involved in crushing any deviant uprisings at home. The Guards report directly to the Supreme Leader and their logo – a bold, geometric design comprising a fist grasping a machine gun in front of a globe and a sheaf of wheat, managing to combine Nazi terror with Communist puritanism – is enough to strike a chill into the heart of any liberal westerner. Only the Quranic motto gives it away as Islamic – 'Prepare against them what force you can'. They are untouchable. It's no wonder they thought it would be fun to mess with me in the traffic jam. Discovering that I was travelling in convoy with a man who had their boss's phone number on speed dial must have really spoiled their fun.

Among the public the general view of the lower-ranking Basij tended towards a wary but dismissive loathing: a bunch of young boys given a uniform and the authority to harass their neighbours at will did not seem to worry the average Iranian; maybe they had got used to their presence, like the persistent irritant of a buzzing fly. The real fear was reserved for the Revolutionary Guards, whose power was most definitely genuine and growing all the time. But their image as moral guardians was considered a farce. Despite their official task of upholding Islamic values, their less official ventures had gained them a reputation as a corrupt organisation profiteering from decidedly un-Islamic activities including the smuggling of fuel, booze and drugs and running prostitution rings. In 2008, when General Reza Zarei, a former Guards brigadier turned police chief in charge of Iran's anti-vice campaign, was arrested in a Tehran brothel with six naked women, the Tehranis were amused rather than shocked. From the conversations I had had with men and women of all ages and backgrounds during my journey, the Revolutionary Guards' suspect operations were common knowledge; a bust in a brothel or a truckload of booze coming over the border on their ticket was simply business as usual. Blind eyes were turned by all, but you crossed the Revolutionary Guards at your peril.

While their morals might be questionable, their power was not, and I could imagine revenge being enacted after today's incident. It was impossible for me to keep a low profile on the bike in Iran, and while most road users greeted me with the usual excitable honking and waving, there was often a police presence at toll booths and on the outskirts of towns, and I felt the eyes following me as I passed through. Omid had explained the multiple factions of the different police and military agencies in Iran and assured me that the traffic cops in their green-and-white patrol cars were the most benign of all, but I couldn't help get twitchy at the appearance of anyone in a uniform.

Alone for the first time in a while and still anxious after the events of the day, I found myself racked with homesickness for the first time on this trip. Would I go home now if I could? I always asked myself this question in times of loneliness or difficulty, and the answer was always no. I knew from my previous journeys that this gloominess was a passing phase, all part of life on the road, but it didn't make it any easier in the moment. It wasn't about being brave, or toughing it out, or any of that air-punching motivational language; all that was required in these moments was to keep plodding on, quietly, resolutely, without fuss or drama. As I rolled along the darkening highway towards Kashan, I thought about home, our little houseboat on a still canal, warm and cosy in a quiet backwater of a benign city, and felt a physical pang of longing. Would I go home? No, I was still excited to be here, trying to unpick this strange land of exotica and intrigue, but I missed Austin and the easy pleasures of domestic life on the gentle English waterways I called home – all so removed from this harsh, scorched landscape I found myself in. But still, I wanted to press on, discover more; I wasn't ready to go home yet. *Fernweh* and *Heimweh*, the words that Germans have to describe these opposing urges; *Fernweh*, the longing for faraway places, and *Heimweh*, the longing for home. Today the endless battle of *Fernweh* and *Heimweh* was tiring and seemingly unwinnable. Could I ever be satisfied, I wondered.

I was heading for Kashan, an ancient town in the desert about 150 miles south of Tehran. The Karkas Mountains appeared on the horizon with Kashan nestled between its two highest peaks. The incident in Tehran had delayed me and the sun was beginning to sink, casting a dusty orange glow over the range. Would I ever manage to arrive anywhere in daylight? The highway was almost empty now and the relief that this day would soon be coming to an end flooded over me. I knew that everything would pass, and accepted that, for now, my bike and this open road was my home, and that was OK.

I had been lost in my thoughts, as is easily done on a long, desolate road, and only a chance glance over my shoulder meant that I saw the vehicle bearing down on me. It was a minibus with blacked-out windows and was barrelling along at a terrific speed. I assumed it would overtake me at the last minute, in typical reckless Iranian style. At the same moment I saw there were roadworks immediately ahead, with the two-lane highway narrowing to one lane. The bus showed no signs of slowing down; in fact, it was speeding up. We were both gunning for the same space. The traffic cones cut across the lane in front of me and the road workers, with a clear view of what was about to happen, waved panicked arms, motioning for me to move out of the way. But with the roadworks looming, there was nowhere to go, no hard shoulder or verge. The bus was gaining on me. For a moment everything went into slow motion; I watched over my shoulder as the bus accelerated towards me, engine screaming. At the last minute my brain snapped into gear and I launched my bike out of its path, crashing through the cones and barriers into the work zone and skidding to a halt, only just managing to remain upright. The bus missed me by an inch, showering me with gravel as it flew past. The road workers stood around me, staring after it, shaking their heads, equally confused by what they had just witnessed.

I limped into Kashan with trembling hands, legs of jelly and a few tears trickling down my dust-covered face. I'd diced with death on roads the world over, but never in my life had it reduced me to tears. Dammit, I'd almost been flattened by a truck in São Paulo and I didn't cry then! But it seemed my British stiff upper lip had eluded me on this occasion. Should I be paranoid? Who was driving that blacked-out minibus? Was this just the usual careless Iranian driving, or something more sinister? I was losing my sense of the line between reasonable wariness and paranoia.

Later that evening I took a walk around Kashan's Fin Garden, a world-famous sixteenth-century example of a classic Persian garden. It was an attempt to soothe my soul. The rose bushes and orange trees cast fragrance and shadows across the grounds, and soft uplighting illuminated ancient, intricate tile work, reflected in the *joobs*, the traditional water channels that bordered the flower beds. The locals promenaded quietly, giving me friendly smiles and snapping themselves on their mobile phones. It was a haven of tranquillity, but, as with everything in Iran, there was another, hidden story lurking beneath. These seemingly innocent gardens had a darker side; an Iranian prime minister had been assassinated here in 1852 on orders from the king, who disapproved of his modernisation plans, the same old story that has been plaguing Iran for centuries. The gardens had decided to memorialise this slice of history with a bizarre diorama in the bathhouse where the murder had taken place.

The display featured mannequins dressed as the key players, entombed in Perspex cases. It must have been a huge political scandal at the time, but this half-hearted homage failed to capture the gravitas. The mannequins were a bit too small, poorly constructed and slightly grubby; some even had body parts missing. When I came upon the *pièce de résistance*, the killer himself, I almost burst out laughing. A five-foot dumpy little figure with a hangdog expression and a droopy moustache painted on his plastic face, draped in Qajar-era robes and headdress, his plastic box bore the unconvincing title, *Secret Agent*. As I stared at this unlikely assassin, I wondered if my tormentors of today would one day end up displayed in Perspex. In 150 years' time, would the Revolutionary Guards and the Basij be considered a curiosity from a brutal bygone age? I hoped so.

It was my second encounter with Iran's secret agents that day, but the first one I'd found amusing. As usual, Iran served to fascinate, terrify and entertain in equal measures. It was all in a day's ride in the Islamic Republic.

11

The Rial Thing

THE HIGHWAY TO Isfahan provided the desert road trip I had been dreaming of: open plains of parched brown with nothing but the faint shapes of distant mountains breaking up the horizon. There were even stretches where I was the only vehicle on the road, a sensation to be savoured in Iran. After the intensity of my time in Tehran, it was soothing to be reminded of the uncomplicated pleasures of motorcycle travel, to revel in its simplicity. I recalled the early days of my first road trips, that heady rush of liberation, not just from my old office job and the tedious obligations of everyday life, but from Stuff. That had been the real eye-opener. Back home my closets still groaned with clothes, handbags, shoes, books, records, knick-knacks; all of it desirable, so little of it actually essential. Here I had everything I needed packed into two bags, and all I had to do each day was find fuel and food. There was nowhere I had to be, no phone calls or emails to return, no meetings to rush around for. My choice of bike, a 250cc trail bike, meant that in theory I could go pretty much anywhere I fancied; no dirt track or sandy trail was off limits. But in Iran it was not quite that simple. While my ability to explore was not hampered by my choice of vehicle or constrained by the timetables and itineraries of public transport, it was tempered by something far more unnerving.

The winding trails that led off the road into the desert were alluring, but upon investigation I would often find they led to anonymous industrial complexes or sinister-looking compounds, ringed by barbed wire, sometimes with tanks guarding the entrance, and I would beat a hasty retreat, remembering Omid's warning about taking photos. Anything linked to the military or Iran's nuclear activities was a definite no-no and I still had enough of the previous day's paranoia coursing through my veins to be wary about making too many off-piste explorations, especially in this area. On the outskirts of Isfahan was a particularly contentious nuclear site, a uranium conversion facility where there had been a mysterious explosion in 2011. The Iranian government initially denied it had even happened, but then amateur footage of smoke billowing from the plant appeared online and Isfahan residents reported their windows shaking. People were suddenly evacuated from their homes amid claims that Israel was to blame, but the truth never fully emerged.

Indirectly, it was Iran's secretive approach to its nuclear activities that was causing me to roam its highways and byways with millions of rials and fistfuls of dollars crammed in my bra and secreted about my bike. Due to the country being cut off from the international banking system, I had entered Iran with the entire funds for my trip in US dollars, changing them into local currency as I went along at the numerous exchange bureaus that were to be found in every town.

It was a strangely quaint, analogue feeling to operate entirely in cash; the only real problem was the sheer amount of notes I had to carry with me. With Iran's escalating inflation rate, the currency had lost so much of its value that the government was considering knocking a zero off. But nobody talked in rials anyway; the numbers were just too big to be practical. With the exception of petrol pumps and the most official transactions, everything was priced in the unofficial denomination of *tomans*, each one worth the equivalent of ten rials. Each morning I would organise my millions, laid out in stashes of peppermint green, candy pink and sky blue, hundreds of different-coloured Khomeinis flashing in front of my eyes like a sinister Andy Warhol collage.

But despite some heavy-duty mathematical DNA in my lineage, I still found myself confused with the sheer number of zeroes and I ended up creating my own do-it-yourself foreign exchange system, colour-coded for dunces: the pink note is twelve quid, the green one is six quid, and so on. As I stowed them about my person I wondered what Mr Khomeini would make of me stuffing his face into my cleavage each morning.

Peeling off from the highway, following signs for the centre of Isfahan, I wondered if I was ready for the onslaught of another Iranian city. But it is impossible not to be charmed upon arriving in Isfahan. Nuclear experimentation aside, and if you ignore the thundering steel industry on its outskirts, this is Iran's pretty city. The former capital during the Safavid empire of the sixteenth and seventeenth centuries, a high point for Iranian art and architecture, during its heyday it was bigger than London. In those days it attracted a steady stream of Europeans, traders, artists and what used to be known as 'merchant adventurers', a most enticing job title if there ever was one. Although Isfahan's political power has waned, it lives on as Iran's glittering jewel, the Rome of the Middle East. Back in Britain, any news story focussing on Iran's nuclear ambitions or politics will be accompanied by pictures of glowering clerics or flag-burning protestors, but a positive piece about Iran will invariably feature images of Safavid-era Isfahan – most commonly the grand Naqsh-e Jahan Square, with its illuminated fountains, or the Si-o-Seh Bridge, its thirty-three spans and covered walkway of stone arches stretching across the Zayandeh River. But despite Isfahan's film-set appearance and the famous Persian saying, '*Isfahān nesf-e jahān*' ('Isfahan is half the world'), the city doesn't seem to engender the love and devotion in Iranians one might imagine. Whenever I mentioned to people that I was heading to Shiraz their eyes would mist over with talk of nightingales, Hafez and the famous charm of the Shirazi people. But Isfahan had the opposite effect; their eyes narrowed amid jingoistic warnings about the Isfahanis and their wily ways.

As I weaved my way through the outskirts, noting, happily, that the drivers were not quite as homicidal as in Tehran, I was greeted by the usual unofficial welcome party of young guys on little Chinese motorbikes. They pulled alongside me at traffic lights, excitement flashing in their eyes at the sight of a foreign bike, inviting me home to meet their mothers and drink tea. But I pressed on into the centre, cruising tree-lined boulevards and passing ancient gardens, mosques, minarets and palaces. Golden domes caught the late afternoon sun, intricate patterned tiles of yellow birds and pink flowers and the classic blue Persian geometric designs decorated every building, and in the warm breeze the fronds of palm trees swayed, casting long shadows across the streets.

Downtown it was clear that all this antique charm, history and exotica in one package attracted tourism dollars. But Iran's pariah status means that tourists are of a certain variety, mostly from the Far East, where visas are easily available and the mention of Iran does not invoke images of terror or come attached with centuries of baggage. Coachloads of Malaysians and Chinese were being bussed around the town, deposited at the key sites accompanied by gentle-voiced female Iranian guides relating historical facts while their charges fiddled with their photo lenses. The other, less common tourist tribe were small scholarly groups of elderly Europeans. A far cry from the dashing merchant adventurers of old, these modern-day Persophiles were mostly Germans in stout shoes and sensible safari-style clothing, frowning over textbooks and making notes. Khomeini could rest easy in my bosom, it would be a long time before Isfahan became a stag-party destination.

The result of all this was that, despite the grandeur and beauty of my surroundings, I felt strangely isolated in Isfahan and I wondered if all those warnings had some basis in fact. Isfahan was known as one of Iran's more conservative cities, but in reality, the unsavoury reputation of the Isfahanis was more likely the result of being the closest thing Iran gets to a tourist town. Here, for the first time during my journey, I was hustled in the street to buy carpets and trinkets and I quickly learned to avoid the eyes of the pushiest of the handicraft sellers, with their obsequious enquiries about the health and happiness of my family and the whereabouts of my husband. One hawker had constructed a line of patter that involved enquiring as to the home country of each female tourist that passed his stall. He would then make a reference to whatever relevant famous countrywoman he could come up with. I heard him comparing a sturdy German woman to Angela Merkel and I thought he might be on to something, but he lost any potential trade from me when he claimed I reminded him of Margaret Thatcher.

The atmosphere in the city centre was a world away from the easy welcome I had experienced elsewhere, and it felt as though the natural warmth and hospitality of the nation was being exploited, although I could hardly blame these guys for trying. Times were tough, sanctions were wreaking the intended results, and a weary *bazaari* told me that in warehouses around the country a surplus of Persian carpets was piling up, unable to be exported to the usual western buyers. Fortunately, travelling by motorcycle provides an excellent excuse for not buying carpets, but he would not be deterred that easily and instead offered me Persian carpet mouse mats, complete with fringing. 'Perfect for carrying by motorcycle!' Impressed at his quick thinking, I bought a bunch of them as gifts. Further guilt-induced, sanction-easing souvenir shopping resulted in an Omidvar brothers situation: how do I get all this stuff home? At this moment, Eman Bakhtiari, a shipping kingpin, import–export guy and all-round useful man about town appeared at my side.

A tubby straight-talker with a tight shirt and a loud laugh, Eman was quick to point out that the Iranian postal system was horribly unreliable and that he could ship my purchases home safely. If I would just like to follow him to his office, everything would be taken care of. It had all the warning signals of a scam-in-waiting, especially considering the Isfahani reputation, but I had a good feeling about Eman. When travelling alone, a well-honed instinct is all the security you have and I had learned to trust mine, especially when it came to choosing which strange men to hook up with, and besides, I was keen to get away from Isfahan's tourist traps and see the everyday life of the city.

Our arrival coincided with lunchtime, which involved the handful of staff and any customers who happened to be in the little shedlike office downing tools and shoving aside piles of paperwork to make room for equally excessive piles of rice, meat and bread ordered in from a local café. We were an unusual dining party: Eman at the helm, keeping everyone fed and in good spirits; Laleh, the competent young office manager who emanated the natural warmth and unspoken solidarity that I had found in many Iranian women; Dariush, an office junior with a puppy-like devotion to Laleh; and a customer who was trying to track down a package that had gone missing en route to his son in France. He was ranting at Dariush, who was attempting to placate him with kebabs.

'That doesn't sound very hopeful,' I said to Eman, who was ushering me to a plastic chair and thrusting a cold can of o.o per cent Carbonated Malt Beverage into my hand, the closest thing you could get to a beer in Iran.

'Ah, don't worry!' Eman assured me. 'This guy is just having a small problem. We can send whatever you want, wherever you want. This is what I do. My main business is in dried fruit and nuts, but I ship everything! Nowadays I have to take whatever work I can, the economy is terrible.'

His brand-new, shiny black SUV parked outside didn't look like the ride of a man who was in too much financial trouble, so I guessed that he was either exaggerating his woes, or that he had fingers in various useful pies. I suspected the latter.

'It is because of the sanctions,' muttered the angry customer, forgetting his missing parcel for a moment. He pointed a bony finger in my direction. 'It is you people that have made all the problems.'

Eman shot me a surreptitious roll of the eyes.

'Well, not me, exactly . . .' I pointed out.

'Please, do not take any notice of him,' Laleh whispered in my ear.

'The sanctions, they are hurting the wrong people, that is the problem,' said Eman, stepping in as moderator. 'The Iranian people are suffering; even the well off. The working families cannot survive like they used to.'

'The cost of food, even milk and bread, is so much now,' said Laleh. 'Me, my mother, my father, we all work two jobs.'

Eman nodded. 'There is so much poverty now in Iran, in just a few years. It is breaking us, as a nation. Something must change soon . . .'

His jolly demeanour struggled for a moment. I got the impression he was speaking from personal experience.

'My wife, she is sick,' he went on, confirming my thoughts, 'we can no longer get the medicine she needs. I am lucky because I know other ways to get it, I have contacts, but now it costs so much!'

'Because it is being smuggled in?'

'Yes, and people are making money out of this problem, of course, and out of all people's problems. Sometimes they sell cheap medicine, from India or China, and they are very bad, they cause bad effects, make people even more ill. But people are desperate. They will do anything. This is what happens. Many people suffer, a few people get rich. Always the same story in Iran.'

'And you know who these people are, the ones who get rich? The police, the mullahs! The sanctions are good business for them!' said the angry customer. 'The people who make the trouble make the sanctions, and the sanctions make them rich! How is this right?'

Everyone at the table nodded and murmured in agreement. More tales of the problems caused by the sanctions emerged from everyone. It wasn't the big issues surrounding business and international trade that concerned them, it was the small details of everyday life: the German-made kitchenware that Eman's wife liked but which was no longer available, the poor-quality cosmetics from Asia that gave Laleh a rash, or the cheap Chinese eyedrops that gave Dariush's father an infection.

'It was not so bad when it was just US sanctions, we are used to that,' Eman said. 'We have those since 1979! But now, the last few years with Britain too, and the European countries, and Canada, Australia, Japan. So many problems now for us; our aircraft cannot refuel in Europe, the airlines cannot buy parts so the aeroplanes are very dangerous. It is so many things, everything is affected!'

'Well, it is looking as though the nuclear deal will work out, so hopefully sanctions will be lifted,' I said.

'It will take a long time to recover but—'

Eman paused for a mouthful of rice. The angry customer filled the space.

'Yes, maybe you will lift the sanctions but why should we always do what you say?' He jabbed another angry finger at me. 'Why should we be bossed about by you and America all the time?'

I didn't have a chance to reply because Eman was shouting through his rice.

'Yes, yes, I agree with you my friend, but this nuclear business, it is a big waste of money! Do you know how much the government spend on this? Millions of dollars! Why? Just to annoy America! But look around us, people starving, it makes me angry. We need more hospitals, better schools, clean air. My nephew in Tehran, he cannot breathe, his chest is hurting all the time. This is my children's future, all this money wasted on this stupid nuclear business. Why?' He banged his fist on the table.

'It is not for America to tell us what we can do!' shouted the other man. 'Israel has nuclear weapons! So do you!' He pointed at me. 'America is holding us to ransom with these sanctions! Now they have the whole world against us!'

The two of them launched into Persian, voices rising, arms waving, but as usual in Iranian arguments, it simmered down as quickly as it started with no apparent fallout, and the conversation and eating resumed as if this was all part of usual lunchbreak activity.

'I used to live in England,' the angry customer said to me, taking a more conciliatory tone, 'in the 1970s. St Austell in Cornwall, do you know this place?'

'Yes, I used to go on holiday there as a child. Did you like it?'

'Ah, yes. I loved it. Cornwall, it is very beautiful. That was a good time . . .' His grizzled expression turned momentarily tranquil at the memory.

'Why did you come back to Iran?'

'Because in Iran in the seventies, there was a lot of money being made, from oil.' He shrugged and his scowling features returned. He looked me in the eye. 'And I wanted some of it.'

I nodded.

'But you were still trying to control it,' he said, back to his combative self.

'Not me. The British government, or technically, the Anglo-Iranian Oil Company.'

I looked him in the eye, wanting him to concede the point. Unlike every other Iranian I had met, he was unable, or refused, to make this distinction. For me this was the most important theme of my journey; the government and its people are separate entities. Making this separation felt important, on both sides. This was the whole ethos of Habib's note that had inspired me to come here.

'You were stealing our oil for years, we made you rich. Very rich. I know because my father worked at Abadan in the 1950s, it was a terrible place to work. If you were Iranian.'

Everything he said was true and I agreed that yes, he was right, the British had been the first to send prospectors here and had made an awful lot of money out of Iranian oil for a very long time. And they had not looked after their Iranian workforce. In the oilfields and refineries of Abadan, the native workers had lived in squalor, shacked up in tin huts on dirt streets with no running water, while the British employees had enjoyed all the usual pleasures of a colonial outpost, with swimming pools, tennis courts and shady gardens. But was *I* supposed to apologise for this now? Then Eman kindly chipped in and pointed out, so I didn't have to, that I was just trying to eat my lunch and send a few mouse mats home. But the other guy was on a roll.

'It was the same with Africa, you stole from them too, made money from their rubber, their sugar, their cocoa. And look at the Falkland Islands! You think you can have whatever you want! Just think what we could have done with all that oil money! Our money! Think what Iran could be like now. Imagine Iran if Mosaddegh had been allowed to rule, like we wanted!'

I nodded again, sympathetically, not sure what else to do. I felt as though I had been teleported into a PressTV documentary. I took a sip of my carbonated malt beverage and wished it was a little more potent than 0.0 per cent.

'And your NHS?' the man continued. 'Your National Health Service that you all love so much, yes? Yes? It is so great, so famous, yes?'

'Yes, of course,' I said, experiencing a simultaneous stir of pride and homesickness at the mention of our most beloved institution.

He jabbed his finger again. 'That was paid for in Abadan. We paid for it. With our oil.'

This conversation was my first experience of blatant anti-British sentiment, but it didn't surprise me. I was surprised it hadn't happened sooner. The guy had a point and it was easy to understand why any Iranian would be aggrieved at how things had gone down between our two nations.

His father was no doubt one of the thousands of workers exploited by the Anglo-Iranian Oil Company, which ran the Abadan oilfields like its own independent state. There were some outsiders, including other western diplomats and American politicians, who had warned Britain that the situation at Abadan was 'deplorable' and foresaw the inevitable uprising. In 1951 an Israeli employee at Abadan wrote a scathing report in the *Jerusalem Post*, describing the terrible living conditions of the Persian workers and how he had tried to convince his British colleagues to improve their lot. Their response was that, 'We English have had hundreds of years of experience on how to treat the natives. Socialism is all right back home, but out here you have to be the master.' Really, it wasn't any wonder this man was still angry.

For the first half of the twentieth century the British had maintained total control of Iran's oil, cutting private deals with tribal leaders of the region and only employing Iranian workers in menial jobs. The Iranian government was kept firmly out of the loop, not even allowed access to the company accounts or details of the production quota; they had no idea how much money was being made or even how much oil was being produced. The British already had a history of slippery business deals in Iran, so this arrangement only served to strengthen Iranians' mistrust of their imperial masters. With anti-colonial sentiment on the rise across the world in the 1950s, it was just a matter of time before Iran made a stand, and Prime Minister Mosaddegh, considered an incorruptible and compassionate leader, even by his adversaries, was the man for the job. He took the plunge and nationalised Iran's oil industry. The British reacted with an onslaught of sanctions, embargoes, industrial sabotage and a fleet of warships to the Persian Gulf, but to no avail. It eventually took the incredibly risky and expensive US- and British-backed coup to get rid of Mosaddegh. The British had successfully secured what they perceived as 'their' oil, but in the process, had unwittingly sowed the seeds of the 1979 revolution.

Meanwhile, back home, the newly formed National Health Service and welfare state were improving the lives of post-war Brits, but nobody was worrying too much about where the money was coming from. Although I had always been aware of these two facts – the great socialist post-war rebuild of Britain, and our exploitation of Iranian oil – I had never put them together or heard the link described as succinctly as it had been by my current dining companion. It was hard to find a case for an argument, so I kept quiet and let the angry customer keep up his anti-British rant.

This conversational turn obviously wasn't part of Eman's hospitality package and I could sense his embarrassment as he tried to butt in and pacify his wayward client. Fortunately, another colleague arrived at that moment with an update about the missing package, and my aggressor was temporarily distracted.

'I am very sorry, madam. Very sorry,' said Eman, suddenly coming over all formal. 'Please, do not think this is what we feel of the British people in Iran. We understand this is not you. You must understand . . .' He gave a theatrical glance around the tiny room and Laleh flashed me a supportive smile. Eman leaned in close. 'This man, he is an opium addict. He is . . .' Eman made the universal sign for loopiness, the twirling finger at the ear. 'Crazy guy!'

'And . . .' He lowered his voice further. 'His missing package, it was his son's iPad, he is a student in France. Yesterday his son phones me from Paris, he says he thinks his father is lying! He thinks his father sold the iPad to buy opium and now he is pretending to him it has gone missing!'

Eman leaned back in his chair, shirt buttons straining, arms expanded, small shiny shoes dangling an inch off the floor, surveying his makeshift domain like a mini-Godfather. He shook his head. 'Ah, the things we must do for money!'

'Oh Eman-*jan*, it could be worse!' said Laleh.

'Look at poor dear Laleh, she would like to be an English teacher but it is not possible. So she must work here with me!'

'Oh, you are not so horrible!' she said and they both laughed.

'Why did you not become a teacher?'

From our few exchanges I could tell her English was flawless and her gentle nature would have made her an ideal candidate.

'I studied English for many years and I applied to be a teacher, but if you want to work for a school, one that is run by the state, they make many checks on you. Not just your qualifications, I mean they find out all about your life. They will investigate your internet history and they will find out about your family. They went to my neighbours to ask about me. I know this because my neighbours told me. They will watch you, see who your friends are and your political views.'

'So, what happened?'

'I was not considered suitable, not Islamic enough.'

'In what way? What do you mean?'

'It is hard to know. They do not tell you the reasons, they just say no. Maybe it is because I do not attend the mosque. Maybe because I do not agree with compulsory hijab and I am very open about this. So they could have found this out from looking at my Facebook or my messages.'

'And that would be enough to stop you getting a job?'

'Oh yes! Now, I can never teach in a public school.'

She gave a resigned shrug. I was amazed at how calmly she accepted that her life's ambition had been thwarted by her government's religious dictates. With typical Iranian resilience, she was just making the best of what had been thrown at her. But so much was beyond her control, I felt frustrated on her behalf and said as much.

'You are lucky, you are free. You want to be a teacher, you study, now you are teacher. Simple,' said Eman. 'It is not the same for us.'

'I teach private English lessons in the evenings, after I finish working here,' said Laleh. 'Some day I hope to come to England, I love your language. All my life I have loved it and studied it. I would like to see London, and to wear my hair free! Really, it is so stupid. I mean what do they think will happen if we have the choice to wear the scarf. That all the men will go crazy and out of control if they see hair! It is just hair!'

Eman, Dariush and even the grumpy opium fiend nodded. At last we had found something we all agreed on.

I ended up hanging out at the office all afternoon, partly due to the archaic amount of documentation involved in sending anything out of Iran, but also at the insistence of Eman. He said it would be good for Laleh to have someone to practise English with and he didn't seem to mind her work being interrupted. I couldn't imagine this easy-going flexibility and impulsive hospitality in a British workplace, but perhaps it was another symptom of Iran's 'realness', the human connectivity that Omid and Hossein valued so highly. Maybe it was a reaction to living under such an autocratic regime that, at a micro level, rules and regulations were fluid or non-existent. As long as everything got done in the end, then why worry about the details or how long it took? There was certainly no talk in Eman's office of targets and deadlines or any such business-speak, but everyone was industrious and in good humour most of the time. Odd as it was, to be in glorious, glittering Isfahan and yet spending the day in a cramped Portakabin rather than in a sixteenth-century palace or a Persian garden, it was the happiest few hours of my time there.

Eman dropped me off later. He was contemplating the remainder of my journey to Shiraz and had fallen into a melancholy, reflective mood.

'Shiraz is the true heart of Iran,' he said. 'This is where you will really know the Iranian people. Where do you go next?'

I told him I was heading west, into the Zagros Mountains, seeking out some fresh air and wilderness. The Iranian cities were starting to wear me down.

His eyes brightened. 'The Zagros, this is the land of my people, the Bakhtiari.'

Bakhtiari was his surname, but they had once been the most powerful tribe in Iran.

'Are there many Bakhtiari living nomadically these days?' I asked him.

'Some, but no, not so many now, not for many generations. But my grandfather used to tell me about the migration and how life was before Reza Shah. Now most of us live in cities but you will see, Bahktiari and Bahktiar, they are common names in Iran. We are still here!'

He fell silent, maybe thinking about the nomadic ways of his ancestors, because after a moment he burst out: 'You are free, really free. You are lucky. It is so hard here now, working all the time, for what? But there is no way out, no choice.'

There was genuine pain in his voice.

'And you know what makes me more angry? My friend, a shipping agent too, he tells me every week, the government people come to him, with crates to send to Lebanon and Syria. Last year, when we think the war is starting for real, it is thirty tonnes a week going out there! Thirty tonnes! He has no choice, he must do what they say. They write *spare parts* on the paperwork. He asks no questions but everyone knows. So much money, but what about the poor people who have nothing, who cannot eat? You know what the politicians say to them?'

He was driving very fast now and looking at me while he spoke rather than at the three lanes of cars, bikes, buses and trucks tearing around us.

'They say, "Allah will provide." And you know what I say to that?'

I could make a pretty good guess.

'I say, "It's bullshit!"' He banged his fist on the steering wheel.

Like Eman, I felt overwhelmed by the hopelessness of it all. He was still talking, as if he couldn't stop now he'd started.

'My mother, she was twenty in 1979, she supported Khomeini, she wanted to throw out the Shah. But now she cries all the time. Ten times a day she says to me, what did I do? What did I do? It wasn't meant to be like this. But there is nothing we can do.'

'What do you think will happen in the future?'

'Ah, nothing will change. People are broken, too scared now.'

He fell into silence for a while, then as we arrived at my hotel he tried one of his winning smiles but it failed to convince.

'You are free,' he said again. 'We have to be careful with everything, who we speak to, what we say in public. I lived in Turkey for some time, I know this is not the same as life in the UK, but it was more free than here. We could enjoy life, I have known this freedom. I know how life can be.'

He turned to me and for a moment all his blustery, wide-boy swagger was gone, replaced by a despairing guilelessness that made him seem suddenly young and vulnerable.

'I would like to go the cinema or a park without fear, like you can. That is what I would like most of all.'

12

Into the Wild

WHEN REZA SHAH came to power in the 1920s, part of his modernisation plan for Iran was to take control of the various tribes that for centuries had been living a nomadic existence. This was what Eman had alluded to during our journey the night before. Many of these tribes, notably the Lurs of Lorestan and the Bakhtiari, made an annual migration to the Zagros Mountains, west of Isfahan, where they would settle during the summer months for grazing before heading to the warmer south-west of the country in the winter. Reza Shah saw the tribes as a threat to his master plan for Iran. To him they were trouble-makers, wild and self-sufficient with their own customs, dress and laws. They ruled over their territories, living in groups of large tents, trading and occasionally warring with other tribes as well as robbing passing pilgrims and traders' caravans that crossed their land.

Their lifestyle and self-sufficiency meant that it was impossible for the government to extract revenue from them. So with his typical heavy hand, Reza Shah set about their destruction, arresting their leaders, forcing the young men into the towns and cities to take part in military service and training programmes, moving families into houses that they neither needed nor desired, and even issuing strict dictates about how they should dress and wear their hair.

Of these tribes the most significant were Eman's ancestors, the Bakhtiari, many of whom landed important positions in government and Iranian society. Their tribal land included the southern oilfields, and, by the time Reza Shah took power, they had already made their own business arrangements with the British, who were busy drilling away and making their fortune in the Persian Gulf. Reza Shah was less than happy about this cosy set-up and his attack on the tribes was swift, unsparing and enforced by laws that he wrote to suit his aims. When his son, Mohammed Reza Shah came to power after the Second World War, his was a less forceful approach, using economic carrots rather than his father's stick – he even ended up marrying the daughter of a Bakhtiari nobleman and appointing a prime minister, Shapour Bakhtiar, of tribal descent. Ultimately his father's goal was achieved. Nowadays there are only a few true nomads left in Iran and most of the Bakhtiari, as well as the other tribes, are integrated in mainstream urban society.

I had first become aware of the Bakhtiari through the 1925 documentary, *Grass*, a black-and-white silent movie made by three Americans who accompanied the tribe on their gruelling annual migration to the Zagros Mountains in search of pasture – the all-important 'grass'. Subtitled *A Nation's Battle for Life*, it is a staggering and nail-biting account of their journey, as gripping as any action movie, but it is the sheer scale of the expedition that is so astounding. Led by one *khan*, the headman of the tribe, 50,000 people and a million animals make the move across the punishing terrain of the Zagros, climbing steep rocky goat tracks, swimming and using rafts to cross the raging Kārūn River and trekking barefoot through the snow. The American film-makers happily join the fray and intercut the end result with Charlie Chaplin-style caption cards, peppered with multiple exclamation marks, finding upbeat humour in what must have been a terrifying reality. Fifty years later, another documentary, *People of the Wind*, narrated by James Mason, followed the same story, this time with the Babadi people, a sub-tribe of the Bahktiari, on the same migration route. This more thoughtful, reflective film shows the nomads' struggles of the intervening years, how their lives had

had to adapt to the modern age, and their problems with in-fighting as well as the ever-present external threat of forced settlement.

Fascinated by the images and myths of these mountains, I decided to head west from Isfahan into the Zagros. It would be a meandering detour before turning east for the desert city of Yadz, my next stop for civilisation, 200 miles south-east of Isfahan. The Zagros had also been on my radar because of Freya Stark's travels. As well as her exploration in the Alborz Mountains on her hunt for the Assassins' castles, she had spent time in Lorestan, a tribal province in the Zagros that at the time was considered lawless and dangerous for outsiders. But she had good reason for going; in 1932, while living in Baghdad, she was approached by a young Lur tribesman with information about a cave in the province containing hidden treasure – twenty chests of jewels, daggers, idols and coins. But she had to move fast, he said, others were searching for the treasure and would stop at nothing – not even murder! – to get their hands on it. How could any sane woman resist? Her quest for this mysterious bounty made her the first western woman to visit Lorestan, but the treasure was never found and her passage through the province was constantly thwarted, not by the supposedly savage Lurs but from officious policemen, who as usual considered her antics to be dangerous and unsuitable for a woman. Although she described the tribes, in her usual blunt way, as 'pathological thieves', she found them on the whole to be more open to her ventures, maybe because Lur women had historically been more liberated than the Persians. Even now, the nomadic women in Iran do not cover their hair.

Leaving behind Isfahan's glistening centre, its western outskirts could have belonged to any modern Iranian city – featuring as they did the usual strip of oily car repair shops, light industry and breezeblock mosques under construction. Ahead of me the land turned rugged. The Zagros range appeared in distant layers of brown, purple and grey, the road emptied and the air cleared. I had no particular place to go, just the urge to ride aimlessly, which turned out to be both a blessing and a curse. As soon as I left the main routes, it was the same old story; my maps failed to match the tangle of roads and the signs dwindled to Persian only, then hand-painted Persian, which was essentially illegible, and then to none at all. Roads, tracks and trails split off every which way, the sun and my compass my only guides. My initial reaction was mild panic at being lost so utterly and suddenly, but I had a whole day ahead of me, the rare luxury of nowhere to be at any time, and an entire mountain range to explore. I breathed deeply and decided to relish the uncertainty, Eman's words ringing in my ears: 'You are so free.' This was the very essence of freedom, and to worry about the minor details of where exactly I was, or where I was going, was to waste the moment.

Riding through the small towns and villages, it was as though I had entered a completely different country to the Iran I had seen in the cities. More so than the Alborz Mountains, where wealthy Tehranis have holiday homes and head for recuperative weekend breaks, the atmosphere of the Zagros was wild and its conurbations makeshift and rundown. For the first time I felt as though I was in a Third World country. This was a land of improvisation, poor sanitation and no services for the traveller beyond the most basic petrol stations with nothing for sale except cheap fuel, hot water for tea and a hole in the ground for a toilet. Building and planning regulations were obviously open to inter-pretation, if not entirely ignored outside of the cities; houses were crumbling, newly built breezeblock walls often comically wonky, and electricity and plumbing either non-existent or improvised. The tarmac extended along the main highways but the side streets of the villages were just dirt tracks. Animals and children grubbed around in the dust and fires burned at the sides of the road, where old women in chadors boiled enormous blackened kettles of water.

One of the most striking aspects of these small towns was the proliferation of street art, murals and enormous sculptures, usually on roundabouts or approaching the town, at road junctions. The clunky eagle at the roundabout in the Alborz had been the first example I had seen, but now, having clocked up a couple of thousand miles, I realised it was a nationwide phenomenon. While a lot of the public art celebrated military endeavours with statues and murals of soldiers and war scenes, there was also a playful element to much of the sculpture. A huge flowery teapot dominated one remote traffic island while a stationery set comprising a stash of fifty-foot pencils, an eraser and a pencil sharpener big enough to crawl inside greeted me on the outskirts of a small town. In one village, an old Paykan had been painted red, loaded with vintage suitcases and jacked up to give the impression of being suspended by a cluster of multicoloured balloons. Often the choice of subject matter related to the town's industry, such as the mammoth cartoon-like pistachio nuts bursting out of a paper bag or the mountaineer figures of the Alborz, but at other times they were comically inappropriate, like the vast, jolly snowman skiing along the central reservation of a parched desert town. Mixed with the moralising billboards and aggressive military murals, these examples of state-sponsored art epitomised Iran's complex and contradictory worldview, as if the combative and the cute, the sombre and the absurd could all coexist without conflict.

Upon arriving in one of the small towns of the Zagros, this one heralded by a concrete soldier shoulder-launching an RPG, I made the mistake of trying to determine my whereabouts. It must be a natural instinct, this need to locate oneself, and I couldn't help but stop at the crossroads that constituted the centre to examine my map. I made my second mistake when I made eye contact with the local policeman as he passed by on his little moped. He stopped, seeming helpful, and we peered and pointed at the map together, but he didn't speak any English and although I had picked up a few words of Persian, it was limited to basic greetings and the standard requests for petrol, tea and water. A crowd had gathered now, emerging from their dark huts. This was probably the most interesting event to have happened in this village for years. My audience was made up entirely of men of every generation: the old and toothless, paunchy and middle-aged, handsome skinny teens, wide-eyed little boys, chattering toddlers. About forty examples of the Iranian male surrounded me, varying expressions on every face ranging from bemusement to wonder, to suspicion. This sudden appearance of his tribe had an effect on the policeman, himself not much more than a teenager, and he turned from inquisitive youth to officious authoritarian.

He puffed out his chest. Then he rapped his knuckles on my number plate and shouted instructions, pointing at my panniers. It could only be a request for money or paperwork, so I opted for the latter. I thought about Freya Stark and how she had dealt with the overbearing interference of the Iranian police as she explored this region. She usually took the bossy approach, and when reading her book I could almost hear her voice in the conversations she described, the commanding, cut-glass accent refusing to kowtow to the petty little men in uniform who believed they knew what was best for her. But these were different times. I did not have the weight of the British Empire behind me, or the breeding that naturally assumes authority over peasant policemen. I contemplated, ruefully, that in some ways this travelling business must have been easier when Britannia ruled the waves. My standard approach, much as it grated, was to smile patiently and employ excessive politeness. The explosion of swearwords I had unleashed on the Basij commander in Tehran was for emergencies only, and we were not at that stage yet. Playing nice and playing stupid were usually the best approaches, and to be fair, Freya Stark used this approach too. As she had observed dryly during her Persian travels, 'The great and only comfort about being a woman is that one can always pretend to be more stupid than one is and no one is surprised.'

Another way to fox a village policeman is with piles of important-looking paperwork in a foreign language. Of this I had reams. His lips moved as he squinted at each page of official documentation, trying to hide his confusion. The men of the village were watching his every move, so he made an exaggerated fuss of comparing my registration plate with the papers, even though he clearly had no idea what he was looking at. Some of the men started calling out instructions or advice, or maybe they were taunting him. It was hard to tell. But his reaction was to start throwing his weight about even more, barking orders at me and waving the papers in my face. I was in the middle of a cockfight for which I had little enthusiasm. But what I lacked in upper-class bossiness I made up for in horsepower. Taking the papers from his hand, I stuffed them down the front of my jacket and before he knew what was happening, I was disappearing up the hill, safe in the knowledge that his little bike would never catch me. I could hear the jeers and a roar of laughter from the crowd as I rode away. I almost felt a bit sorry for him.

Alone again, apart from the occasional horn-honking trucker, I meandered deeper into the mountains, awed by their scale. This was a land where at last my bike could really come into its own, a land made for motorcycling with sweeping curves and enticing trails that were unlikely to lead to any contentious military outposts. It was as if I'd entered a whole new world, but on this little detour of mine I would see only a fraction of the Zagros' thousand-mile range. From the north-west of the country, the mountains run parallel with Iran's border with Iraq to the Strait of Hormuz in the Persian Gulf, and I was now deep in their central section. Bare hills swept up and away from the wide flat valleys where oaks and mulberry trees clustered around green pasture and wide rivers flattened out along the valley floors. Out on the open hills, and sometimes blocking the roads, were Bakhtiari shepherds, grazing their sheep and goats in enormous flocks. The nomads, who consider these mountains to be sacred, appeared out here as if from another age, dressed in their traditional clothing of black baggy low-crotch trousers with matching short jackets and skull caps, with no signs of modern life. Some of the older men wore a woollen tunic with a woven pattern in indigo and cream and carried tall wooden crooks. But there was nothing anachronistic about them; they were working men, walking and herding all day in these clothes, and I supposed they had looked like this for centuries.

The hills and roads were dotted with Bakhtiari men of all ages, the older guys on donkeys and the younger men on little motorbikes. But it wasn't until I entered a particularly isolated valley that I came upon one of their encampments. Sited slightly away from the road, I spotted the large black tents and pulled over on the verge. Their wild, ragtag camp with a couple of beat-up old motorcycles, a fire and animals running freely reminded me of how I used to feel as a teenager when the fair came to town. The same seductive image of freedom, the physical connection with the outdoors and the exclusive tight-knit self-sufficiency of living and moving together in a group had stirred something in me as a child – a longing for the same autonomy in my own life – and had probably contributed to my decision to live a rootless lifestyle aboard a boat in my early twenties. Now, gazing at the Bakhtiari camp, I was thrilled to catch a glimpse of their world and inspired by their resistance to outside pressures. A woman stepped out of one of the tents to tend to the fire. Even from this distance I was awed by her presence; she stood tall, wild and bold. Her hair hung long and loose, a great cascade of black over her shoulders. After being surrounded by so many headscarves, it was almost a shocking sight, and the image of this unknown Bakhtiari woman remained with me.

The Bakhtiari were the main tribe in this region. Further north were the Lurs and north again were the Kurds, with their own Iranian province of Kurdistan. The general attitude to the tribal groups in Iran seemed to be positive; people spoke of them as gentle, noble people, the only exception being the Kurds, who seemed to be viewed as trouble-makers. An independent state of

Kurdistan had been promised when the Ottoman Empire had broken up after the First World War, but this never materialised and when the land was carved up the Kurds ended up straddling the borders of Iran, Iraq, Turkey and Syria. They have never given up the fight for their own nation and occasional uprisings have flared up in all the territories over the last century. Their fight for independence, although not as strident in Iran as in Turkey or Iraq, has never gone away. 'They all carry guns in Kurdistan,' Omid had warned me, urging me to avoid the region, while inadvertently making it sound like an enticing adventure. I thought about Aheng, the teenage Kurdish girl I had met at the roadside hotel, with her sharp opinions and bold professional ambitions, and wondered how she fitted into the tribal stereotype. I came to the conclusion that it was impossible to classify anyone in Iran, and herein lay its fascination.

These days the few remaining true nomadic tribes were left to their old ways by the authorities, and even wheeled out on occasion for touristic duties. But there had not always been this respect for their traditions. I recalled Freya Stark's reports from the early 1930s of seeing government men who had been sent into the tribal lands by Reza Shah under instructions to cut the long hair of the nomadic men, dress them in western trousers and jackets and replace their turbans with his standard issue Pahlavi hat, a round peaked cap that was enforced by law on the male Iranian population to prevent their foreheads touching the ground during prayers. All part of Reza Shah's wider move to westernise and secularise Iran.

Riding along the main routes, I would occasionally come across small villages of flat-roofed, blocky little mud-brown houses, nestled in the foothills and dwarfed by the mountains that loomed behind them. But the deeper into the Zagros I went, the sparser the land and the less frequent the signs of civilisation, until, after climbing for several miles, I was alone under a vast sky in a wide-screen panorama. I came to a stop, switched off the bike and soaked up the silence. In the distance I watched a shepherd moving his flock across the empty hills, tiny black and white specks disappearing over the horizon until they were gone and there was not another living soul in sight.

But allowing myself to get well and truly lost turned out to be harder than I imagined and I couldn't quite give up hope of orientating myself. I slipped off the road down a small track to a stream, taking shade under an oak, where I decided it was probably safe to dare to bare my hair and feet while I studied the map. Late afternoon sun threw long shadows in the grass and I began casting my eyes over the jumble of routes and the multitude of little towns and villages, making uneducated guesses about a suitable destination for the night. I realised then, sitting silent and alone in the wilderness, that it wasn't just the traffic, noise and pollution of the cities and highways that I'd found wearing, it was also the sensation of being constantly on display, even if the attention I attracted was almost always well-meaning. Iran is a country of, and for, extroverts, and although I would consider myself in that category most of the time, I could hear the repressed introvert in me crying out, *Can we just hide away for a bit, please?* The familiar oak leaves made me feel at home and I shut my eyes, leaning back against a grassy bank.

First I heard the rustle of footsteps among leaves, then the sound of soft breathing above my head, and then a tentative 'Hello . . .'

A young man, probably in his late teens, was standing beside me, beaming. My first instinct was to throw my headscarf over my hair, but he waved his hand as if to say, don't worry about that. He stood next to me, smiling shyly, and said again, 'Hello.'

'Hi,' I said back.

'Hello,' he repeated, not making any attempt to move.

I wondered where this was going. I felt no danger. He had a childlike expression of wonder that radiated from his face; there was no threat of menace or even a hint of wariness or cynicism in his eyes. It struck me how rare a sight this was. I could not think of a time when I had seen such an open, unguarded face on a young man.

'Do you speak English?' I asked him.

'Yes. A little.'

'What is your name?'

He told me he was called Alan. My first thought was that this was an unusual name for a Bakhtiari shepherd, but I didn't press the point. He said he lived in a town further north with his family, but they had come out to the country to help his uncle with the herding. He wore the traditional baggy trousers but no hat, and he had topped off the outfit with an army surplus jacket over a grubby faded T-shirt bearing a cheesy montage of a Union Jack, a Routemaster bus and Big Ben. I wondered if I had stumbled on the only teenage anglophile in the Zagros Mountains. He saw me looking at his T-shirt and grinned.

'London!'

'Where I live,' I said, and his face practically exploded with delight.

'Where did you get this?' I said, pointing at his T-shirt.

'In my town there was a man from Australia. He stayed with our family. He gave it to me. And books. This is how I learn English, from him and the books. Harry Potter. And a dictionary.'

Who was this mysterious Australian? I wondered. Probably some young backpacker making his own traditional overland migration to the mother country, or back home again, scattering Harry Potter books and tacky T-shirts in his wake. Where was he now and did he realise the effect he had had on one young boy in a small Iranian town that most people couldn't find on the map? I was suddenly, acutely aware of how every interaction makes an indelible mark. I smiled at Alan and introduced myself.

Behind him appeared an older man in the full traditional Bakhtiari dress, carrying a staff, who I guessed to be the uncle. He was welcoming towards me too, but his manner was more reserved. Daylight was running out and I made a move towards packing up the bike, but Alan had already made plans for me. He spoke eagerly with his uncle in a dialect I didn't recognise.

'My uncle has house here in the village. You will meet my family, my mother.'

As usual in Iran, there was no discussion required and I sensed it would have seemed strange, and possibly rude, to refuse their hospitality. So I agreed to follow them, safe in the knowledge that if things turned strange, I would be out of there in two shakes of a Bakhtiari lamb's tail.

'We bring the sheeps in the village,' said Alan, as we emerged on to the road to see his uncle coaxing his flock into line. 'They sleep with us too. Tomorrow we bring them out again.'

The uncle was one of the settled tribesmen, his home one of the low, flat-roofed breezeblock dwellings I had seen throughout the mountains. Located on the edge of a small village, it comprised just two rooms and a small outbuilding containing a squat toilet and a cracked sink with one tap that offered an occasional trickle. Behind the house was a well-tended, bountiful vegetable garden with squash and beans and fruit trees. Inside the building, the rooms were bare except for the worn but still beautiful rugs on the floor, and what I guessed to be Quranic verses pinned on the wall. There was no furniture; we sat on the floor around the rug, where the women – Alan's mother, his aunt and grandmother – surrounded by a handful of children whose various relationships I could not quite grasp, served us tea and bread and white cheese. The women wore long full skirts and removed their headscarves once inside the house. The three of them made an imposing sight of matriarchal power; they were well-built women with strong jaws and rough hands who would have looked equally at home in charge of a herd of goats, a swarm of children or an AK-47. But when they greeted me their tanned faces opened easily into toothy smiles. They were warm and welcoming and seemed unperturbed by my arrival; I parked my bike in the yard and was simply slotted into the proceedings.

During her expeditions to the Zagros, Freya Stark spent most of her nights in the tribal camps and gave much thought to their laws of hospitality. Her interpretation was that the nomads consider a stranger to be an enemy until they enter the sanctuary of someone's tent. Once they enter the tent, however, the host takes his role very seriously, accepting ultimate responsibility for their comfort and safety, as well as assuring the rest of the tribe that they are not a threat. The adoption of a guest is therefore a considerable responsibility and one that is usually taken only by an important member of the tribe. I wasn't sure how much of this remained in twenty-first-century Iran, but the tradition of hospitality certainly ran deep in every strata of society. In all the social situations I had found myself, my hosts had been exceptionally gracious and conscientious in their role, often going way beyond the call of duty, but never showing any sense of being burdened. It was one of the most notable and endearing elements of my journey, and I wished I could import this easy selflessness back home to our time-poor, suspicious little island.

Nobody spoke English except for Alan, so he was tasked with translating and explaining, to the women mostly, why I was travelling without my husband and why I didn't have any children. Their smiles were replaced with expressions of confusion and pity at my child-free status and at my errant husband who allowed me to travel so far and so dangerously without his company. As usual, I responded politely, privately amused that seventy years earlier, and just a few miles north of here in Lorestan, Freya Stark had been answering these very same questions from the Lur tribes-people. I expect she gave them short shrift and I wondered if there would ever come a time when women could wander the world freely without having to explain their marital status and breeding habits. Probably not in my lifetime. So I resigned myself to gamely carrying on with the courteous responses required for social harmony.

My suspicions about my new friend's name turned out to be

correct. He revealed that Alan was the name of the mystery Antipodean, but that in some kind of divine serendipity, his given name was Ali, so he had since taken on a kind of anglicised version. They were 'brothers', he said, with a nostalgic smile.

'Have you ever been to the USA?' he asked me quietly.

I told him I had and he nodded in deep thought, as though this required some real consideration.

'I have never left Iran,' he said eventually.

I asked him if he considered himself primarily Iranian or Bakhtiari and he looked almost confused by the question.

'Both. I am both. I cannot choose one only. I think it is possible to be different things. Do you agree?'

In this one, awkwardly translated statement in his hard-won second language, I saw another side of Alan. A thinker, maybe an outsider even, rejecting the very notion of tribalism here in his own tribal lands. A citizen of the world, although he would not describe himself as this. I asked him what he would do after he left school and he said he was going to study English, adding, 'I will be the first of my family to attend university.'

He was vague about the rest of his family's employment. He had a younger sister who was here, sitting with their mother, and he mentioned two brothers, but they were back in the town. He didn't mention his father and I didn't want to ask in case there was some strangeness or tragedy involved. Families are tight in this part of the world, and the father was notable by his absence. Instead I asked him what he wanted to do for a job after he left university.

'I am not sure,' he said thoughtfully. 'I think maybe I would like to become a teacher. There are not many opportunities for work here, it is not easy. Many people are unemployed. The people I know, some of my friends, they make their money from smuggling. You see the trucks, yes?'

I said I had seen a few of the ubiquitous blue Zamyad pickups thundering past in both directions but I hadn't realised their mission. Now it made sense.

'Yes, you will see them more often at night, with oil drums in the back. Diesel going to Iraq. Fuel is cheaper here. They come the other way with alcohol.'

With the Iraqi border running along their western edge, the Zagros Mountains had long served as a smugglers' paradise. In Freya Stark's day it had been cloth, tea and sugar. Under the Islamic Republic it was cheap fuel one way, whisky and vodka the other.

I bid my farewells in Persian, '*Khoda hafez!*', and Ali responded with an unexpected 'Cheerio!' as I wheeled my bike out of the yard and rode away down the bumpy road into the darkening mountains. That night I made my own camp in a moonlit, silent valley, huddled up in the lea of the hills. At dawn I was woken by the sound of a hundred sheep bleating gently and their bells chiming as they passed along the valley floor.

13

Dark Times in the Desert

I SPENT A few more days winding south through the Zagros Mountains, revelling in the wild scenery and marvelling at the good fortune that had landed me in such a striking and remote landscape. It was a simple routine: exploring any track or trail that took my fancy, invariably getting lost and stopping to picnic, Iranian style, on flatbread and white cheese, on the banks of winding rivers and small rocky streams. It was easy to picture the nomads treading these routes before the tarmac and steam-rollers came along, making their encampments of tents around communal fires with their hordes of animals grazing on the open land, the last gasps of a centuries-old lifestyle that was already on its way out.

Eventually, though, modern life snapped me back into reality. Just as the nomads had been crushed into submission by the fist of centralised bureaucracy, I too was a slave to Iranian officialdom. I had a ticking visa and I didn't fancy finding out what fate awaited an overstay Brit. Shiraz was now firmly in my sights; I could have made it there in a couple of days if I'd wanted, but first I was heading east to the ancient city of Yadz, at the heart of Iran's two great deserts, the Dasht-e Lūt and the Dasht-e Kavīr.

With the mountains behind me as I entered the fringes of the Dasht-e Lūt, I thought about Alan and his family, and Habib and his note, grateful to them both for what I now understood to be a typically Iranian gesture, although many thousands of miles apart – a heartfelt offer of hospitality and a desire to communicate, connect and exchange ideas, simply as one human being to another, away from politics, religion, tribe or any other identifying label. Finding Habib's note in the heart of hectic, cynical London had seemed strange, incongruous even, but now, after spending time in his home country, I could imagine most of the people I had met here doing the same thing. Here in Iran, among Iranians, it seemed a perfectly natural response, and I was struck again by the easy openness, the joyful hospitality of this nation. No wonder Habib had been so distressed by our diplomatic spat.

After meandering my way out of the mountains with the usual navigational challenges, I was running low on fuel and daylight, and I headed on to a main highway to make up some miles and fill up my tank. Although the road was empty, it was still a shock to the system after the timeless tranquillity of the Zagros. Dirty industry and litter-strewn verges made for a bleak backdrop. This was not a picture-postcard desert of dunes and palm trees but flat, empty parched land where nothing grew and nobody lived. The roadside was lined with shredded tyres, unidentifiable scraps of ill-fated vehicles and the occasional abandoned wreck. Brown and grubby, the featureless plains stretched out for miles in every direc-tion but, unlike the Zagros, the emptiness felt forbidding rather than exhilarating. With the sun moving westwards and a dwindling tank of petrol beneath me, I became increasingly uneasy. The only evidence of human activity was a factory spewing out fumes far away on the horizon and a vast scrapyard, piled high with canni-balised Zamyad trucks, smashed-up old Paykans and a mountain of twisted little motorbikes that rose up from the sea of metal like a bad omen; a funeral pyre for motorcyclists foolish enough to take on Iran's drivers. I stilled my silly, fitful imagination and focussed on the most pressing issue. I needed fuel.

Strangely, for a country that produces millions of gallons of its own cheap petrol, Iran's filling stations are few and far between and it was not uncommon to see queues at the pumps. I had last filled up the day before at a small village garage in the mountains and had expected to find a service station once I hit the main highway, but I had been going for hours now and so far, nothing. I estimated I could eke out another fifty miles at the most, but on a long desert road that would pass by in a flash. A few little settlements were marked on the map, but they turned out to be nothing but abandoned truck stops or collections of rundown shacks with no signs of life, just scatterings of broken glass and unintelligible graffiti. I was becoming increasingly jittery, riding at a strict fifty-five miles an hour, recalling some ancient parental advice that this was the best speed for optimum fuel efficiency. Who knew if it was true, but at least it gave me the sense of having some control over my situation. As a last resort I supposed I could flag down a passing car and syphon a few litres in exchange for some *tomans*, but the idea did not appeal out here. I felt a powerful need to keep moving until I reached some kind of civilisation. Although I had spent much of the last few weeks marvelling at the hospitality of the Iranian people, this deserted highway was not the kind of place I wanted to stop and accost a stranger.

It was hard to know if I was being unduly paranoid. While the culture of hospitality is indelibly imprinted into the Iranian DNA, and I had reaped the rewards of this tradition, there were definitely places that were not so female-friendly. While I was always welcomed and treated courteously in public locations such as shops, markets and hotels, where it was conceivable a solo foreign woman would be likely to make an appearance, I had the sense that certain places were out of bounds, to any woman. Sometimes this was obvious and enforced by law, such as the men-only tea houses where signs above the door explicitly banned females from entering, but more often the segregation was implied rather than imposed. I had discovered this on my wanderings in the towns along my route, when I would find myself straying accidentally into what I had come to refer to as 'Man Street'. Every town had one; a shopping street dedicated solely to building equipment or car parts or tools, where the working men's club atmosphere spilled out from the shops on to the pavement and my appearance raised suspicious looks amongst the proprietors and their customers. Just by being there I had broken a social code. The babble of conversation would stall in an uncomfortable silence as I picked my way past pallets of car batteries or bags of cement and other such male ephemera, feeling their eyes burning into my back.

This highway I was riding along now was one giant Man Street. The only women I had seen were a couple of chador-clad passengers in the back seats of passing cars, squinting at me as they sped past. A few tyre repair workshops cropped up in the middle of nowhere and I thought about stopping but there were no petrol pumps, just guys kicking around outside the corrugated iron sheds or spannering on beat-up trucks, smoking and watching with unsmiling expressions as I rumbled by at my sedate, fuel-saving speed, eyes firmly on the road ahead. These semi-industrial badlands were most definitely a man's world, and not the men of the cities with their shiny shoes and fitted shirts, hair slicked back, iPhones in hand. It was not even the men of the mountains with their quiet welcome and weather-worn faces. It was a world of men in poorly paid, dirty manual labour in a harsh climate with no comforts. In my darkest imagination it was a world where deals went down, where home-grown justice was meted out, where anything or anyone could disappear, and nobody could hear you scream. I tried to stop my mind inventing such lurid scene-setting, but this was definitely a side of Iran I had not encountered up close before, and not one in which I wished to linger.

With every mile, I watched the odometer make its dreadful turn and imagined the endless repetition of the four-stroke cycle happening beneath me, using up my precious petrol. Suck, squeeze, bang, blow, the actual process of my last gasps of fuel flowing into the carburettor, exploding and ultimately disappearing out of the exhaust, each thump of the piston emptying my tank, little by little. But the horrible truth about running low on fuel is that there is nothing else for it but to keep going, and hope.

Mercifully, a few miles later, on a long and particularly lonely stretch of highway, the familiar slab of a petrol station roof loomed into sight. It was so incongruous in this wasteland that it appeared like a crash-landed alien craft. My heart leapt with relief and I whooped out loud, punching the air in triumph and delight. The station stood alone on a strange little spit of land between the two carriageways, requiring me to veer across the lanes and ride over a piece of rough waste ground to reach it.

There were two pumps but only one man working them, a young, regular-looking guy, clean-shaven, short-haired, dressed in jeans and a checked shirt who was busy filling up a truck as I pulled up alongside the vacant pump. The truck driver gave me a wave and a smile from his cab, but as soon as the pump attendant turned his attention to me I knew there was something wrong. I could not say why or what, but I just knew. Over the years I had learnt to trust this instinct and had come to respect my gut reactions as the ultimate self-defence tactic, far better than any gun or knife. I didn't know how it worked; I could only assume it was true animal instinct − the sixth sense, the most essential survival skill of all.

The pump attendant stared at me myopically behind his glasses, and abandoned the truck to come to my side. He stood too close and grabbed at the map on my handlebars, speaking fast and erratically in Persian. I didn't need to understand what he was saying to know that my instinct was right. There was something very wrong here and where I would normally take the opportunity of a fuel stop to get off the bike and stretch out my limbs, I was overcome with a powerful sense that I should remain sitting on the bike. Pointing at the tank, I requested *Benzin* but the truck driver was calling him back to finish filling up his tank, so I stayed sitting there, uneasy, waiting. Every bone in my body told me to leave, but I desperately needed the petrol. I considered my options and concluded that I had to take the risk and fill up. Another petrol station could be a hundred miles away. As I waited I was aware of being hyper-alert, like an animal under threat, but I couldn't quite identify the source of my unease; the guy seemed a bit unhinged but he was obviously capable of doing his job and that was all I needed. Twenty litres of petrol and I would be getting the hell out of here.

The trucker, all filled up, drove away down the dirt track. I watched him disappear in a dust cloud and felt a creeping fear. It was now just me and the pump attendant in the middle of this desert. I heard his strange shouts first and turned. He was coming at me, eyes wild, yelling. In what I hoped was a calm but authoritative manner I said, '*Benzin*,' pointing at the tank again. But he ignored my command and I was suddenly knocked off balance as he threw himself on to me, screaming words I didn't understand. The force of his attack caused me and the bike to almost fall but I just managed to stick out my right leg and stay upright. Trying to remain vertical while fighting him off, I shoved him as hard as I could, succeeding in pushing him away for a brief moment. Stable again, I yelled '*Benzin!*' in between a volley of English swear-words. It was as if he was deaf to my instructions. Still ignoring me, he lunged at me again, his full body weight on mine, almost succeeding in toppling me over this time. Again, I just managed to stay on the bike and again shouted, '*Benzin! Benzin!*' But it was time to give up on that plan. There was no way he was going to stand there and patiently fill my tank, not now. His face was in mine, screaming and spitting, his arms pinned on my bike and his torso shoved up against mine, writhing. I pushed at him harder, yelling in his face, 'Get the fuck off! Fuck off! Fuck off!' but it was no use. He was solid, heavy and stronger than me. We grappled for a moment, but it was almost impossible to push him away with the sideways force of his weight against me while trying to keep the bike upright.

There was only one thing for it. I jumped upwards, on to the footpegs, surprising him, and in that moment, balancing on the right peg, I high-kicked my left leg with all the force I could muster, into his stomach. He staggered back, winded and roaring, but in the moment it took him to recover I had hit the start button and was ripping it up across the forecourt, out on to the waste ground and back on the highway, engine screaming, back wheel skidding in the gravel, kicking up a cloud of dust. I had never been more grateful to whoever invented the starter motor. That little button had saved my life.

Out on the highway I could barely think straight. I looked down. My legs were visibly shaking, trembling in that jelly-like way that comes only from true shock. Both furious and distressed, I had no choice but to keep going, but I needed fuel, and badly. That had been the first petrol station I had seen all day. What was the chance of finding another one now? And it was getting dark. The thought of running out of petrol here, at night, in this godforsaken desert, was the worst situation imaginable in my current state. Now, with the light fading, everything seemed sinister, every passing car, every shape, every shadow. As I pondered the miserable possibilities, my bike spluttered and choked with the familiar warning sound that told me to switch over to my reserve tank. I had a couple of litres left at best.

As one is inclined to do after an alarming incident, I replayed the scene in my head, again and again. What troubled me most was that I couldn't make any sense of what had happened. A plain old robbery, a stick-up for some dollars, I could understand; hand over the cash and off you go. Likewise, a straightforward sleazy grope and an opportunistic lunge would have been unpleasant but it wouldn't have been quite as disturbing. That kind of thing is par for the course unfortunately, and most women will have fended off such attempts by the time they reach my age, at home or away. But there was something different about what had occurred in the petrol station. It had felt sexually motivated but there was something else too, something disconcerting; the crazed ranting, the deranged eyes, the refusal to even attempt a greeting or acknowledge my initial request for fuel. I wondered if he was on something. Alone, pumping gas in the desert all day, drugs would keep you occupied. At first glance he had appeared unremarkable. He was young, reasonably well turned out and, if anything, a bit chubby and nerdy looking – not the kind of person I'd imagined as a threat. I wondered if his anger was ideologically motivated. Maybe he was a hardline Islamist, but it seemed unlikely, although, again, I was basing this assumption largely on his appearance. My only whiff of that kind of hostility had been limited to a few disapproving scowls from robed mullahs as they passed me in the street. This kid in the petrol station had looked like every other guy his age, and they didn't tend to take such a stance. On the contrary, they tended to be friendly and welcoming.

I thought about the last few weeks and calmed myself by recounting all my positive experiences with Iranian males; even in my state of distress, I was rational enough to know that this could have happened anywhere in the world. On the whole I had been treated with great courtesy by the men here, of every age and status, from truckers and shopkeepers to students and high-flying businessmen. But I had to admit that the business of male–female relations in Iran was still something I had not quite unpicked, and it remained a constant source of confusion to me.

Because unmarried men and women are forbidden by law from mixing together, schools are segregated, and women are banned from activities as innocent as riding a bicycle or attending a male sports game, an unnatural air of exoticism and mystery surrounds matters relating to sex. Many of the Iranian women I had spoken to about this believed that it contributed to the common harassment they experienced in public, compounding the underlying sense that women were somehow apart, another species. Several women, when telling me tales of being hassled in the street or on public transport, had assured me that as a westerner I was actually less likely to be harassed openly, and it was true that I had not experienced much in the way of outright pestering or catcalling.

But for Iranian women, discrimination goes way beyond the odd lewd suggestion shouted from a building site or a grope on the Metro – it is embedded in the fabric of society and written into the law of the land. Only recently, a conservative newspaper associated with the office of the Supreme Leader had questioned the wisdom of sending an Iranian delegation to take part in a UN summit on women's rights, stating that gender equality was 'not acceptable to the Islamic Republic'. But what was curious from my outsider viewpoint was that these laws of the land – controls on women's hair, dress, behaviour, social life and even the need for the approval of a father or husband when applying for a passport – seemed to have little impact on the private, professional and even public lives of Iranian women. I remembered Shirin, who I had met in the Hotel Alborz. 'Difficult times make you stronger,' she had said. It was true. The women I had met over the last few weeks, of all ages and social classes, were bold, fun-loving, vocal, educated, opinionated, and did not in any way behave like an oppressed group. This was especially true of the urban, liberal classes and the younger generation, who socialised in mixed groups and viewed the battle for women's rights as a crucial element of their anti-regime stance. Although my travels by their very nature meant that I was less likely to find myself mingling with conservative hardliners, when I had come into contact with older, religious or more traditional women, they did not exude oppression either. Women in Iran certainly had plenty to complain about but they did not behave like victims. I could only put this phenomenon down to what I saw as the great Iranian spirit, the embedded sense of self that ran through the core of the nation, and that refused to be crushed.

But despite the outward appearance of Iranian women being strident and confident, I was still aware of a pervading, institution-alised sense of their second-class status, which filtered down from the men at the top and the religious establishment. What made this more insidious is that it was frequently dressed up as chivalry. In Tehran I had ridden one of the public buses where women are sealed off at the back in their own section. It was for their safety, I was told by a man, they needed to be protected. 'From what?' I asked. 'From bad men,' he explained. He was speaking as a good man who would step up to defend a woman. The sentiment was well meaning, but this gallant chauvinism disturbed me. The Iranian women I had encountered seemed perfectly capable of looking after themselves. It seemed the whole nation was in the grip of some entrenched Freudian Madonna–whore complex and, most tellingly of all, nobody ever suggested that it was the men's behaviour that needed changing, rather than the women's.

As I continued along the darkening highway, eyes darting left and right for somewhere or somebody selling petrol, I remembered something a female Iranian friend in London had said to me before I left. 'People will be very friendly, but be wary of the older guys. They are not always so pleased to see you, they are from another time.' Omid had made a similar comment when some grizzled old men in south Tehran had shouted lascivious comments at us in the street. 'This country will be better when all those old guys have died off,' he had muttered. I realised that part of the shock of what had just occurred in the petrol station was that it had involved a young man, a person who normally would be welcoming, open and respectful.

As I watched the dwindling sun, I could not ignore the ever-increasing digits ticking by on my odometer. There was nothing else for it but to pull in at one of the sketchy roadside mechanic shacks and hustle for some petrol. I sat on the bike, still nervy and shaky, while two silent, suspicious-eyed guys sloshed the contents of a jerry can into my tank in exchange for a fistful of rials that I didn't even bother counting. As I rode off to find somewhere to stay for the night, I accepted I would never know the motivation behind the young petrol station attendant's attack. My guess was some combination of drugs, mental instability and a generous helping of testosterone, a miserable cocktail to be found the world over. I was just thankful I had got away safely, and for that I gave my ever-reliable bike a grateful pat; it gave me autonomy, speed and a sense of empowerment that no other form of transport could provide.

14

Hotel Nish-Nush

D UE TO MY fragile state, I elected to spend the following day
in hiding in a hotel. The outside world held little appeal,
and I knew there was no value in forcing myself to keep pushing
on. The desire to hit the road would return soon enough and a
day in bed watching cable television seemed like the most appealing
option right now. A channel beamed in illegally from Dubai
provided me with me an Arabic-dubbed *Downton Abbey* followed
by a gruesome *X-Factor*-style show, infuriatingly titled, *Arabs Got
Talent*. I whiled away a few hours composing a complaining letter
to the production company regarding apostrophe crimes.

When the excitement got too much I strayed down to the lobby
to chat with the receptionist, Nahid, the daughter of the ageing
hotel owner. She was a sympathetic woman in her forties who,
like many Iranians, worked two jobs, her other being in a hair
salon. Over the obligatory glass of tea she asked me about my
journey and after talking to her for a while, I told her about the
incident of the night before, intrigued as to what she would make
of it. She was commiserative but not particularly surprised.

'Ah, this is the *shishe*,' she said with a knowing nod, but I did
not recognise the word.

'*Shishe*, in English it means "glass". It is what you call crystal
meth, yes? It is a big problem in all of Iran but here, very much.
The road you travel on yesterday, there are many places where
they make it. Because it is desert, very empty. No police.'

I didn't realise I had been in Iranian *Breaking Bad* territory, but now it all made sense. The skinny, rough-looking guys with their wary eyes, the deranged behaviour of a young guy, bored out of his skull in a remote desert petrol station. I thought about the shacks I had seen off in the distance; the vast open spaces made a perfect environment for meth labs. My creeping sense of unease and the atmosphere of lawlessness that I had dismissed as the product of an overly dramatic imagination had been spot on after all.

'I am very sorry for this to happen to you in our country,' Nahid said, taking my hand and looking genuinely chagrined.

Like all the Iranians I had met, she shouldered the responsibility of my experience. I assured her that all was fine, and that meth-head pump attendants aside, I had fallen in love with her country. She looked relieved but still worried.

'Please be careful, it is not safe for a woman to be alone some-where like this. I would not go in my car for *benzin* to this place alone. Only with my father or my brother.'

I sighed, wondering if those chivalrous chauvinists had a point after all.

'There are many bad people,' she continued, 'because of the drugs. It is a very big problem.'

I asked her advice about reporting the attack and she said she would speak to her father about it, as he knew the local policeman personally. I suggested I could save him the trouble and report it directly to the police station myself, but she shook her head.

'He is an old friend of my father,' she said. 'He will know what to do. It is best if he asks.'

It was a relief to rest my body and mind for a while, to not have to think or do anything. The hotel was located in a small, unremarkable town with no attractions that tempted me outside to explore, and for this I was oddly grateful. I had a sensation of being over-stimulated; every one of my senses had been on high alert for weeks; every night my nerves tingled and my mind raced. This urge to hide away for a while was an almost primal need for shelter; I recognised it from my previous motorcycle journeys and

I knew it was a temporary craving, it was simply a response to always moving on and being outdoors day in, day out, weathering the elements and a continually changing environment, forever in the company of strangers, assessing and constantly making decisions, every minute of every day.

There was no chance of being pestered here. I was the only guest at the hotel, and it didn't look as though they were expecting any more. It was clean but musty, as if the rooms had been closed up for a long time, and I wondered how many visitors came through these parts, and who they were. I couldn't imagine anyone stopping here for business, and certainly not for pleasure. I was used to people being surprised when I showed up out of the blue, but Nahid had given the appearance of coming out of retirement when I walked in, literally dusting off ledgers and scrabbling around for a pen.

When I asked her that evening about dinner arrangements she made no hesitation in inviting me to eat with her and her family in their house that backed on to the hotel. It made more sense than opening up the hotel kitchen to cook for one guest, she explained. One of the many crumbling brick cubes that serve as basic homes in Iran's boondocks, the house was connected to the hotel by a narrow, rubble-strewn alley strung with sketchy-looking electrical cables. Although the house was as weary as the hotel, inside it was spacious, clean and tidy, if lacking in homely comforts. The walls were bare and on the floor of the living room the seating area comprised the standard arrangement of a few cushions around a worn-out rug. In the corner was a low single bed where Nahid's father, a balding, wizened little man with smiling eyes, reclined, his manner resigned but peaceful, as though he hadn't moved from this position in years. Nahid's older brother, a gaunt, rake-thin man in his fifties, sat by their father, the two of them speaking quietly together while Nahid prepared dinner.

I joined her in the kitchen and she explained that her father was unwell.

'He has pains in his body,' she said. 'My brother helps but he has problems too.'

I nodded sympathetically. She was keeping it all together without complaint, running the home and the business, working two jobs, cooking and cleaning.

'My brother, he is a good man, very kind, but he has treatment for heroin addiction for many years.'

That explained his ravaged appearance. I asked her if this was a common problem and she nodded, and then proceeded to list a catalogue of assistance that he received courtesy of the state. She told how he was supported by a local treatment centre where he was given methadone, and there were also needle exchange programmes, support groups and help for addicts in prison.

'This has saved his life,' she said simply.

She didn't seem embarrassed or ashamed by her brother's situation and spoke about it more as an illness, taking a resigned but practical view, as one would with a relative suffering a long-term chronic ailment. In a society with such strict social codes and morality-based laws, these policies seemed at odds with everything else I had seen and heard from the Iranian government. Once again, I found myself confounded by the apparent contradictions all around me.

Neither Nahid's father or brother spoke English, but after eating they attempted to engage me in conversation. It seemed to be some kind of invitation. They were motioning some kind of activity and laughing. Nahid laughed too, translating: 'They are saying, do you want some nish-nush?' Her brother added something, prompting more laughter.

'Special Iranian tradition!' she translated. She leaned towards me to explain: 'Nish-nush is opium. My father, he smokes it, for his back, for the pain.'

The brother was busying himself preparing a brazier, a large round metal dish of charcoal that he placed next to the bed so it was within reach of his supine father. It took a little while for the coals to heat up, but once they had become red hot he picked one up with a pair of tongs and held it over the end of an ornately carved, foot-long pipe. At the end of the pipe was what appeared to be a small clay bowl, but when he showed it to me I saw it was more like a bulb with a small hole in it. Over this hole he pressed the opium – a small, sticky brown lump that looked as innocent as chocolate. As he held the charcoal over the opium, he blew hard, causing the coal to glow red hot and in turn, the opium to bubble and crackle. A sickly sweet smell filled the room. He took a long inhale of the pipe and leaned back against the wall. Next he passed it to his father, who remained lying on the bed, taking his time, blowing and sucking in silence. Nahid, it seemed, did not partake in this Iranian tradition, so next, it came round to me.

I'd chewed coca leaves in Bolivia, eaten camel in Algeria, drunk moonshine in the Appalachians. Hell, I'd even had colonic irrigation in Los Angeles. Once again, it was time to do as the Romans do . . . I exhaled down the pipe, watching the sudden burst of oxygen give life to the lump of charcoal that Nahid's brother held, gripped by the tongs, carefully over the end. The opium softened, melting under its heat. He was giving me instructions.

'Now breathe in,' translated Nahid.

As with most substances that make you feel good, the taste was unpleasant. Bitter and pungent. I kept going. I took my time, making my breaths slow and steady, but Nahid explained I was doing it wrong, translating her brother's directions: 'It is better if you breathe more hard, more fast.' I had been approaching it as one would smoke a joint, but apparently the more effective method was to exhale and inhale with shorter, quicker breaths. 'But not too much, because you have not done this before, it might make you sick,' Nahid warned.

While the pipe was passed between the three of us, Nahid went to the kitchen and returned with plates of sweets, pastries and fruits. 'The opium make your blood pressure low, it can make you faint. So you must always eat sweets and drink tea when you are smoking it.' Next she brought glasses of tea with sticks of crystallised sugar. They looked like little magic wands of precious jewels, coloured pink and yellow and flavoured with cardamom and cinnamon. She stirred them into the tea and they melted away. The sugar brought a welcome, heady rush to my bloodstream.

A knock on the door brought some friends of Nahid's father, who joined in the smoking without ceremony. They were an elderly couple too and this was obviously part of their culture; it was not seen as a big deal or a source of illicit excitement in their world – it was no different to passing around a joint or, indeed, sharing a bottle of wine. They laughed and chatted in the way of people who have known each other a long time, and Nahid's father admonished them for smoking cigarettes. They were arguing good-naturedly. Nahid was translating for me.

'He is saying to them it is bad for them to smoke.'

The irony of her father lecturing them on the evils of tobacco while sucking on an opium pipe was not lost on Nahid, and she smiled, shaking her head.

'And he will not eat salt in his food, he says it is bad for his health!'

For the first time in a while, I felt pleasantly relaxed and at ease. All the tension in my road-weary muscles was seeping away and I was aware of a dreamy sense of well-being. Nothing mattered now. I leaned back on the cushions and suddenly understood why in all those pictures of antique opium dens, people are lying down on beds. A mild euphoria washed over me. But I didn't feel spaced out or trippy, I was still coherent, and everyone else was chatting away as normal, nibbling on sweets and sipping at their tea. It was as though life's edges had been sanded away, no aches and pains, no anxieties, no problems . . . what a wonderful world! After the third round of the pipe I succumbed to the overwhelming desire to get horizontal. My bed had never been so appealing, even the slightly sagging, fusty one that awaited me. Thanking my hosts, I returned to my room and lay down, no longer worried by the past or the future. I wasn't bothered by the attack at the petrol station, or by the thought of getting out on the road again tomorrow, or whether my bike was making funny noises, or any of the usual things that eat away at one's night-time mind on a lonely road trip. I zoned out in front of the television, no longer perturbed by the weirdness of Hugh Bonneville speaking Arabic; I wasn't even fussed by *Arabs Got Talent* and their crimes against punctuation. All was well with the world.

15

Yadz: How Iran Lost Its Religion and Found Air Conditioning

I WAS ROUSED from my opiated sleep the next morning by a knock on the door. It was Nahid, saying her father had spoken to his friend in the police. I snapped awake, excited for news of the manhunt. But her voice sounded apologetic rather than triumphant.

'I am sorry, Lois. He told him what had happened, and the policeman, he said, "Well, what does she expect if she goes riding around Iran on a motorcycle by herself?"'

We looked at each other. Neither of us said anything; there was nothing else to say. As I packed my bike outside the hotel, I asked her if the policeman's response was typical. Nahid shrugged, apparently resigned to the reality. As an Iranian woman she had no expectations of equality or justice, but neither did she show any signs of outrage at her second-class status.

'Yes, what the policeman said is not a surprise to me. Once, in Tehran, I was on the Metro, and a man, he is touching me, but people say it is my fault for being in the mixed carriage. If I don't want to be touched, they say, I should be in the women's carriage.' She shook her head and shrugged again.

I loaded my luggage on to my bike, aware that in the last forty-eight hours I had just got a little closer to unpicking the reality of women's lives in Iran.

I busied myself with preparing my bike – checking the oil level, chain tension and tyres, focussing on methodical, practical tasks. It was my daily routine and an effective way of distracting my mind from any anxiety about getting back out on the road. Nahid insisted on flitting around me with well-meaning warnings, interrupting my Zen-like attempt at motorcycle maintenance.

'Do not stop until you get to Yadz,' she said as I packed away my tools and made my swift swap from headscarf to helmet. I started up the engine, keen to get moving now. 'Do not speak to anyone. Sometimes they will wave and try to stop you, they pretend they need help. But if you stop they will rob you. There are many robberies on this road. You remember what I told you last night, about the *shishe*?'

I nodded, knowing she was trying to help, but wishing she would stop talking. The opium-induced bliss had most decidedly worn off, and it had taken all of my will to force myself out of my room and back out on the road again. Truthfully, another day of *Arabs Got Talent* and some nish-nush was far more appealing than braving the desert meth-heads. My trip was coming towards its end, these next few miles to Yadz and then on to Shiraz would be my last days of riding in Iran. I wanted to go out on a high! What I needed right now was an air-punching pep-talk about what a great day I was about to have, not all this anxious soothsaying.

'Please be careful. It is not safe for a woman alone' were the last words I heard as I rode away.

I waved Nahid goodbye, faking a winning smile as much for my sake as hers. The sun beat down, the heat fierce and angry, even at this time of the morning. Leaving behind the small town, the road was as bleak as before amid the scorched, rubbish-strewn desert. I had only gone two miles from the hotel when I realised I was being followed. Over my shoulder I could see two men in one of the blue Zamyad trucks that I had come to associate with either reckless manual labourers or smugglers. I was one of the slowest vehicles on the road, the highway was empty, and there was no need for them to be tailgating me. They could have easily overtaken my bike but they stayed close, just inches away. I couldn't tell who they were, or what they wanted. Were they *shishe* guys after money, or were these finally the angry Islamists I had been warned about by everyone back home? Yadz was supposedly a more traditional, conservative city than Tehran or Shiraz, and maybe I would not be so welcome here. As usual, it was hard to judge the situation. All I could do was ignore them, staring doggedly at the road ahead. I had enough fuel to get me to Yadz, and once I was in the thick of city traffic I would shake them off easily enough.

My plan would have worked if they hadn't started a cat-and-mouse game. My heart quickened as they overtook me before suddenly swerving into my path, trying to force me to stop. I dodged around them and kept going. They dropped behind again but stayed close, sticking behind me for another mile or so. Then they were pulling in front of me again, giving me no choice but to veer off on to the rocky verge. The road was empty, no other vehicles, no signs of civilisation in sight. I felt sick with fear, wondering what to do, imagining the worst and reliving the attack at the petrol station. I wanted to scream *Just leave me alone!* Then they came up alongside, lowering the window, shouting and motioning for me to pull over. They were so close, I could have reached out and touched them. Suddenly, without warning, they swung in front of me, forcing me to plunge down the bank to avoid smashing head first into the side of their truck. I came to a wobbly halt at the bottom of the ditch and looked up to see that they had stopped ahead of me and were now reversing back at speed. I was stuck in the gulley, trapped. Then the two men jumped out of the cab and came running at me.

In moments of fear, time can seem to freeze or go into slow-motion, but in this instance, the opposite happened. Everything moved quickly, like a film on fast-forward. They were racing towards me, gabbling as if the sound had sped-up too, their arms outstretched, holding something I could not make out. My fear turned to anger and I started shouting and swearing at them to leave me alone. I'd done too much of this lately, too much shouting and swearing. I was sick and tired of it all, sick and tired of being alone and exposed, intimidated and stared at, and these guys were going to feel the full force of my anger and fear. I yelled at them again to back off. Then I saw them shaking their heads, their faces breaking into great dazzling smiles, their eyes eager, sparkling with excitement. And then I saw what they were holding in their hands. And I cringed.

The younger man stopped in front of me. He was skinny and ragged, visibly poor. He spoke a few words of English.

'We see you. We like to speak with you. We have food for you.'

He thrust two bags of fruit into my hands. The older man had bottles of water for me.

'Welcome . . . to . . . Iran,' said the older man carefully, as if he had been practising the phrase for the last two miles.

The seesaw of emotions was too much. Now I wanted to laugh and cry and hug them. I settled on the first option. Then we were all laughing and making jumbled introductions as we attempted to find places to secrete ten pomegranates, eight peaches and two bottles of water in my overstuffed luggage. I ended up barely able to move, with fruit bulging out of every one of my jacket's pockets.

'Please, we take photo?' said the young man.

They took it in turns to stand next to me, almost hysterical with amusement and excitement as they snapped away on an ancient Nokia phone. When the older man dared to rest an illicit arm on my shoulder, they both broke into uncontrollable schoolboy giggles. I was giggling too, thankful to them, not just for their generosity and kindness but for the timely reality check.

'What do you think of Iran?' asked the younger guy from the cab before they drove away, wide earnest brown eyes meeting mine.

'I love it,' I said. 'I really love it.'

He touched his hand to his heart and bowed his head before careering back on to the blacktop, driving like a maniac. I gunned the bike out of the ditch and up the bank, and watched them disappear into the distance, making a mental note to self: *When other road users in Iran appear to be trying to kill you, rob you or kidnap you, normally they just want to feed you. Now for heaven's sake, stop worrying about everything.*

The road took a majestic turn as it approached Yadz, emerging on to a scene reminiscent of the American West. Flat scrub transformed into high desert, with mountains on the horizon and great towers of rock in stripes of red, yellow and golden brown lining the route. The highway now twisted around these formations, providing some much needed motorcycling thrills. My mood soared as I swept through the curves of this startling multicoloured landscape, flicking the bike from side to side. The similarity to Utah or New Mexico was uncanny, but it wasn't the only aspect of Iran that reminded me of America. The two countries had far more similarities than either would care to admit; both maligned and misunderstood, tarnished in the eyes of the world by a minority of religious fundamentalists and obstreperous politicians, but in truth, populated by generous, hospitable people, endlessly innovative and industrious with a truly astounding capacity for vast portions of food. The meth-cooking drug labs of their respective deserts were another more recent and unfortunate similarity. *Shishe* had come late to Iran, in the last decade, but was ripping through the country, overtaking heroin as the drug of choice among disaffected youth and even upper-class women looking for a quick weight-loss plan.

In keeping with his revolutionary rhetoric, Khomeini had blamed the Great Satan for Iran's drug problems, claiming that global heroin distribution was part of a US-inspired conspiracy, and made possession of even a few grams a capital offence. Unfortunately for him, and every Iranian leader since, being positioned between poppy-growing Afghanistan and the lucrative drug markets of Europe made for big problems, with Iran at the heart of two major smuggling routes. Over the last few decades Iran has stepped up its own war on drugs and the border with Afghanistan has become a battleground, with tribal groups and the Taliban cashing in on the smuggling action. Fighting off the Revolutionary Guards with RPGs and machine guns, the traffickers transport hundreds of tons of opium and heroin across the frontier, even resorting to using camel trains on ancient back-country routes to avoid the Iranian authorities. The Revolutionary Guards give as good as they get, treating it as a jihad, a holy war on the traffickers, and operate on an officially sanctioned shoot-to-kill policy. Iran claims to have the highest rate of heroin seizures in the world, but it comes at a cost; it is not unusual for officers' bullet-riddled corpses to be found lying burned or beheaded in the lawless border country.

As Nahid had attested, Iran's heroin problem has become one of the most severe in the world, partly because of the easy access from Afghanistan, but she also blamed the inevitable fallout of a large, disillusioned youth population with high unemployment and a bleak future of seemingly endless repression, where the creating of music or art, or even dancing, is under the control of the authorities. Khomeini's zero-tolerance approach to drugs during the 1980s had little effect, and since reformist president Khatami took power in the 1990s, Iran's official approach to its addicts has been to offer help rather than punishment. Nahid had taken much pride in stating that Iran is now considered to have one of the most progressive treatment programmes in the world. It even has an English-language website devoted to its efforts – the Iran Drug Control Headquarters – with the baffling subtitle Resistance Economy; Action & Proceeding, and with therapy programmes based around contrived Persian-themed acronyms such as PERSEPOLIS – Participatory ExpeRienceS for EmPOwering Local InitiativeS. This strange bureaucratic waffle is about as close to bleeding-heart liberalism as the Islamic Republic

gets, with references on the website to 'outreach teams' and 'thera-
peutic communities'. But while it may not be making much of a
dent in the number of addicts, it has at least reduced the stigma
of being one, as was clear from Nahid's openness about her
brother's situation.

Yadz came as a blessed relief. The city was about as far from
the rubbish-strewn drug highway as I could have imagined.
Despite being cursed with the usual Iranian traffic on its outskirts,
its centre oozed antique charm and the timeless tranquillity of an
ancient desert citadel. I was immediately at ease as I walked around
the mud-walled old town with its winding alleys and adobe-type
houses with their domed roofs and ornate wooden doors. Marco
Polo had come to Yadz in the thirteenth century, describing it
as a 'good and noble city', and something of that atmosphere
remained even now. There was a gentler, more subdued atmosphere here, compared to Isfahan, and certainly to Tehran, although
some of the residents I spoke to, mainly young women, bemoaned
the lack of action. But I was glad of the respite. In Yadz there
was a tangible feeling of being in one of the oldest cities in the
world. Iranian ingenuity was visible at every turn, from the *qanats*,
the underground water channels invented by the Persians in the
first millennium BC, to the *bâdgirs*, the square brick wind-catchers
that make up Yadz's unique skyline. These are the most striking
feature of the city and a source of great pride to the Yadzis, who
love to explain their inventive form of air conditioning. When I
admitted my ignorance on the subject, a taxi driver insisted on
taking me free of charge to the Dowlat Abad Garden, where
an eighteenth-century pavilion boasts Iran's tallest *bâdgir*.

My self-styled host was, I guessed, in his late fifties, a thin,
slightly bowed figure who walked with a limp and took a formal
approach to our relationship, giving his name only as Mr Yadzani
and making his introduction with a respectful bow. When not
driving a taxi, he worked as a librarian, where he had taught
himself English and, like many Iranians, was keen to test it out

on a real person. Thankfully for me, he wasn't at the stage of seeking answers to complicated grammatical conundrums.

'You can feel it, yes?' said Mr Yadzani, as we stood in the centre of the pavilion underneath the *bâdgir*. I gazed up inside the hundred-foot tower to the chink of daylight above, aware of the gentle movement of wind being channelled down through the tower's vents and then up again, cooling the air around us. At our feet was a small tiled pool, its still turquoise waters evaporating and further lowering the temperature of the air as it made its way up and out.

'Yes, I can. But what happens when there is no wind?'

'Today there is only a little wind but as you can feel, even a small breeze from any direction will be caught by the *bâdgir*,' he explained. 'And if there is no wind, the heat from the room rises up the tower so inside the building stays cool at all times, and the water here, this also helps to make the room cool. It is a great Persian invention, used in desert countries all across the world,' he added with a serious nod.

Sun streamed in through a huge stained-glass window scattering a multicoloured light show across the floor, and outside, through a row of perfectly formed archways, I could see lines of cypress and beyond, pomegranate trees, their shiny red fruits catching the sun and reflecting in more pools of water. The garden layout, the design and proportions of the pavilion, the ingenious *bâdgir*, all of it was a triumph of Persian ingenuity, but I couldn't help look at the beauty around me and be bewildered by the contrast not just to the chaotic scenes of Iran's street life and its homicidal highways, but also to the brutality meted out by the people in charge of this nation over the centuries. How could a people who are capable of inventing and creating to this level of perfection also be responsible for so much cruelty and carelessness? I was standing in one of the most exquisitely designed places I had ever seen, in a country that pollutes its air to lethal levels, litters its countryside, crushes artistic endeavours and executes more people than almost anywhere else in the world. It was as though there was no middle ground; both ends of the spectrum of the human condition represented, both taken to the extreme.

After my experience in the desert petrol station, Mr Yadzani unknowingly continued to restore my faith in the Iranian male. A gentle soul, he insisted on becoming my unofficial guide to Yadz. I wasn't sure if he felt sorry for me being alone, or if this was a form of *ta'arof*, but there was no mention of a fee and when I tried to establish a financial arrangement, he protested so vehemently that I ended up leaving banknotes secreted around the interior of his car. The most important thing for me, he said, was to come to his home to meet his wife, but on the way we had to stop off at the Zoroastrian Temple of Fire.

'Here the flame has burned for fifteen hundred years,' he assured me.

I was dubious about that claim but I kept quiet. Surely in fifteen hundred years, I thought, someone would have nodded off on the night shift and let it go out. I imagined a lackey hastily relighting it the next morning and hoping nobody had noticed. The temple was small and unassuming and only the Zoroastrian symbol, a winged figure above its entrance, gave a clue to its significance. I realised that I had seen this image all over Iran, sometimes worn by people as a pendant or carved into the walls of buildings, or even used in company logos.

'This is the Faravahar, the symbol of Zoroastrians,' said Mr Yadzani. 'But Reza Shah, he made it the symbol of all Iran. Now people use it for many purposes, even people who are not Zoroastrians.'

I asked him what it symbolised. It comprised an emperor-like figure in profile with a fanned tail and wings.

'A Faravahar, it is, how would you say?' He thought about the English word for a moment. 'Soul. Your soul. Always there is a battle between good and evil, between light and dark, this is what Zoroastrians believe. This is why fire is important.'

'Are you a Zoroastrian?' I asked him. He shook his head.

'No but my brother's wife, she is Zoroastrian.'

'Is that unusual, for her to marry outside of the religion?'

'No, not so unusual now because there are not very many Zoroastrians left in Iran, but some people, they do not think it is good. And their children cannot be Zoroastrian because it is only through the father, so his wife's family, they were not so happy about this. My brother met his wife in Tehran, but they come to live here in Yadz. There are many Zoroastrians in Tehran too, maybe more than Yadz, but here, there is the fire temple. This is very important.'

I mentioned the Bahá'ís I had met on the train from Turkey and their tales of persecution and discrimination, but Mr Yadzani seemed dismissive of them, as if they were a bunch of newcomers, trouble-making upstarts. The Zoroastrians, he assured me, were greatly respected in Iran because it was the original religion of the nation, and even though they were prevented from taking certain positions in government and universities, they did not suffer harassment or abuse in the community. The way he described it was as though they were regarded as the venerable, if slightly quaint, elder statesmen of Iran. Although, he was quick to point out, it had not always been this way. For centuries the Zoroastrians had been victims of oppression and massacres and forced conversions to Islam, he said, looking pained. He had a particularly expressive face and every story or opinion was amplified by a glint or squint of his eyes, the raising and furrowing of his eyebrows, and a whole range of frowns and smiles. A quiet dissenter, he was a vocal admirer of the Pahlavis, and put the change in the Zoroastrians' fortunes down to Reza Shah and his enthusiasm for a unified Persian identity.

'He understood it was important to honour the ancient Persian kings like Cyrus. He knew the Zoroastrians were important to Iran, to all Iranians. He brought the country together. Now many young people in Iran, they are thinking this way too, they wish to convert to Zoroastrianism,' he said, 'because they do not like

Islam, because they are angry with the Islamic Republic. But you cannot convert to Zoroastrianism, you can only be born into it. But the young people, they see that it is the real Persian religion, Zoroastrians are their ancestors, before the Arabs came.'

Despite the fact that the Arab invasion of Iran had happened nearly fourteen hundred years ago, he uttered the word *Arabs* in a tone of voice that made his opinion on that topic clear, and I recalled the gentleman in Tabriz who had invited me to eat with his family on my first day in Iran, and his words of advice for my onward journey: 'Whatever you do, you must never call an Iranian an Arab!'

On our journey across town Mr Yadzani expanded on the merits of Zoroastrianism. 'Good thoughts, good actions, good words,' he repeated, and I got the feeling he would have liked to have converted if it had been allowed. At one point he stopped the car, causing a minor traffic jam while he exchanged a few words with a priest he knew from the temple, but nobody seemed to mind being held up, or at least there were no more honking horns than usual. 'And you know, in Zoroastrianism, that women can also be priests,' he added with a proud nod as he set off again, effortlessly rejoining the tangle of cars. 'Not like Islam.'

At the next junction he saw a group of his taxi-driver friends, waiting for fares, and called out a greeting to them, holding up the traffic once more, but again it was of no particular concern to the other drivers. Mr Yadzani insisted on taking us through the centre of the city, to see the Amir Chaqmaq Square and its mosque. Here, among the promenading families and groups of boys messing about on sun-bleached, clapped-out mopeds, there were several men dressed altogether differently to anyone I had seen in Iran, bearded and sandalled, in flowing white *shalwar kameez*. A few of them were lounging in the alcoves that surrounded the square, escaping the mid-afternoon heat, while others walked the streets by the bazaar.

'These are Baluchi, traders from Baluchistan,' said Mr Yadzani when I asked him about them. 'From near the border with Pakistan, they come to Yadz to sell many things, food and clothing. And they take Iranian goods into Pakistan. It is a very poor part of Iran, life is difficult there, and there are many people smuggling oil and drugs, but these men, I know them. They are good men.'

One of the Baluchi men was standing on the pavement outside a hardware store, rolling out a bolt of patterned pink cloth for two women in black chadors, who fingered the fabric, running appraising eyes over it. If it hadn't been for the tower of Chinese plastic storage boxes behind them, it could have been a scene from any time in the last thousand years.

'In this area,' said Mr Yadzani, pointing down a nearby street, 'there are also many Afghans living, and Iraqis too; they came during the Imposed War and they stay since then.' I asked Mr Yadzani if there were any problems with the Afghans and Iraqis being Sunni Muslims, but he just shrugged and shook his head and said, 'No problems, no.'

In the southern desert areas I had seen many more Afghans than in the north of Iran, and their lot was not generally a happy one. The men were viewed by many Iranians as a source of cheap labour, but out on the highways it was more common to see the women, always with children in tow. They stood out from the Persians with their darker skin and traditional dress of brightly patterned, wide skirts. But despite their colourful appearance they made for a pitiful sight, often to be seen begging for food and money outside truck stops and petrol stations. They were usually shooed away in no uncertain terms by the proprietors before they could get anywhere near me, and when I asked the men at the truck stops about them, they dismissed them quickly as pests or worse, often accompanying their comments with a look of disgust and a dismissive gesture. This was their lot out on the rough, tough gritty highways; but Mr Yadzani took a more generous view of all visitors to his country. He was notable as one of the few people who did not speak disparagingly about the Afghan refugees when I asked him about them.

Mr Yadzani's kind heart meant it took a while to arrive at his house as he kept seeing people he knew, resulting in frequent stops to exchange pleasantries, enquire after the well-being of family members, diagnose a mechanical fault in a colleague's taxi and commiserate with all about the state of the economy. The car windows remained open to necessitate this mobile socialising, and as we drove through the streets the city drifted into our cab on the warm desert air; wafts of kebabs, dust, exhaust fumes, blasts of horns, snippets of conversation and the occasional sweet hint of an unidentified flower, the scents and sounds of Yadz. Mr Yadzani, true to his name, had taken on the character of his city: calm and reserved but warm and accepting. He did not speak much about himself, and I wondered about his bad leg and his auto-didactic English learning, and whether he drove a taxi through financial necessity or as a way to stay connected with his city and its people. His wife, Sara, he told me with a glow of pride in his voice, was a researcher at the local hospital, so I assumed she earned enough to keep them both, but he struck me as someone who felt the need to keep both brain and body active.

Like many middle-class Iranian homes, Mr Yadzani's stood behind a high wall that gave little clue as to what lay beyond. The electronic gates slid open to reveal a small courtyard for car parking and a modern block of ten storeys. A sleepy doorman rose to his feet when we entered the building and greeted Mr Yadzani like a prodigal son. There was much hand holding and touching of each other's arms as they exchanged greetings and enquiries as to each other's health. I noticed the doorman was also injured and moved slowly with an awkward gait. As we stepped into the lift, Mr Yadzani said: 'He was also in the war. He lost a foot. This is why we are like brothers, it is the same for all soldiers who fought.'

Outside the door to each flat were collections of shoes, neatly lined up, giving clues as to the inhabitants. Mostly they illustrated the Iranian nuclear family; one pair of men's, one women's and two children's of varying sizes, sometimes including the scuffed, worn-down trainers of a teenager. Only one door had a single pair of men's shoes outside, and as we passed by, a familiar smell seeped into the hallway from underneath the door. Mr Yadzani wafted the air and wrinkled his nose.

'He is always smoking opium,' he said, shaking his head sadly rather than disapprovingly. 'He lives alone,' he added, as if this was the unhappiest situation imaginable for a man. Then quietly, almost as if a reminder to himself, he said, 'I will visit him tomorrow.'

Outside the Yadzani residence the more socially acceptable line-up of family shoes greeted us and the only smell seeping out under the door was the unmistakable aroma of *ghormeh sabzi*, the classic Persian green stew. Mr Yadzani aligned his black leather slip-ons and I dutifully placed my incongruous dusty motorcycle boots alongside.

16

Half a Million Martyrs

I GUESSED MR Yadzani had forewarned his wife, Sara, of my arrival, as she welcomed me like an old family friend with much ado about what a delight it was to host me. I was immediately invited into the kitchen where preparations for an elaborate dinner were already underway. Whether this was business as usual or related to my visit I wasn't sure, but from what I had seen in other Iranian homes, the rigmarole of cooking an enormous multi-course meal each night was standard procedure. The kitchen buzzed with levels of multitasking that would have sent me into a panic but that Sara orchestrated with effortless calm. Huge bunches of herbs were being chopped for *ghormeh sabzi*. Garlic and onion sizzled in an iron pan, a bowl of tiny dried limes awaited their fate and a mountain of rice was steaming away in butter under a cloth to achieve *tah-dig*, the typical Persian style made by crisping it ever so slightly on the bottom of the pan. Slices of fresh watermelon appeared, then little bowls of dried fruits and nuts to keep us busy until the main event. There was no alcohol in the Yadzani residence; instead we drank chilled *doogh*, a salty yoghurt drink flavoured with mint. I sat at the kitchen table, next to their youngest son, eleven-year-old Amir, chirpy, polite and fluent in English, who was busy alternating between his maths homework and sketching the fascinations of a contemporary Iranian boy: luxury sports cars, the BMW roundel and masked gun-toting terrorists.

'These are the speciality of Yadz,' said Sara.

For a moment I thought she was referring to her son's artwork, but was relieved to find her presenting us with a plate of tiny decorated sweets and pastries. 'And this is also why in Yadz, we have the highest rate of diabetes in Iran!' she laughed. 'I work as a dietitian so I see this problem every day, many overweight people, eating Yadzi sweets all the time!'

Their flat was decorated in a mixture of western and Iranian styles. The main living area, like every home here, was dominated by a large Persian rug. A few cushions were placed around the edges but also a squashy leather sofa facing a wide-screen television. Here we flumped, in post-prandial, pre-diabetic stupor. Or at least I did. My hosts were obviously accustomed to ingesting such vast amounts of calories, although they somehow remained trim. I, on the other hand, after a month of Persian food and sitting on my bike every day, was struggling to fit into my jeans. I surreptitiously undid the top button and, for once, wished I was still wearing my shapeless manteau. Mr Yadzani had made a big deal about me removing any Islamic-imposed clothing as soon as the door had shut behind us, insisting that my headscarf and manteau were exchanged for loose-flowing hair and a T-shirt. He didn't say as much, but I sensed this was not merely a desire to make his guest comfortable but also his own quiet way of showing me his opinion of the regime. As a fifty-something war veteran, with his reserved, old-school demeanour he seemed an unlikely spokesman for women's rights, but he talked with great pride about Sara's career and studies and, as ever, I was reminded how it was impossible to pigeonhole any of the Iranians I had met. Whenever you thought you had a handle on them, they came out with an unexpected opinion, thought or statement. It was one of the most intriguing elements of my journey; I never quite knew what was going to happen next.

Amir was talking me through the display of family photos. 'This is Mehdi, my big brother,' he said. 'He has gone to university now.'

'I had Mehdi when I was very young,' said Sara. 'This is him when he was ten years old.' She was showing me a picture of Amir as a baby in the arms of his older brother. 'Now Mehdi is at university in Tehran. I began my studies when he was a baby and qualified when he was five.'

'That must have been hard work,' I said.

'I looked after him while she studied,' said Mr Yadzani with a hint of pride in his voice.

'Yes,' said Sara, 'and my family helped a lot and most of my tutors and colleagues were very understanding. But you know, nothing is easy in this country, especially for women.'

She said this as a plain fact, with no self-pity. After being in her company for just a few hours, I was already impressed by her quiet strength of character and intelligence and, like so many of the Iranian women I had met, this resilience, which would have been impressive alone, was accompanied by a natural warmth and kindness. You could see it in her face, her easy welcome and her affectionate interactions with her family. She smiled a lot, laughed easily and listened intently when others spoke. She had been battling the system her whole life, but it had not made her bitter. To me she was the epitome of the modern Iranian woman – a generous heart and an inner core of indefatigable strength.

'At university we would be harassed all the time,' she said, offering me another plate of Yadzi sweets. 'After I qualified I also worked at a university in another city in Iran, but the universities, they are controlled by the state, and when Ahmadinejad became president everything was much worse. He did not think it was good that more women go to university than men, he wished to see women in the home, only having children. For the first time in many years, maybe even since the revolution, they tried to segregate the classes and they stopped women from studying certain subjects. But, you know, women in Iran are very educated, they did not like this.'

'Even Khomeini wanted women to be educated,' added Mr Yadzani.

'Under Ahmadinejad it has been terrible,' said Sara. She shook her head in distress. 'First, they tried to segregate the students, and even the faculty. But this was not possible, they had to give up, because the staff, we have to speak to each other! It was crazy, it could not work. But it was not only this problem; they would come to me, asking me to tell them about my colleagues' behaviour, to inform on them.'

'About what kind of thing?'

'Un-Islamic behaviour, maybe if they drink alcohol at home. Or if they said things against the government, this kind of thing. I said I would not do it, they are my colleagues and my friends too, and then they tried to make me leave my job. They followed me, they disciplined me for wearing jeans under my manteau. Ah, it was a very bad time. Now I have a new job at the hospital.' She fell into silence for a moment, then continued. 'But it means you never know,' she said. 'You can never really know about other people, the people you work with, people you may think are your friends. How can you ever know? Who is watching, who is listening?'

I remembered Omid making a similar comment, about how Iranians cannot easily make new confidants, how they cannot risk exposing their opinions or behaviour to anyone they don't know intimately, preferring to stick with their close groups of truly trusted friends. It was as if all the openness and tolerance I had witnessed was reserved for outsiders, but could not be extended to their fellow countrymen.

'Then, nine years after Mehdi, we had Amir. So there is a big gap between them but they are very close.' She ruffled her son's hair. 'He misses his big brother, now he has gone away to university, don't you?'

Amir looked up from his latest sketch of a Kalashnikov-wielding figure and gave another of his dazzling smiles, nodding and expressing his love for his absent brother before cuddling up against his mum and adding the finishing touches to his drawing – a cascade of bullets flying out of the muzzle of the rifle.

The Yadzani residence was a spacious but homely apartment with framed pictures of family members on every wall and surface, and decorated with antique Persian handicrafts and traditional soft furnishings. After the rigours of the road, I revelled in the simple comforts of a family home, full of food and warmth and affection. I thought about the lonely, opium-smoking neighbour on the other side of the wall with his single pair of worn-out shoes, and felt a wave of gratitude for Mr Yadzani's natural empathy and his kindness, which had brought me here into his home.

On a shelf, among the family photos, was an old grainy snapshot of Mr Yadzani in his youth. His arm was slung around the shoulders of another young man who looked so similar I guessed them to be brothers. They were bearded and bare-headed but dressed in the army uniform of the 1980s that I had come to recognise from the martyr portraits I had seen throughout Iran. These portraits had become one of the defining features of my road trip, appearing literally everywhere. In the smallest mountain village, on the most remote desert highway and in every street of every town and city, each one of the boys or men who had died in the Iran–Iraq War of the 1980s was officially commemorated by a portrait in their home town. It was a lot of paintings; the total number of Iranian deaths during the eight-year conflict was estimated at half a million. I had vague memories of the war from the news bulletins of my childhood, and was aware of its scale – eight years of fighting, making it the longest conventional war of the twentieth century, with a million fatalities across both sides. But what I had not been aware of was this graphic phenomenon of the Iranian martyrs and their significance in the nation's consciousness.

Over the course of my journey I had found myself strangely affected by this unrelenting parade of strangers' faces that accompanied my ride. Sometimes the portraits took the form of a vast mural accompanied by a revolutionary message, especially if the deceased had been a high-ranking official, but the majority were simple painted portraits of regular soldiers, the conscripts, reservists and the thousands of teenage volunteers who had signed up to fight against Saddam Hussein. Their faces appeared mounted on lamp posts and fences, in rows along central reservations or on roundabouts, painted on the walls of cafés, shops and government buildings or on the sides of family homes. Very occasionally, in rural areas I had seen framed or laminated photographs tacked on to wooden posts, but this was rare; more often the images were excessively decorative with soft-focus backdrops of doves, roses and fluffy clouds. The war martyrs were accorded the greatest respect and their portraits, shrines and cemeteries were always kept in tip-top condition by the authorities. Like the vintage propaganda of the DOWN WITH USA murals in Tehran, there was a retro charm about the airbrushed eighties style of the portraits, which, combined with the fact that Iranian men are on the whole a handsome bunch, made for a compelling spectacle. A million soulful brown eyes and chiselled cheekbones lining the highways and byways of Iran.

'Is this your brother?' I asked Mr Yadzani.

He nodded, picking up the framed photograph, looking at it with an inscrutable expression. 'Yes, we were twins. He was martyred. In the Imposed War. This is 1981; we were nineteen years old in this picture.'

Like all Iranians, Mr Yadzani referred to the conflict as 'the Imposed War', a reference to Saddam Hussein's initial invasion. Iran had not been in prime fighting condition in 1980; the country was in post-revolutionary chaos and Khomeini had publicly executed most of the army's leaders, fearing their loyalty still lay with the Shah. Across the border in Iraq, Saddam saw his neighbour's moment of military weakness as an ideal opportunity for an easy land grab along the frontier. What he hadn't counted on was the revolutionary fervour that burned in the hearts of so many young Iranian men at that time.

'We all wanted to be part of it,' said Mr Yadzani, still staring at the photograph. 'I was lucky, just my foot.' He motioned to his bad leg. 'From a landmine, this was very common. My brother, he was not so lucky. Operation Ramadan, in 1982, many Iranian martyrs from this battle, thousands. It was a terrible thing, with the Iraqis using chemical weapons, you know, mustard gas?'

I nodded. Mr Yadzani added, 'We did not use chemical weapons. Khomeini said it was un-Islamic.'

I found this a peculiar notion, that certain weapons of war were acceptable in Islam but others not so much. And what of the tear gas used on the Green Revolution protestors just a few years ago – was that considered to be 'Islamic'? Who made the rules? There were so many aspects of this story, of this nation's mindset, that confounded me. Indeed, the very concept of martyrdom was almost impossible for me to comprehend. Did people really believe in it? Had Mr Yadzani and his brother believed it? Much had been made in the western media at the time about the Iranian child soldiers who went not just willingly, but enthusiastically, to battle, believing that if they died fighting for the Islamic Republic, they would be granted a place in heaven. Pictures showed troops praying in the trenches and corpses lying on the battlefields with the Quran and other holy books tucked in the pockets of their uniforms. Footage showed Iranian child soldiers in their thousands, charging towards the Iraqi army, shouting *'Allah Akbar!'* in the infamous 'human wave' attacks. It has been said that Iraqi troops were so appalled by the phenomenon of thousands of young, often unarmed Iranian boys marching towards them in a state of religious ecstasy, that it affected their morale and ultimately their defence; they simply couldn't stomach it.

In Iran, these men and boys, some paid-up members of the Revolutionary Guards but most volunteers of the Basij militia, became not just heroes of the war but symbols of the revolution. As I now saw all across the country, the Islamic Republic has never stopped promoting this image with its relentless stream of soft-focus glorification; the martyr portraits, the endless documentaries and feature films about the war, books and photo exhibitions, television shows, concerts and parades. In only a matter of weeks, I had seen references to all of these, still being churned out, thirty years after the event.

I asked Mr Yadzani about the 'plastic keys to paradise', a story that had taken hold in the western news during the war and come to symbolise the Iranian child martyrs. Thousands of golden plastic keys were supposedly manufactured by a toy company in Taiwan on the orders of Khomeini. He had issued them to the young *basiji*, on the promise that if they wore them around their neck as they charged in their human waves, should they be killed, these keys would 'unlock' the gate to paradise. It was a suitably horrifying and provocative image for the western media, who leapt upon it as a perfect example of the inhuman 'otherness' of the Iranians. Britain and the US were still reeling in shock from the revolution, and this only added fuel to their anti-Iranian fire. The plastic keys entered western popular culture, they even had songs written about them, but the reality is that there is no evidence of them having existed. They do not appear in any photos or footage from the war. Were they a reality or just a piece of propaganda invented and exaggerated by a western media hungry for stories that further demonised Iran? Mr Yadzani was listening carefully as I spoke, silently chewing at his bottom lip, brow furrowed in one of his great expressive frowns.

'I have heard something like this once before but no, I never saw such a thing. We had metal ID tags around our necks of course but no, no plastic key.'

I wanted to ask him if he and his brother had truly believed the propaganda, if they believed that they would go to heaven. He had referred to his brother being 'martyred', but the word was so much part of the vernacular in Iran that I wondered if it no longer implied true belief in the concept of martyrdom. So much of Iranian speech was emotive, infused with dramatic, religious language; even the surviving war veterans were referred to as '*Jan bazan*' – 'those who risk their souls'. I feared digging into these deeply entrenched beliefs was too delicate a subject. I was still wary of discussing religion unless someone else laid their cards on the table first, but Mr Yadzani saved me the awkwardness.

'It was not like this for us, about going to heaven,' he said, shaking his head, as if he could sense my bewilderment. 'Maybe for some people, yes, but we just wanted to be part of it. All our friends were going to the war. We did not want to be left behind. We had no idea of what would happen, how it would be. Of course, we heard people talk about being martyrs, but I did not really understand what this meant. It is hard to believe now, but we had no fear. No fear at all. We thought it would be a good game, yes?'

'This is how boys think!' said Sara, shaking her head.

'The Imposed War,' said Mr Yadzani, 'it was a terrible thing. Because it touched everyone. Everyone in Iran still, they will know someone who fought or maybe died, a relative or a friend. But it was also a great time for Iran. It is hard to remember that now.'

'What do you mean?'

'It made Iran strong. In all of history, for hundreds of years, thousands of years, Iran has been invaded, controlled. The Arabs, the Turks, the Soviets, the Americans, the British . . .' He smiled at me. 'Sorry.'

I smiled back.

'The revolution had just happened. It is hard to think like this now, but everyone thought this was a great new start for our country, we had thrown out the Shah, and then we had this chance, to fight, to show the world, to show Saddam about the new Iran.'

'But there was no real winner, am I right? It was a ceasefire?'

In 1988 Khomeini had likened the signing of the UN-mediated truce to 'drinking a cup of poison', so it was hardly a triumphant victory, but I didn't mention his famous quote, not wanting to rain on Mr Yadzani's patriotic parade.

'Yes, this is true, but what is important is that we fought back and we defended Iran. Saddam had the backing of America, but we had nothing. The war brought the country together.'

'So when you signed up, you were part of the Basij?'

'Yes, all the volunteers were *basiji*. Hundreds of thousands of us. We had a uniform, a gun, grenades. Some had RPGs.'

'But the Basij is different now,' Sara added quickly. 'Then they were only to fight the war. Now it is terrible, how they treat people, the things they can do . . .'

She drifted off, shaking her head, her feelings written all over her face, reflecting the general impression I had got from everyone I had spoken to in Iran about this subject, this mixture of anger and revulsion at any mention of the Basij.

'They tried to make Mehdi join. I begged him not to. They came to his university; they have a special branch for students, to keep watch on the other students, and if they are making trouble against the regime, to report them to the university.'

'Did he want to join?'

'No, thankfully, no. But they gave him a lot of pressure. And it is easy to see why some boys want to, especially if they come from poor families. They will be given food at the mosque, they are looked after, given uniforms, sometimes weapons. This is very attractive for a young village boy with nothing. As a *basiji* you will be taken care of in all ways, a place at university, maybe a government job after studying. Many things like this, so these families encourage their sons to join.'

'It is not only about these things,' said Mr Yadzani. 'It is the power. Suddenly you have power, the power to stop people in the street because of their clothes, their hair, young people like them, old people, women. It has gone too far, it was not like this when the Basij was created. We were supposed to fight for the Islamic Republic, against Saddam.'

Khomeini's original vision for the Basij, had been to create a 'twenty-million man army', a volunteer militia force, the Organisation for the Mobilisation of the Oppressed, made up of almost half the population, reporting to the Revolutionary Guards and loyal to the Supreme Leader. Originally created to quash uprisings among the Kurds and other tribes, within a year of the Islamic Revolution, Iran was at war and the ranks of *basiji* swelled as their duties extended to the battlefield, although it never got anywhere close to Khomeini's fantasy of 20 million. Women were originally encouraged to join, but with the war underway, the force was largely made up of young men and boys, mostly poor, rural and illiterate, seduced by the romantic notion of seeing some action or martyrdom, or both. Mr Yadzani obviously despaired at what the Basij had become over the intervening decades – essentially a thuggish, home-grown militia of ignorant bullies.

'So what happened? What changed?' I asked him.

'It was always different, depending on who was president, but it became very bad when Ahmadinejad was in power.'

'Yes, now they are everywhere,' said Sara. 'Harassing people in the street for everything! This is when they tried to make Mehdi join. Our neighbour's son was threatened by a *basiji* in Tehran for having gel in his hair – he had a spiked haircut, they said it was too western. This kind of thing suddenly happened more and more, they would ride around on motorcycles, stopping cars to find out what music was playing, or if they saw a man and woman together who they thought were not married. They would smell people's breath to see if they had been drinking alcohol, even elderly people.'

'So do you think the Basij will be scaled back now, under Rouhani?' I asked.

'Maybe, yes, I hope. I think the feeling is changing now. Because of the protests in Tehran in 2009, after the election. The Basij were shooting into the crowd, beating people in the street, young boys just like them, and girls too, beating them with iron bars and sticks. After this, even some ayatollahs spoke out against them. It was too much to see this. People were killed, young people, sons and daughters. You know about Neda Agha-Soltan?'

I nodded, recalling the chilling video footage that had shocked the world – the death of Neda Agha-Soltan, a young music student shot in the chest from a rooftop by a *basiji* at the Tehran protests of June 2009. Fellow protestors had captured her death on their cameras, her last breaths and blood pouring out of her mouth as she lay in the street, in broad daylight. I thought about Aheng, the young sparky schoolgirl I had met on the road to Tehran who had protested that day with her parents, joining the thousands marching down Azadi Street. It could so easily have been her, killed by some boy of her own age, cocky, brainwashed and trigger-happy. Instead it had been Neda. She was not the only one, but it was Neda who became the international face of the protests, the martyr of the Green Revolution and, as is the way with twenty-first-century revolutions, a hashtag, #Neda, that had swept across the internet.

Mr Yadzani was tiring now and made his excuses as he rose slowly from his chair.

'He likes to go to sleep early,' said Sara, an affectionate smile across her face, patting her husband's arm as he limped off to bed. 'But he is much older than me,' she added, her smile turning to a cheeky grin. He smiled back and kissed her on the head.

I watched him go, scooping up a sleepy Amir on his way, and wondered how he remained so gentle and kind after the horrors he had witnessed in the war, the death of his brother and his own injuries that clearly still caused him pain. There had been no need for him to look after me today; he could have seen it as an opportunity to squeeze a hefty 'tourist tax' from me for his taxi services. He hadn't needed to stop to help his friend with the broken-down car, or make his quiet pledge to check on his lonely neighbour. It wasn't the first time I had marvelled at the remarkable humanity among the people of this country. Was it against all odds, or a result of their situation? The question remained a mystery.

17

Persepolis: Empire and Excess

As I left Yadz, I was aware that I was embarking on the final leg of my Iranian adventure. Shiraz, the city that had been calling me for so many months and thousands of miles, was finally in sight, no longer a mysterious faraway place but an achievable goal, just 300 miles away now. I allowed myself the thought that I really was going to make it.

Wanting to make the most of every precious day of my visa, and reluctant to retrace any of my route back north to the Turkish border, I had planned to end my journey in Shiraz with just enough time to ship my bike home from there. My final plans were still undecided, and I mulled them over as I studied my route to Shiraz, plotting a purposely meandering course for my final days on the road. I settled on a network of back-country roads that took me over a vast dry lake bed, its salt crystals sparkling in the sun, before crossing a flat, rocky plateau with the remains of ancient forts and abandoned wells dotted along the roadside.

A remote but well-travelled dirt track delivered me over one more mountain range into a lush river valley. This source of water and greenery was obviously so rare and revered that it warranted its very own brown tourist signs, the first and only time I had seen them in Iran. *Behesht-e Gomshodeh – The Lost Paradise*, they promised. I followed these signs for miles, with no idea what such an enigmatically titled place could be but intrigued by the notion. My mind ran wild with its own version of such a fantasy, and I wondered when this mysterious tourist attraction would appear.

I even wondered if it was some kind of theme park; I imagined crystal grottos, palm trees, scented tropical flowers and warm turquoise lakes. It was only when the signs ran out that I had a *Lost Paradise? You're standing in it* moment and admonished myself for feeling slightly disappointed. Beautiful as it was, it was essentially no more than a particularly verdant valley that had been bestowed, in typical overly dramatic Iranian style, with a flowery title. But once I'd recalibrated my expectations, I came to value the Lost Paradise as much as the Iranian tourist board obviously did. Its empty roads, shady rest stops and cool, crystalline rivers were a welcome relief after so many miles in the harsh, baking climes of the Dasht-e Lūt and so long running the gauntlet on Iran's violent highways.

Before I landed in Shiraz, I had a small but important detour to make that would satisfy a long-held fascination. The story dated back to before I was born, to France in the autumn of 1971, where the Parisian elite were up in arms. *Quelle horreur!*, their restaurant of choice, Maxim's, had closed suddenly for two weeks. And should they have resorted to their second, third or even hundredth choice of dining establishment, they would have found themselves out of luck too. For one fortnight in October of that year, 160 of Paris's top chefs had been transported 3,000 miles to the Iranian desert, where they were cooking up a storm, in more ways than one.

As the French chefs toiled and sweated in the desert heat, spooning Caspian caviar into thousands of quails' eggs and artfully arranging the tails of fifty foie-gras-stuffed peacocks, they had no idea that they were participating in the fall of the Pahlavi dynasty. To them and the other Europeans who had won the lucrative contracts for the catering, decorating, horticulture and costume design, they had struck gold. Here was the chance of a lifetime, to work on the biggest party the world had ever seen: the Shah of Iran's celebration of 2,500 years of the Persian monarchy. The location was Persepolis, the world-famous ancient ruins of the empire's former capital near Shiraz, and the next destination on my Iranian road trip.

From late 1970, over the course of a year, 160 acres of barren desert land next to Persepolis were transformed into a luxurious tented city, created in the shape of a star around a central fountain. The interiors were styled by the Parisian design firm, Maison Jansen. Crates of Porthault linen and Limoges tableware were shipped from France, and from Germany, a fleet of 250 Mercedes limousines to transport the guests from the airport. Trees, shrubs and flowers were flown in from France to recreate the site as it would have looked 2,500 years previously, but modern conveniences were not overlooked; each tent was air-conditioned and installed with a direct-dial phone and telex line to the guest's respective home country. A different vintage wine was selected to accompany each course of the banquet, and 5,000 bottles of champagne sat on ice, awaiting a guest list of 600 members of the world's royalty, presidents and prime ministers. The airport at nearby Shiraz was souped up accordingly and a brand new highway constructed to Persepolis. True to the traditions of Persian hospitality, the guests' comfort and security was of the utmost importance, and with this in mind, the Shah ordered that the area surrounding the party site was cleared of snakes and vermin, both literally and metaphorically.

In the days running up to the event, while hundreds of lowly rat-catchers scurried around the desert, killing off any animal threat, the Shah's secret police, SAVAK, were busy taking care of the human equivalent. This constituted a process of 'preventative arrests', targeting anyone they considered to be anti-Shah, who could potentially use the opportunity of the party to cause trouble, even if there was no evidence they were hatching such plans. As a result, in the week before the celebrations Iran's prisons were heaving with thousands of innocent citizens. And they weren't the only ones unhappy about the Shah's plans. Ayatollah Khomeini, in exile in Iraq at the time, publicly denounced the party, describing it as the 'Devil's festival' and its attendees as 'traitors to Islam and the Iranian nation'. By now he had built up a loyal following, particularly amongst Iran's poor and pious, who were equally resentful of the Shah's decadence and what they saw as the increasing 'westoxification' of Iran. A few years previously, the Shah had had Khomeini arrested, causing an uprising in the religious city of Qom, and although his Islamic revolution was still eight years away, the seeds had been sown. The Shah's decision to hold such a lavish and ostentatiously expensive gathering turned out to be the catalyst for his downfall, and ultimately, the Islamic Revolution of 1979.

This image of the fallen king, and his terrible misjudgement that would eventually lead to his undoing, had always fascinated me. And now Persepolis was just down the road, less than forty miles from Shiraz. I was keen to see the ancient ruins, of course, but the site of the party to end all parties was equally as enticing. Leaving behind the soothing habitat of the Lost Paradise, the land turned harsh and rocky once more, the sun blasting out of the sky, cooking and cracking the earth, and overheating me and my poor air-cooled bike. No wonder the Shah had insisted that the tents were fitted with air con.

After getting mildly lost in the streets of Marvdasht, a grubby little dustbowl town on the approach to Persepolis, I was beginning to wonder if I'd misread my map. It was hard to believe that the great ruins of the former capital of the Persian Empire were to be found up the road from this collection of shuttered shops and litter-strewn gutters. I doubted the Shah and his guests had come this way in their limousines. There were no signs for Persepolis, just a few sun-bleached martyr portraits and the usual moralistic billboards warning against the perils of social media, qalyān pipes, lipstick or whatever else the government feared was in danger of corrupting Iran's youth. I rode around the half-abandoned streets, trying to find a passer-by to ask directions, wilting between the relentless sun and its reflected heat rising up from the tarmac. But the town was deserted and all I could do was keep blundering around the unmarked roundabouts, hot, bothered and fighting my innate cynicism regarding visiting world-renowned tourist sites.

I was steeling myself for coachloads of visitors, pushy tour guides and unctuous souvenir sellers, but Persepolis, when I finally found it, brought none of the tourist tackiness I had feared. Tall cypress trees lined the wide approach road and an ethereal calm that felt as old as the ruins themselves hung in the air. Most strangely, the site was almost empty of visitors. Officially, the Islamic Republic do not approve of anything relating to the Persian monarchy, which may account for the low key, uncommercial atmosphere. Originally, a complex of palaces, it was built by the Persian king Darius around 515 BC, and housed various monarchs until Alexander the Great destroyed most of it nearly two hundred years later. Its association with the ancient dynasties did not chime with the worldview of Khomeini, who described the concept of monarchy in his typical histrionic style, as a 'shameful and disgraceful reactionary manifestation'. I doubted many contemporary Iranians felt this way about Persepolis, their very own UNESCO World Heritage site. The two people I did encounter wandering around the ruins – a teacher leading a school trip and a young guy selling a half-hearted collection of fridge magnets – spoke of the site with a rousing, almost chest-beating pride, describing it as the true heart of Iran and Persian culture.

'Persepolis has no connection to the Islamic Republic,' explained the fridge magnet man in a conspiratorial whisper. 'This is why I like to work here. It reminds me where we are from, this is real Iran. It is like an escape for me.'

I wandered among the fluted columns, up staircases decorated with bas-relief carvings of Armenians bringing wine to the Persian kings, and around the tombs of the ancient rulers themselves, passing immaculate stone horses' heads and imperious griffins. Passing through the vast entrance of the Gate of All Nations, I marvelled inwardly at the skill and intricacy of the carvings, and laughed outwardly at the discovery of some less-skilled handiwork, a prime example of British graffiti. Admittedly, it had distinguished provenance, dating from 1870 and having been scribed by the hand of explorer, Henry Morton Stanley. Apparently defacing ancient monuments was all the rage in those days; the famous gate was covered in the names of various nineteenth-century Europeans – a collection of diplomats, archaeologists, merchants and statesmen, their motivation no different from the urge known to teenagers the world over to etch one's name into a park bench or tag a railway carriage *I was here*.

As I completed my tour, I caught sight of what appeared to be a collection of derelict structures in a large patch of wasteland just a short walk from the main site. The area was nestled among the tall evergreens and half hidden by overgrown brush, but as I studied the view, I could just make out the shape of a skeletal metal framework poking out from the untamed bushes. Here it was, the remains of the Shah's tent city, ramshackle, forgotten and consumed by nature. I walked into this eerie nether world, tiptoeing among the long grass, occasionally tripping over cracked concrete slabs hidden beneath the scrub, and thought how peculiar it was to be among these two symbols of fallen dynasties, built nearly 2,500 years apart: one still breathtaking in its grandeur and ambition, the other reminiscent of an abandoned provincial garden centre.

Standing inside the metal frames of the circular tents, I imagined them as they had once been, swagged in brightly coloured cloth, visiting nations' flags flying outside each fringed doorway, hastily planted palm trees swaying in the breeze, and uniformed servants on hand at every turn. I tried to picture Princess Anne getting stuck into the 5,000 bottles of champagne and Haile Selassie telexing back to Ethiopia from his tent, and wondered how many pairs of shoes Imelda Marcos had brought with her, and if she had cut a rug with President Mobutu of Zaire with his leopard-skin hat and Coke-bottle specs.

Queen Elizabeth had turned down the invitation, officially due to security concerns, but Public Record documents unearthed since reveal that the palace feared the festivities would be 'possibly undignified' and described the guest list as a 'motley collection of heads of state', further adding, with a disdain only the British establishment can muster, 'or more likely, their representatives'. Not considered a hot enough ticket for the Queen herself, Prince Philip and Princess Anne were sent in her stead. Adding insult to injury for the Pahlavis, President Nixon and France's Georges Pompidou also declined the invitation, sending underlings in their place. I wondered if the Shah was at all put out by these snubs, from the leaders of the countries he most sought to impress. Like many powerful but vain men, his ego was frail and the final guest list, of lower-ranking officials of western countries and a throng of Third World dictators, was not quite the glittering A-list he had hoped for.

The Shah's plans were well intentioned: the event was designed to show off Iran and its grand civilisation to the world. But at home it only served to demonstrate how alienated the Shah was from his subjects. In the early 1970s, despite the previous efforts of his father, Reza Shah and his own 'White Revolution' – the programme of reforms that had been designed to propel Iran into the modern age – much of the population were still illiterate and living in poverty. Meanwhile the new young Shah and his cronies were jetting around Europe, skiing in the Alps and even flying into Paris for lunch on a whim. When the Shah was to be found at home, he remained aloof from his people, preferring to funnel vast amounts of money into his favourite hobby, outfitting the Iranian army with a seemingly endless supply of weapons, tanks and aeroplanes, happily provided by Britain and the US. In this climate the announcement to spend tens of millions of dollars on a three-day celebration, with its five-and-a-half-hour feast, sound and light shows, specially composed music and numerous military processions, all for the benefit of the world's super-elite, failed to inspire patriotic pride in the hearts of the Iranian people. The sop they were offered was that the celebrations would be filmed and screened at cinemas around the country. Unsurprisingly, the resulting movie was a box-office flop.

In the wake of the party, the tent city continued to be used for government events but it was not long for this world. When the Islamic Revolution swept through the country in 1979, it was looted by Khomeini supporters who attempted to burn it to the ground. Local residents fought them off and it stood half wrecked for years until it was commandeered as army barracks during the war with Iraq. Now, standing amongst the weeds and cracked concrete, even its ruins felt temporary and cheap, a reminder that nothing lasts and that maybe, one day, even the Islamic Republic would be no more than a memory.

'What's going to happen to it?' I asked my fridge-magnet man, who was taking a moment in a quiet corner of the Persepolis café to do a stocktake. Neat piles of miniature plastic Azadi Towers and griffins' heads sat at his feet. He finished his counting and shrugged. 'Ahmadinejad wanted to restore it about ten years ago, but it did not happen.'

'Ahmadinejad? Really?' I was surprised. I would have thought that of all people, he would have wanted to erase it forever, a symbol of the western decadence that he so enjoyed denouncing in his colourful language. But it seemed this was part of his confused plan to attract more tourists while maintaining the ideals of the Islamic Republic.

'This was his idea, to use it to show the world the excess of the Shah, to remind the people of those days and why the revolution happened. I saw the pictures and the plans when they came here to make the announcement. But it never happened.'

'Why not?'

'People liked the idea, but not for the reason Ahmadinejad liked it. Nowadays people have good feelings for the Shah, and they think this party was a great thing to happen. They would love to have a party like this again! They do not want to be told "This is evil." People are tired of this message now. I think this is the reason.'

I could see his point, but it seemed Iran's rose-tinted glasses were at work again, and I wondered how the people who had been 'preventatively arrested' felt about the original celebrations now. I also wondered if in forty years' time the country would have been blown apart once again, and if the Iranian people would ever be nostalgic for the good old days of the Islamic Republic and get similarly dewy-eyed about Khomeini – 'Oh, he wasn't that bad.' It seemed unlikely, right now, amongst all the seething anger and frustration of twenty-first-century Iran with its impassioned, forward-thinking youth. But who knew what the next regime would bring? Iran's tradition of tyrannical leaders went back centuries and seemed set in stone, destined to endlessly repeat itself. As if the fridge-magnet seller was reading my mind, he said quietly, almost as if to himself, 'More Cyrus, that is what we need.'

I nodded. He was right, Cyrus the Great had been Iran's one and only benevolent leader, founder of the Persian Empire and an early proponent of human rights who had helped establish the national identity of Iran. I agreed with my new friend, admiring his sage-like wisdom and analysis of Iran's political and social history, until I realised he was talking about his stocktake. He only had two Cyrus magnets left.

Down the road from Persepolis was a small campsite with cabins and manicured plots set among rose bushes and more tall pine trees. I rolled in to be met by excitable pointing and gesturing from the two men at the reception. I couldn't understand what they were trying to tell me, their English being as non-existent as my Persian, but when I ventured into the campground I was greeted by the sight of two BMW motorcycles, clad in the familiar battered luggage and country stickers of the overland traveller. It was a blast from another world, another life almost. For the global motorcyclist, it was not uncommon to bump into other riders on the road, to hang out or ride together for a while. On my first journey through the Americas this had been a defining feature of the experience, connecting with a worldwide tribe of adventure riders. But during my trip through Africa I had met only one other motorcyclist plying the classic Cape Town overland route, and in Iran I had not met another western traveller. I realised just how immersed in my surroundings I had become. Isolated by sketchy, restricted internet access and making only scant connection with home, I had been cut off. I had relished this immersion but now, shaking hands, and even exchanging furtive hugs with the owners of these two bikes, Georg from Switzerland and Jacek from Poland, I slipped into the welcome, easy patter of motorcycle travellers the world over.

We compared routes, exchanged border-crossing horror stories, discussed bikes and equipment (theirs big and blingy, mine little and lo-fi). They had been on the road for several years, most recently in Africa, before coming east across the UAE and arriving in Iran's port of Bandar Abbas on the ferry from Dubai. They were on the home stretch now, the last leg to Europe, and they had little interest in any Iranian meanders. They had wives, families and, in Jacek's case, a sock empire demanding attention. I could see the calling of home in their eyes and hear it in their voices when they talked about the road ahead. They were done. It was a feeling I knew well from my own journeys, though I wasn't quite there yet.

In the otherwise empty campsite we sat beneath the tall pines, cheerfully bemoaning the lack of a cold beer that contained more than 0.0 per cent alcohol, while they cooked me a pasta dinner on their petrol stoves and, in a heart-warming display of chivalry, refused to let me do the washing-up. The camaraderie was familiar and comforting, and when we strolled around Persepolis and spent the next day riding together, I was aware of how different my Iranian experience was in the company of two strapping European males. At petrol stations and cafés, they did all the talking. But I didn't mind. For the short time we were together, I decided to consciously relish the protective shield of their presence. Tomorrow I would be back on the road, alone again for my final day's ride in Iran.

18

Shiraz: Poetry and Pomegranates

As I MADE my way through the dry, rocky hills approaching Shiraz from Persepolis, I envisaged the city that Habib had painted so enticingly all those many months ago in his strange scrawled note on a cold winter's day in London. I could hardly believe how that incident had spawned this incredible journey. Rolling down the steep, sweeping descent towards the city, Shiraz appeared in front of me, full of promise. A jumble of the ancient and the new, dusty brown blocky homes, modern high-rise hotels and offices, sixties tower blocks, domes, minarets and flyovers – all nestled together in the rocky folds of the surrounding hills and dotted with bursts of green, parks and trees bringing life to the arid cityscape. I was picturing an Iranian San Francisco, a hip city of rebels, lovers and poets, founded on the passionate words of Hafez and Saadi, on an ancient tradition of wine and rowdy taverns (no longer, of course) and compounding its reputation with the recent student protests. As for its inhabitants, I had given much thought to the mysterious Habib and the archetypal Shirazi I heard so much about, the easy-going, laidback lovable jokers of Iran.

I soon discovered that their relaxed nature did not extend to their driving skills. The fringes of Shiraz consumed me like every other Iranian city; sprawling, manic multi-lane chaos. Horns, shouts, car radios and flashing neon Persian pounding my senses. Thick diesel fumes mingling with the sweet ripening fruit of roadside stalls, piles of shiny pomegranates at every junction, and trucks kicking up so much dust you could taste it in every breath. My heart gave its usual thud as I spotted a police car full of uniformed officers parked by a set of traffic lights. Did the Shiraz police force also live up to this laidback reputation? My thudding heart sank as the lights turned red, forcing me to sit there, next to the police car, while the traffic streamed and weaved across the junction in front of me for what felt like an age. But the police weren't interested in me. It was the fruit seller next to them who was staring, mouth agape. He edged closer, eyebrows knitting in bemusement that verged on disbelief. I did my best to ignore him. Then he turned to the police, waving to attract their attention, then back to me again. I stayed focussed on the road ahead, a nervous jiggle taking over my leg as I silently urged the lights to change. Hassle with the Iranian police was the last thing I needed at the end of my journey.

Red turned to green and I pulled away with a spurt of nervous throttle, glancing back over my shoulder. The fruit seller was pointing after me, and now he had the policemen's attention; they had stepped out of the car. I just caught the amazement in his expression and the laughter erupting on the policemen's face as the fruit seller pointed after me, made the universal motorcycle throttle action and then squeezed an imaginary pair of breasts on his chest. As I disappeared into the turmoil of Shiraz traffic, I noted with pleasure that his fruit stall had consisted of nothing but an enormous pile of melons.

So here I was at last. Shiraz. The city that had summoned me. It felt livelier, louder and tattier than Isfahan with its refined boulevards, or Yadz with its tranquil antique alleyways. This was a working, moving, living city. As I picked my way through its streets, watching its men and women going about their business, chatting, laughing, shouting, shopping, bartering, I thought about Habib, and wondered if he was here somewhere amongst its 1.5 million citizens.

I was eager to explore but a motorcycle is no way to get to the heart of a city, so I parked the bike in the underground car park of a hotel and set out on foot. I had long got over my Londoner's discomfort about being approached by strangers; there was no place for that kind of personal privacy in Iran. But the Shirazis took it to a new level. I could not walk a block without being greeted by passers-by with varying levels of English. Often it was just the standard 'Hello! How are you?' as taught in schools and evening classes the world over.

A middle-aged couple who spoke no English at all invited me to eat with them, beckoning and miming the process of putting food in their mouths. It was well meaning but so hopeless a lunch date that they settled for a selfie with me instead and left me with a pomegranate in each pocket. At the next block a young, irrepressibly camp guy in tight T-shirt and skinny jeans popped out of his mobile phone shop to hijack me for a quick English refresher.

'I am studying your language but I forget a word, the word for when something is not straight. Please can you help me?'

'Wonky?'

'Ah yes, *wonky*, this is it. *Wonky*. Thank you!' He touched his hand to his heart.

But whenever I stopped for longer than a minute in a shop or café, or just to buy a bottle of water or a freshly made juice at a roadside kiosk, I was inevitably cornered for more meaningful conversation.

'What do people think of Iran in your country?' and 'What do you think of Iran?' The same questions I had heard echoing across the country. I tried to explain that people at home in England didn't really know very much about Iran, that it wasn't our fault, we'd been fed misinformation, for years, decades, centuries even. I thought back to my own feelings and misgivings before I left home and cringed at my ignorance.

An elderly but sharp-witted woman took the opportunity to boast in the most charming manner about the academic successes of her children, all doctors and lecturers at Harvard, MIT and other faraway universities. She longed for them to return to Iran and bemoaned the situation that kept them away. 'Things are bad here, the economy is bad. Everyone clever, everyone young goes away to America. This used to be a good place to live. If you had come here before, you would see it was different . . .' she tailed off. I thought she meant before the sanctions, but when I pursued the subject she waved her hand as if to suggest the distant past and said, 'Oh, no, no. Before 1979.'

But not everyone had got away. The results of Khomeini's revolutionary breeding programme were on full display in Shiraz. Young people filled the streets, particularly around the university campuses and in the tranquil corners of Eram Botanical Garden, the latter of which was known as a hotspot for furtive trysts. But their intentions were hardly the traditional teenage knee-trembler of a British alleyway, constituting nothing more shocking than an arm around a shoulder in a shady corner or a walk, hand in hand, through the flower beds.

'This is illegal in Iran if you are not married,' said a man's voice behind me as I stood surveying the scenes around me. His name was Ahmad. He was taking a walk in the gardens with his wife and they offered to show me around. They pointed out groups of architecture students, sat on the grass, sketching the eighteenth-century pavilion, its reflection perfectly still in its ornamental turquoise pool. Later we strayed into the darker corners of the garden where less studious visitors had headed for the shadows, risking a chaste kiss beneath an overhanging branch. Peaches and the ever-present pomegranates hung like jewels around them and tiny birds darted among the bushes. The air was warm and fragrant, the atmosphere relaxed and unashamedly romantic.

'*Eram* is from an Arab word, it means "paradise" or "heaven",' said Ahmad. He motioned towards a young couple sitting close together, hand in hand, on a rock beside a small man-made lake. 'This is why people who are not married come to Eram, they know they will not be arrested.'

'But surely the police know about this? They could come down here any evening and arrest everyone, couldn't they?'

'Ah, not in Shiraz. It is different.' He smiled. 'The police would not do that here. People are more relaxed here, even the policemen.'

I told him about the car full of laughing policemen and the melon seller that had greeted me upon my arrival, and he laughed, nodding.

'Yes, this sounds like Shirazi policemen, it is not like in the north of Iran, where I come from. They raid houses there, for parties and alcohol. Even in Tehran the police will arrest women because of their clothing every summer. This is why Shiraz is the best city in Iran. Here we like to talk, to read poetry, not to work too hard, and of course to eat. We are so relaxed here, we have a saying, "Eating a meal is like taking a bullet, you must lie down immediately."' He laughed again out loud. 'Come to the tomb of Hafez, it is not far. Here you will understand about Shiraz.'

As we walked, Ahmad spoke of his love for his adopted city but was equally passionate about his desire to get out of Iran. He was yet another of Iran's young, urbane computer programmers; there seemed to be a glut of them. Almost every young man I spoke with worked in the tech business, and all were desperate to ply their trade in the free West.

'I email my resumé to a company every day,' he told me. The weariness of his fruitless campaign showed on his face and in his voice.

'Where to? Where do you want to live?'

'Anywhere. I apply to firms in America, Canada, Australia, the UK, France, Germany . . .' he tailed off. 'I will go anywhere.'

He said his best chance was Canada or Australia, where they had programmes for accepting skilled workers. Some of his friends had made it to Toronto, and some distant members of his family had sought asylum in London after the revolution. I told him about Hossein, who I'd met in Ramsar and who had made the journey to a new life and a highly paid tech job in

Canada, but who'd returned home after four years, pining for the 'real life' of Iran.

Ahmad was dismissive. 'Hah, he will change his mind soon enough.'

We were walking through the packed, brightly lit streets. Ahmad said it was like this every night, that Shirazis liked to get out and enjoy themselves, this is what they lived for. Restaurants were full, shops still buzzing after dark, and of course picnickers making the most of every patch of grass. Ahead of us a crowd filled the pavement and I realised we had arrived at the site of Hafez's tomb.

It was not until I saw the throng that I fully grasped the significance of Hafez in the everyday lives of Iranians. His name and poetry had cropped up everywhere along my journey; on ornamental tiles on grand buildings and in the most rundown hotel, and the book of his poems, the *Divan-e Hafez*, was to be found in everyone's house, no matter what their political or religious inclinations. His lines were dropped into conversations and newspaper articles, used as sayings and proverbs, and pinned on walls of cafés and shops alongside quotes from the Quran and pictures of Khomeini, although unlike these two other omnipresent icons of Iran, Hafez seemed to have the effect of unifying the Iranian people. His poems epitomised the Iranian mindset; passionate and opinionated but laced with humour and a lust for life. His moral and religious messages had elevated him to oracle status, but they sat comfortably alongside admissions of human frailty and decadence, including plentiful references to desire, wine and drunkenness. And just like the twenty-first-century Iranians I had met, from tech-savvy young guns to devout traditionalists, Hafez's world was a harmonious blend of the mystical and the human, as if no conflict existed between the two.

The crowds milled peacefully outside the entrance to the tomb, while inside the gates families, friends and couples walked together around the small pillared mausoleum, many of them holding the

SHIRAZ: POETRY AND POMEGRANATES

Divan, opening it randomly and whispering his words to each other, using them as a prophecy. All around me, people of all ages were huddled on benches in the surrounding garden, performing the same ritual. I could not imagine such scenes at Poet's Corner in Westminster Abbey or Shakespeare's tomb at Stratford-upon-Avon. This was a joyful, egalitarian celebration of art and life, with none of the stuffiness or elitism we associate with poetry back home.

'There is a tradition we have, it is called *Fal'e Hafez*,' explained Ahmad. 'It means "Ask Hafez". Every year, on the first day of winter, the shortest day of the year, we gather with our families, we eat pistachio nuts and fruits and we say, "*Fal'e Hafez*". Then we open the *Divan* to see what he says about our future, or to seek his advice about our problems.'

'What kind of problems?' I asked.

'Oh, any kind, all things . . . work, love, family, life . . .'

Outside on the street, old men and young boys were making half-hearted attempts to hustle the crowd. They had little yellow canaries on their shoulders and were calling out, '*Fal'e Hafez!*' In their hands they held a small wooden box stacked with coloured cards. I handed over a 'one Khomeini' note, and waited as the boy, a ragged kid no more than ten years old, motioned to his bird. It took a couple of muttered instructions but eventually, alighting from his master's shoulder, the canary landed on the box, pecked at a card and held it in his beak, head twitching. The boy passed it to me with a smile that failed to hide his tiredness and boredom, his eyes as dull as the canary's were bright.

Staring at a mass of illegible Persian squiggles, I asked Ahmad to translate Hafez's prediction for my future. He read it through silently first, then translated, slowly, phrase by phrase: 'All your friends will abandon you . . . everything you try will fail . . . But . . . this is OK, because . . . it is God's will.'

'Well, that's the last time I bloody well *fal'e Hafez*,' I said.

Despite Ahmad's gloomy translation of Hafez's prediction, I

took him and his wife for a meal, escaping the heat of the night in a cool cellar restaurant. I warned them that I would have no truck with *ta'arof*, a stance that caused much concern and flapping around among the staff when it came to paying the bill – whispering to Ahmad, 'Your guest is trying to pay!' We lounged against cushions on the traditional low bedlike seats, our food spread out over the faded carpet before us, and talked of everyday life in Iran. Ahmad bemoaned the poor wages in the IT sector, the lack of opportunities, the restrictions and repression of life in the Islamic Republic, even here in laidback Shiraz, where he and his wife had both migrated in the hope of grasping some small freedoms. His wife, who had a stylish geek-chic look going on with vintage heavy-framed glasses, chunky jewellery and Converse hi-tops, bemoaned the sartorial dictates of the ayatollahs.

'We are not religious, you see,' said Ahmad.

I was surprised. It was the bluntest statement of atheism I had heard in my time in Iran. Most people who spoke about such matters fell into the category of the 'secular Muslim', a loose description that allowed them to enjoy un-Islamic activities and criticise the government, but meant they still tipped a respectful nod to their upbringing and culture. But Ahmad put me straight on that right away.

'Most people of our age are not religious. Why would we want to be? Look around you.'

'Were you brought up as a Muslim? Are your parents religious?' I asked.

'Yes, we both were brought up as Muslims. But we have seen what religion does. I do not want any part of this. We have a young son, he is seven years old and we are not bringing him up to be religious. My parents understand this, they do not mind. Lots of young people feel like this, especially in Shiraz, and in all the cities.'

I was intrigued at how Shiraz had acquired this reputation as Iran's liberal enclave. Ahmad was a straight-talking, rational-minded westernised software developer with an eye permanently fixed on the outside world, and this aspect of the city was the main reason for his move here. I asked him how this image of Shiraz had formed, expecting him to provide me with some analysis about the effect of the university and its large student population, or how, as the home of Hafez and Saadi's poetry, Shiraz had attracted artists over the centuries and formed a creative hub. Or even how the rebellious Bahá'í religion had begun here. But he leaned back into the cushions and made an expressive wave of his arm.

'It is because, to the south of Shiraz,' he said, gazing into the distance, 'there is a great salt lake, Maharlu Lake. The water is pink and when the air is hot, special fumes rise and float into the city. These make the Shirazis very dreamy and relaxed and it has a special effect on our minds.'

I had a feeling that Hafez would have been proud of him.

Wishing Ahmad and his wife goodbye and good luck with his job applications, I took a cab back to the hotel, passing the sixties modernist university campus set high up in the hills, jutting out of the cliffs like a futuristic sculpture. Although late on a week-night, every street still teemed with life and traffic. We joined the cars shunting bumper to bumper on the bridge over the dried-out rocky bed of the Roodkhaneye Khoshk, the seasonal river that bisects the city, before passing the Arg-e Karim Khan, the late eighteenth-century citadel in Shiraz's central square, gloriously exotic with its softly illuminated turrets and towers. The taxi driver was cheery and valiant in his attempts at English, and when he stepped out of the cab, unusually, he shook my hand as he said goodbye. This had happened a few times in Shiraz and I wondered if it was a conscious move on the part of the Shirazis to demonstrate their liberal, anti-establishment credentials.

'My name is Habib,' he said after he had wished me good luck for my onward journey

My heart gave a little jump. 'Habib! Really?'

'Yes . . .' He looked amused, if a little confused at my sudden interest.

'Have you ever been to London?'

He shook his head and repeated the same mantra I had heard all over the country: 'No, I would very much like to visit London. I have never left Iran, it is very difficult to travel with an Iranian passport.'

I told him about my Habib and he smiled. 'I think there are many Habib in Shiraz, maybe many thousands of us. And many in London too.'

I nodded. 'You'll do,' I said.

Before he got back in his cab he removed his house keys from their key ring, passing it to me and touching his hand to his heart. 'From the people of Shiraz to the people of London,' he said. The key ring was a miniature model of Hafez's tomb. Habib, my Iranian everyman, disappeared into the traffic with a clatter of loose exhaust brackets and a lungful of black smoke, waving out of the window all the way.

As I had discovered over the last 3,000 miles, Iranian hospitality knows no bounds, and is inevitably extended to friends, family and associates who are rounded up to take care of you, passing you along from post to post, like a package on the Pony Express. In the spirit of this tradition, Omid had offered to put me in touch with an old friend of his in Shiraz, a former army general who had fought in the Imposed War. He had not been as fortunate as Mr Yadzani, and an explosion in a minefield had destroyed both his legs. He lived with his wife but in a semi-hermit state, supported by a military pension and prosthetic limbs.

In the spirit of my 'say yes to everything' ethos, I had accepted the introduction, but I admitted to Omid that I was slightly wary. I imagined a grizzled veteran, outwardly and inwardly broken. What common ground would we find? I wondered. This was a military leader who had fought against Saddam Hussein and risen to the highest rank of the Iranian army; how could he be anything but a conservative hardliner? I saw myself through his eyes, the eyes of a battle-hardened, double amputee who had lived through a hell I could not even begin to imagine. Wouldn't he think me a dilettante, a frivolous westerner, an irritant dropped into his world for a day or two?

With just a couple of days left in Shiraz, it was time to grasp the nettle and make contact with my army general. We arranged or, to be more accurate, I was instructed, that he would pick me up at the hotel. From there we would go to his apartment, and then out for dinner, where we would be joined by his wife. And, he told me on the phone in gruff, halting English, I would stay with them for the rest of my time in the city. It was not so much an invitation, more a command. As I approached him in the hotel lobby I was struck by the full force of the man. Despite missing both legs, he exuded power. His upper body was stocky and strong, his grey hair cropped short, his eyes dark but behind the penetrating gaze was a kindness and even, I detected, a flash of mischief. It wasn't until I went to check out that I discovered he had paid my hotel bill in advance. Out in the car park, without telling me, he commandeered a taxi driver and hired him as my personal chauffeur for the rest of my stay. It was made clear that while I was in his charge, as his guest, all my needs would be taken care of. I was in the company of a man who was used to getting things done, to having people fall into line, and who did not need to seek approval or permission. I made my protests but it was no use. This was *ta'arof* on a military scale. There was only one response to this state of affairs: surrender.

The general lived with his wife on the ninth floor of a modern block of flats not far from the city centre. His English was limited, enough to hold the most basic conversation but not much more. His wife spoke fluent English, he told me. She worked as a doctor in the main hospital and would meet us this evening for dinner. Like Mr Yadzani, the general was very keen that I relax in an un-Islamic fashion. This meant an almost forceful removal of my headscarf as soon as the front door closed behind us, and being presented with a selection of his wife's clothes to choose from. Unfortunately, she was a dress size smaller than me so I plumped for the largest offering I could find, a still-too-tight Minnie Mouse T-shirt. Looking in the mirror, I was shocked to see the outline of my body and my loose hair; I had almost forgotten what I looked like. Weeks of being swathed in either motorcycle gear or my manteau and headscarf, as well as sporadic access to full-length mirrors, had resulted in a lack of preoccupation with my looks. As I examined my reflection, I was struck by three thoughts: how much time I spend thinking about my appearance back at home; that the straining Minnie Mouse T-shirt was verging on the obscene; and, as I made an ungainly twirl, that the Iranian force-feeding programme was starting to take its toll.

The general was a gracious host and I was a polite guest, but his difficulty in moving around coupled with our language limitations made for an awkward settling-in process. Unlike every other Iranian I had met, even those with limited English, he did not appear to have any desire to discuss politics, religion or how Iran was viewed by the rest of the world. He did not talk about the economy, the sanctions, whether life was better or worse under the Shah or the imminent nuclear deal, all standard topics in every social setting I had encountered up until now. And he certainly didn't mention the Imposed War. Unlike Mr Yadzani's apartment, there were no grainy eighties photographs of young men going off to fight.

After half an hour of stilted small talk on the safer subjects of our respective families and the weather in England, I was relieved when it was time to head out for dinner. We were meeting his wife at a Lebanese restaurant in the city centre and the driver that had been commandeered at the hotel was on hand and waiting for us outside. The general said he didn't like to go out much, without adding further explanation. But I could understand why. He never made any reference to his disability but it was easy to see how venturing into the swarm of Shiraz would be a challenge.

Iran's streets were hazardous, even for an able-bodied person, and I had seen little evidence of ramps or dropped kerbs and even less evidence of disabled people out and about in everyday life.

Fortunately, his block of flats had a lift, but as we stepped in and began the slow, silent descent the intimacy of the tiny lift only served to amplify the awkwardness of our pairing. To break the silence I practised my Persian numbers, counting down the floors as each number lit up. The general joined in with his limited English. There was a palpable sense of relief. Now we had an activity we could do together!

'*Hasht* . . .'

'Eight . . .'

'*Haft* . . .'

'Seven . . .'

'*Shesh*.'

'Six.'

We got through five and four and then, as we reached the third floor, the general stopped counting. He turned his steely gaze on me, our faces just inches away from each other. In his heavily accented English, he made a short, staccato announcement, 'It's the final countdown.'

His eyes stayed on mine. I gave a polite, nervous laugh that I hoped hid my discomfort and silently prayed for this lift journey to be over. For this whole visit to be over. What had I been thinking! Eyes still boring into mine, he spoke again. 'Was that by Europe?'

I studied his face – it was still inscrutable but his tone was questioning. It was a genuine enquiry. Could it really be? Pop quiz time at last!

'Yeah, Europe. December 1986, it was number one when I was at school.'

Our eyes met. We didn't need to speak. We both knew exactly what to do. *Da-da-dah-daah* . . . We were singing in unison, at the top of our voices.

The lift doors opened on to the lobby. We had arrived on the ground floor. Zero. *Sefr*. We punched the air simultaneously as we reached the chorus: 'It's the final countdown!'

My singing general ushered me out of the lift, grinning. '*Bezan berim!*'

'What does that mean?'

'Let's go!'

I decided I liked Shiraz. And at that most brilliant and bizarre moment, I had never been happier to be in Iran. Thank you, Habib, wherever, whoever you are, I thought. I am so glad I took you up on your curious invitation.

Our cab driver was waiting for us outside. He couldn't understand why we were laughing and singing all the way to the restaurant.

19

Neither East Nor West

A s I spent my final days in Shiraz, reflecting on my journey and the strange course of events that had brought me here, one thing became clear to me – I had to come back to Iran. I needed to delve deeper, discover and understand more. My visa was about to expire and I was frustrated at having to leave. I had clocked up over 3,000 miles, but this country was huge. There was so much more to explore, more people to meet, to talk with, and try to make sense of in this intriguing, confusing and most beguiling of countries. I had taken a tantalising sip and was now being wrenched away.

I decided to take a fast train back to Tehran with my bike in the goods wagon, and to leave the bike in Tehran over the winter with a plan to return the following spring for another road trip. Omid, my trusty friend and saviour in Tehran, sprang to my assistance in his indomitable can-do way, and magicked up storage for the bike in the back room of a friend's car showroom. I stowed it away in a corner, and although I am not one for getting senti-mental about vehicles, I gave it a fond pat on the saddle. It had been a trusty friend, starting every morning without fail, and not a splutter or groan throughout the entire journey. Nothing had broken or worn out, it still had plenty of miles left in it – and I would be coming back for those miles. It had made me friends, encouraged conversation and allowed me to see parts of Iran that would otherwise have been impossible to reach. It had allowed me to get under the skin of this country in a way that no other form of transport could. But, most of all, it had saved me, possibly even saved my life, enabling me to nip out of the way of a lumbering blacked-out minibus and to escape the crazed lunge of a whacked-out petrol station attendant. It had been the tough, loyal companion I had needed all the way, and for that I was grateful.

Omid drove us back through Tehran's wild streets. My flight home was that night; this would be my last view of the city in daylight. I was careful to soak it all up, every texting smoking moped rider, every mammoth Khomeini mural, every horn blast, every near miss, every futile *Please Drive On The Lane* road sign. The main routes were as slow-moving as ever, so we cut through the backstreets of south Tehran, but quickly came to a halt, our progress stalled by a funeral procession.

The crowd of mourners was immense – there were more than a hundred of them. They filled the entire street, the men in the front carrying the coffin and the women following behind, all cloaked in black, moving at a solemn pace. We wound down the windows as we waited and the women's wailing filled the car, echoing off the buildings. Stuck in this slow-moving melee of bodies and vehicles, there was nothing to do but sit it out. I studied the scene. There was something mesmerising yet disturbing about the communal crying and chanting. Some of the men, their faces grave, carried a shrinelike structure on their shoulders in the form of an ornate metal cage decorated with mirrors and illuminated by light bulbs. Others carried posters of the dead man's portrait. It was a young face; no more than early twenties.

'This is called a *hejle*,' said Omid, pointing at the shrine. 'You used to see a lot of them during the war. It is for when young men die unmarried. *Hejle* is actually the same word as for a bride's bedroom. So they make them for young men who never made it into the real "*hejle*", if you know what I mean.' He gave me one of his cheeky grins. I was going to miss Omid.

The crowd continued their steady procession. We sat and

watched in silence. Then the mass of bodies broke apart. Something was happening. A surge of movement, a flash of metal. A terrible sound, a cry that I could not identify. The crowd had parted and I could see one of the men was holding a knife. In his other hand he held a sheep by its neck, one foot on its lifeless body. He had slashed its throat. Right here in the street of a twenty-first-century capital city, in broad daylight. Blood was pouring across the road. I had never seen so much blood. I found myself wondering how one sheep could contain it all. It splashed on to the wheels of parked cars and ran in great rivers down the gutters. The road turned red.

'It is to stop other deaths taking place,' said Omid, 'that is why they sacrifice the sheep.'

He was unperturbed, laughing at my reaction, amused at my shock and my squeamish, British animal-loving ways. I remembered how he had told me of the public execution he had witnessed as a child growing up in this city; the death of a sheep was nothing to him. None of the mourners or the pedestrians or the other car drivers waiting for the procession to pass seemed fazed by this animal sacrifice.

I was aware of being very far away from home. My entire time in Iran had been like this; great lurches between a sense of intense connection and love for the people and this nation, and moments of deep discomfort and incomprehension. My responses bounced all over the place, mirroring the contradictions of Iran as well as my own nature. I couldn't work out what I felt from one moment to the next. Both ends of the spectrum were extreme. At one I had never felt so engaged with my fellow humans; the Iranians represented the very best of humanity with their effortless warmth and kindness, their desire and innate ability to connect on a meaningful level and to find humour and fun in all situations. Their lust for life ran through their very core and I had thrived on being amongst it. I admired them, was envious of them even, this ability to simply feel and express oneself without fear or shame. But at the other end of the spectrum, these great gushes of emotion were not just reserved for the good times, and it was this that left me feeling exposed; there was no stiff upper lip or sarcastic humour to hide behind when things got sad, bad or scary. The rough and the smooth had equal billing in the hearts of the Iranians and every emotional response was laid bare. I suspected this was the true essence of being human, but also I feared it would take a while for my uptight British soul to assimilate, if it ever could.

We eventually edged our way through the backed-up traffic. The wailing receded, subsumed into the usual Tehran traffic noises, and as I watched the black-clad figures and the red-stained street disappear behind us, I wondered if we could ever truly understand each other, and if not, did it matter? Maybe that was where we had been going wrong all this time, always trying to understand, to make sense, to control, to fit Iran into our own frame of reference, instead of simply accepting? And I wondered if this went some way to explaining the enduring British fascination with Iran – this simultaneous sense of connection and disconnection; at once so like us, yet so disturbingly 'other'.

This public, daylight outpouring of emotion and the ritualistic slaughter of the sheep had been shocking, alienating even. Lobbed like a grenade into the mass of already heightened emotions surrounding my final day in Iran, it had brought into sharp focus the differences between our worlds. But as we drove away from the scene, I looked back at the weeping women and the sadness etched on the faces of the men and I knew there was much more that connected us than separated us. The details and differences did not seem as important as when I had arrived just a few weeks earlier.

I flew home with Iran Air, which gave me six and a half hours to truly appreciate the impact of the international sanctions first hand. The scratchy seat fabric, cigarette-burned plastic washbasins and whiff of engine oil throughout the cabin reminded me of late seventies coach travel, which was probably the last time these planes had had a facelift. I tried to convince myself that Iran Air had prioritised the maintenance of engines and safety features over the interior decor but I wasn't convinced, especially when the seatbelt refused to budge. The in-flight entertainment had certainly been spared an upgrade, consisting of one small television at the front of the plane showing repeat screenings of a gentle propaganda film featuring chador-clad women gazing at waterfalls and flowers with an appropriately tinkly soundtrack. The stewardesses' outfits were suitably dreary too. Reflecting Iran Air's status as the national carrier of the Islamic Republic, they were of course modest to the point of unflattering, with not a single glimpse of neck or hair visible beneath the military style cap and hijab. As we took off, I examined my fellow passengers. Nobody was praying and as soon as we were airborne, every female passenger removed her headscarf without ceremony.

The man next to me was reading a newspaper. From the pictures I could tell it was an article about the nuclear deal. The composite images of Rouhani and Obama were still considered press-worthy weeks later; after all, this was the biggest international story to happen in Iran for decades. The debates continued to rumble on; hardliners resisting, the moderates trying to move it forward. I wondered how it would all pan out. Would the Islamic Republic 'open up' as western commentators were predicting, and if so, what did this mean for us watching from the other side of the world? And more crucially, what did it mean for the Iranian people? The lifting of sanctions was the big deal, bringing trade, business opportunities and of course tourism. It would be a long time before Iran became a hen-night destination, but even so, I was ashamed to find myself contemplating that for the traveller, Iran's charms lay in its isolation. This was not a mindset I liked, or approved of; I didn't want to be like the smug backpackers in *The Beach*, trying to keep their special place a secret. I wanted the Iranian people to reap all the benefits from engaging with the world and for the rest of us to wake up to the reality that Iran is not a nation of desert-dwelling terrorists. But I guessed it would be like everywhere else in the world – a tourist trail would appear, attracting the hustlers and the unscrupulous, as it always does. But the real Iran would always be there, with its warmth, hospitality and humour; you would just have to stray a little further from the trail to find it.

Snacks and drinks more associated with an eight-year-old's birthday party – imitation Coca-Cola and the Iranian equivalent of Wotsits – were handed out as I watched Tehran's messy sprawl appear below me, and as we climbed higher, the deserts and mountains beyond. Cutting across the empty plains to the south, I could see the straight scars of roads that I had been riding just weeks before. From here they looked empty and enticing, a thrilling desert highway, but their reality was still embedded in my bones and nerves, and probably would be forever. But still, I wanted to come back for more. Why?

I smiled inwardly at the thought that I was becoming another Persophile Brit – an *Iran-doost*, friend of Iran – joining a long and not always illustrious tradition. Iran has this effect on people, particularly the British. It sucks us in, fascinates and appals, confounds and charms in equal measure. Its subversive contradictory nature appealed to my own; I liked that I could not quite understand it, that it kept me guessing and that each time I thought I was making sense of it, something happened to blow my theories and expectations out of the water. I loved that the Iranians never quite did what you thought they were going to do, or even, what you wanted them to do. The whole damn place reeked of cheeky bad-boy charm, and to this, I was not immune.

Our stormy relationship must play a part in the British fascination with Iran, linking us forever like a permanently warring couple, a geopolitical version of 'Can't live with 'em, can't live without 'em'. And like all torrid couplings, I had noticed many similarities as well as differences. As two former empires, both with distinct identities and a strong sense of national pride, there is an island mentality in Iran that feels strangely familiar, a perverse pleasure to be found in going it alone, not being bossed around. Neither nation is particularly comfortable with the idea of mucking in with its neighbours – Britain with its scepticism towards Europe and inflated sense of importance in the world; Iran, an island of Shi-ite Muslims surrounded by Sunnis, geographically in the Middle East but definitely not Arabs – always, defiantly, neither East nor West. But there were gentler similarities too; an appreciation of the absurd and a sense of humour that celebrates the subversive and the silly, a love of the outdoors and an illustrious history of mountaineering and climbing, the national penchant for picnics and a profound appreciation of nature. Even the strange formalised politeness of ta'arof reminded me of our own British rituals of insistence and refusal when passing through a doorway or our habit of apologising when bumped into by a stranger. And, of course, our mutual inability to do anything without a cup of tea.

I had not expected to find any of these reassuring footholds when I arrived in Iran. I am ashamed to say that despite my conscious mind taking an open-minded approach to this journey, my subconscious had prepared for the worst. When I had turned up at the border I had been bracing myself for all the horrors as predicted by the doom-mongers back home. I was steeled for the onslaught of angry Islamists who would shun me (or worse) for being British/western/an infidel/female – take your pick. But instead I had been hit with a tidal wave of warmth and humanity to a degree that I have never experienced anywhere else in the world. Now I wanted to step off the plane when we landed at Heathrow and start whispering to people, 'We've got it all wrong! We've been lied to! Come with me, let me show you!' I wanted to round up all those doom-mongers on the next Iran Air flight to Tehran, and tell them, 'Ignore the dodgy snacks and the in-flight entertainment, this place will blow your mind, you will never think or feel the same way again!'

Iran had altered me in some essential way. It had recalibrated my brain, my heart and soul, which is surely the best possible outcome of any adventure. As we ascended into the clouds and Iran slipped away from view, I knew I would come back, again and again. And I remembered Freya Stark's words on the purpose of travel: 'To feel, and think, and learn – learn always, surely that is being alive.'

Epilogue

Summer 2016

T HE TAXI DRIVER spoke no English but his intentions were clear from his hand gesture. Two fingers. Two minutes. 'OK!'

We were making an unscheduled detour on the standard run from Tehran airport into the city centre. I had no idea why we had stopped but he had ducked down a side street and now he was out of the car, disappearing at a light jog down the road. The familiar raucous jostle of south Tehran swarmed all around, the morning air already thick with dust and exhaust fumes in the summer fug. It was going to be a hot one. The driver had vanished from view. I guessed he had an errand to run, some other sideline, a typical Tehrani, on the hustle, running two jobs. I wound down the window, breathing in, tasting the familiar tang, letting the noise rush in from the street. I was in no hurry. Then he came into sight in the wing mirror, bounding back towards the car, youthful, eager, long-legged. He seemed to be carrying something in each hand. His face appeared at the window, smiling. No words, just an ice cream cone thrust into my grip, huge sticky swirls, laden with chocolate sauce and sprinkles, already melting in the morning sun. He jumped into the driver's seat, and we were off again, slipping back into the throng. It was good to be back in Iran.

I returned to Iran the following spring after my first trip. All I had to do was dust off the bike; it started right away and I picked up where I had left off, exploring new territory but also returning to favourite haunts and visiting some of the friends I had made the first time. Not many months had passed since then, and the mood on the street was much the same as it had been the previous autumn. Negotiations over the nuclear deal were rumbling on but looking hopeful, and while there were all the usual complaints about the regime, there was still a sense of optimism in the air. I had managed to get a visa without any trouble this time, and I hoped that maybe it was true what they said, that Iran was 'opening up' to the world.

But then, halfway through my trip, I received news from home that things had changed, at least for me. British citizens would no longer be allowed to travel independently in Iran. From now on they could only enter the country as part of an organised tour group or if accompanied by a government-approved guide. I was in a café in Tehran when I received the news and I surveyed my surroundings with fresh eyes, aware that every remaining moment was to be savoured now. I had been very fortunate, one of the last few Brits to have entered Iran unaccompanied, able to roam freely under my own steam. This new ruling seemed to have come out of nowhere, although there were mutterings that it was in response to a comment made by David Cameron at the UN criticising Iran's human rights record; yet another point scored in our tradition of tit-for-tat diplomacy. I kept my head down for the last few weeks of that journey and sent my bike back home by Iran Air Cargo. The era of independent overland travel in Iran was over for the foreseeable future.

My guess back then, in April 2014, was that this new rule would soon be reversed. Iran has a history of inventing peculiar restrictions to its visa policies on a whim, and I guessed this would all blow over soon enough. I hoped so – I had big plans for future Iranian adventures. So, in a replay of my first trip, I waited and watched. But nothing budged. The consulates in London and Tehran remained closed and the travel restrictions stayed firmly in place.

Then, in July 2015, after years of tortuous negotiations, and amid much clamour and celebration, the deal on Iran's nuclear programme was approved. Twelve years of international sanctions were lifted and the Iranians took to the streets in their thousands to celebrate. In Tehran they cruised up and down Valiasr Street, honking their horns, waving 'V for victory' signals out of their windows; there was even dancing in the street. The 'morality police' turned a blind eye for a night.

Back home the Foreign Office changed its travel advice for Iran, swapping 'no-go' red for 'go for it' green and suddenly you couldn't move for broadsheet travel features gushing about the ancient treasures of Persia. Iran was suddenly 'safe', although the reality was that nothing on the ground had changed at all; to the visitor, Iran was just as safe or unsafe as it had been a week earlier. And upon closer examination, these newspaper articles were nothing but thinly disguised adverts for tour companies, whose bookings were going through the roof because, despite all the 'opening up' of Iran, British citizens could not get in without joining one of their authorised excursions. The embassies quietly reopened but the consulates that issue visas remained firmly closed. Everything had changed but nothing had changed.

I continued to wait and watch. I wondered what Habib was making of all this. Was he still writing imploring notes to strangers? Was he happy how things had turned out? Most of the Iranians, both at home and abroad, appeared pleased; a great new dawn of opportunity awaited their land, they believed. Only a few of the old hardliners protested, comparing the nuclear deal to Khomeini's famous 'drinking of the poisoned chalice' truce that ended the Iran–Iraq War. I thought of the petrol-pumping psychology student I had met on my first journey – 'Our countries are going to be friends!' – and of Raha, the glamorous luxury brand management queen with a penchant for Stoli, who had decided to stay and carve her career in her home country. I hoped their dreams and ambitions were coming to fruition.

So I kept an eye on the situation, and not just on what was happening in Iran but also here at home. There was a shift in mood and I noticed a new response to talk of visiting Iran. Less of 'What d'you wanna go there for?' and more, 'Oh, how fascinating!' There was a new flurry of broadsheet stories, now focussing on Iran's underground scenes – the music, the parties, the drugs. The underlying message being, 'Look, they're just like us! They want to have fun too!' But in Iran the fun continued to reap the same reactions as usual – the arrests, jail terms and lashings continued. Executions for drug offences were at their highest level ever.

Still, the consulates remained closed and the visa restrictions didn't change or at least, not for Brits. In the wake of the lifting of the sanctions, citizens of every other European nation were now allowed a visa on arrival but the UK remained out in the cold. But in the summer of 2016 I managed to find a way to wangle my way back in. Travelling with my husband Austin this time, we flew into Iman Khomeini Airport, or 'Tehran International Airport' as the pilot preferred to call it when he announced our arrival in English. I noticed its official title was used in the Persian announcement that followed.

We were greeted by a looming Khomeini and Khamenei, of course, frowning over the baggage carousel as if they were looking out for their missing suitcases. But the immigration guards were cheerful and at the bureau de change the teller waxed lyrical about his long ago university degree in English literature, quoting a few lines of Milton as he counted out our millions. 'Your English pounds are so much nicer than our money,' he added.

I agreed that the rials' multitude of zeroes made my head spin.

'No, I mean your notes don't have pictures of an idiot mullah on them!' he said with a grin, loading me up with the familiar pastel-shaded wads of cash. Half an hour later we were shunting and weaving our way up Valiasr Street, ice cream and chocolate sauce melting all over our hands. I realised I had missed this place, these people.

Unable to bring our motorcycles into the country, we hired a car for our road trip this time. Surveying our dented, scratched and bird-shit-splattered Hyundai saloon, we suspected we were at the vanguard of Iranian car rental. It came with a Quran in the glove compartment and a hire agreement that began with the line, *In The Name of God*. As I peeled out into the familiar highway madness, there was a sense of joyous, if slightly hysterical, abandonment about being back on the road in Iran. The two of us with our scrappy motor and no idea what was going to happen next, a Persian version of the *Blues Brothers* scene – there's 106 miles to Qom, we've got a full tank of *benzin*, half a pack of pistachios, it's sunny out, and I'm wearing a hijab. *Bezan berim!*

The plan was to hit the road and take the temperature of the nation in its new dawn. I had not fully realised on my first trip just how significant a moment in Iran's story I had been witnessing back then. The UN talks and the phone conversation between Obama and Rouhani had been a monumental turning point in Iranian history, and now, three years later, on my third visit, I could see how that moment had shaped my experience. The optimism had been tangible.

But now, sadly, within days of arriving, there was a distinct sense that not all was working out as hoped. People were frustrated. Nothing had changed, they said. 'Yes, the sanctions have been lifted but that was a year ago, when is it going to make a difference to our lives?' they wanted to know. On the surface, Tehran seemed to be teeming with business conventions, their bilingual vinyl banners splashed across office blocks and hotels throughout the city, from oil industry conferences to book fairs. In swanky restaurants serious German businessmen were attempting to cut deals with their bored-looking Iranian counterparts on everything from soft drinks to stationery. Further south, in Yadz and Shiraz, the tourist industry was making hay, with groups of awkward hijab-wearing Australians and Europeans being bussed around the place. A handwritten sign outside a budget hotel in

Shiraz shouted in a most uptight, un-Iranian style, *Persepolis Tour leaving 7.30 a.m. DO NOT COME LATE.*

But the reality for most regular Iranians was the same as it ever was. High unemployment, low wages and no sign of all the promised opportunities any time soon. 'It will take a while for the world to trust Iran,' explained one Shirazi businessman over a hotel breakfast. 'America and Europe are still wary of doing business with us, this is the problem. The banks are allowed to trade now but everyone knows that many of the big companies in Iran are owned by the Revolutionary Guards, or connected with them in some way. If foreign companies are found doing deals with them, they can still get a big fine because it is seen as doing business with sponsors of terror. I mean a really big fine.' He shook his head. 'It is not worth the risk for many. But people here thought everything would change overnight. Now they are angry when their lives are the same as before.'

We caught up with Omid and Tala in Tehran. It was the last time we would see them here, but we would be seeing a lot more of them in the future. They were busy packing their belongings into boxes, getting ready to return to the UK, this time for good. Tala couldn't have been happier. Her dream of Sorena attending school without a headscarf would come true.

'I've had enough of Iran, it's getting me down now,' said Omid, flumping down for a moment among a pile of crates and cardboard. 'And people are getting jealous here, that's a new thing. If you're seen to be doing all right, they don't like it.'

Omid and Tala were the fortunate ones, with British passports and friends in the UK. I was happy for them and excited to have them closer to home. But for millions of others, the options were not just limited, but non-existent. They were stuck. The older Iranians were more resigned to the situation; they had ridden many a wave in Iran's tumultuous history. But the younger generation were visibly, vocally frustrated. Ahmad in Shiraz was still desperately pitching his CV to every western IT firm, and Aheng was still plotting her escape to an American university. The more pragmatic still believed change would come but slowly, more connection with the world would eventually bring more opportunities, and most importantly of all, more freedoms – to the internet, the press, their social lives. It would be a gradual affair, there would be no revolution, they said, but it was better this way.

In one of Tehran's new fashionable coffee shops, all exposed brick walls and mismatching cutlery, the young guy behind the counter engaged us in conversation. He was the new breed of Tehrani hipster who wouldn't have looked out of place in Brooklyn or Hoxton; long-haired, artfully unkempt, the opposite of the typical highly groomed Iranian male. Gypsy jazz was playing over the speakers and he was carefully arranging a selection of French cheeses on the counter. I wondered if they were a new, post-sanctions arrival on Tehran's culinary scene. He said yes, it was easier to import the cheese now, and talked me through the merits of a newly arrived Comté and a particularly pungent Normandy Livarot.

'Is it your first time in Iran?' he asked. He was erudite and charming and, like all Iranians, eager to engage with visitors to his country.

I explained it was my third visit, and that Austin had first come here in 1984, as an eighteen-year-old, making his way to India.

'You like it? You like Iran?'

We both gushed. Oh yes, we love Iran.

He looked me in the eye but his expression did not reflect my enthusiasm. 'I hate it.'

It was like a blow. We were free to come and go. He was not. The words remained unspoken, but that was the nub of it. I had encountered many emotions from Iranians about their country – frustration, anger, despair, disgust – but I had always found the negative to be countered with a profound passion and love for Iran that somehow managed to transcend the travails of everyday life. It was as if they were able to separate their own personal experience under the Islamic Republic from the wider, grander picture of belonging to an ancient, sophisticated civilisation. But not this guy. He just wanted to be French.

'I would like to live in Paris,' he said.

Now the cheeses made sense. He would fit in a treat on La Rive Gauche. And it broke my heart that his dream would probably remain unrealised, that instead he was creating his own mini-Paris, with his coffee and Camembert and his forbidden Django Reinhardt, here in a backstreet of Tehran.

'Have you ever been to Paris?' I asked him, but I already knew the answer. He shook his head.

'You know of Joseph de Maistre?' he asked.

It was my turn to shake my head.

'He was a Frenchman, a philosopher.'

No, I said. I didn't know him.

'He is the man who said that a country gets the government it deserves.'

This time I nodded. I knew the saying.

'But he is wrong.' He looked me in the eye again. 'We do not deserve ours.'

Acknowledgements

MY JOURNEYS IN Iran and this book could not have happened without an enormous amount of help and friendship from so many, both at home and in Iran.

Firstly, thank you to Austin and Mum, for supporting the plan from the get-go, for being fearless, and for never being naysayers. And to Austin, thank you also for the endless reading, re-reading, talking, brainstorming and your unwavering belief in me.

To the wonderful trio of Sina, Avid and Ava who were so integral to my journey and have gone on to enhance my life in so many ways. Thank you, my dear friends! I could not have done it without you.

A huge debt of gratitude is due to the inimitable Antony Wynn, chairman of the Iran Society (www.iransociety.org) who generously offered to read and fact-check the first draft. Thank you for amending my mistakes, correcting my Persian and enlivening my margins no end. Any errors to be found are mine.

To Zohreh for being the kind of woman who can make anything happen. You are the true embodiment of the great Iranian spirit.

To Laudan Nooshin for making what I now know to be a very Iranian gesture of assistance to a total stranger. I'm glad you were listening to the radio that day.

To Lisa Harrison and Eleanor Crow for reading early drafts and for your sound advice, friendship and encouragement.

To Suzi Searle and Marcus Ackerman for the Tehran connection.

To Ruth Killick for putting me in touch with Nick Brealey,

the man who really got the book off the ground and worked hard to make it happen.

At Nicholas Brealey Publishing/John Murray Press, big thank you to my editor, Kate Hewson, for her sensible suggestions and snappy asides in the margins. To Ben Slight and Louise Richardson for their unending positivity and enthusiasm for this book, and to Ruby Mitchell for her tireless work in promoting it. It has been a real pleasure to work with you all. Big thanks to the powerhouse that is Melissa, Alison, Michelle and Tess at Nicholas Brealey Publishing in the US. You guys rock.

A big مرسی to the formidable Masih Alinejad and Ahad Ghanbary for their ongoing support. Great Iranians, both. And to Nader Omidvar for his positivity and kind words, and chasing up his dad for me.

To my fellow author and two-wheeled globetrotter pal, Ants Bolingbroke-Kent for writerly support and chai. To Shirin Shabestari, Iranian adventurer, climber and my Iran-*doost* in London, thank you for your enthusiasm and good energy. And to Raha Kamezi for early encouragement and top tips – *seer shodam merci* – it didn't work.

And on the road, big thanks to my fellow motorcycle travellers, Andreas in Ankara for his help and hospitality, and to Polly, Ivo and everyone at Motokamp in Bulgaria for looking after me on my way east.

There were many Iranians who gave so much of their time and energy to help me during my journey but who cannot be named – you know who you are. مرکشتم

Finally, thank you to the people of Iran who welcomed me so wholeheartedly and unconditionally. You have taught me so much. And, of course, thanks to Habib for the invitation . . .

Timeline of Significant Events

1906   First parliament formed and constitution created.

1908   The British discover oil in southern Persia and form the Anglo-Persian Oil Company.

1921   Reza Khan, a soldier, takes control of the army in a coup.

1925   Reza Khan crowns himself the first Shah of the Pahlavi line and begins his modernisation programme.

1935   Reza Shah changes the country's name from Persia to Iran.

1941   Reza Shah is exiled by British and Soviet forces due to perceived support for Nazi Germany during WWII. His son, Mohammed Reza, becomes Shah.

1951   Nationalist Mohammad Mossadeq is elected Prime Minster and proceeds to nationalise the oil industry.

1953   The CIA and MI6 coordinate a coup to oust Mossadeq.

1963   The Shah implements his 'White Revolution' series of reforms, improving women's rights and eroding the power of the clerics, tribes and powerful landlords.

1964   Ayatollah Khomeini is sent into exile in Iraq for criticising the Shah and the USA.

1971   The Shah throws a lavish celebration at Persepolis to celebrate 2,500 years of the Persian monarchy.

1978   Anti-Shah protests erupt in Tehran. The army shoot and kill protestors.

1979   The Shah flees Iran. Khomeini returns from exile to tumultuous support. The Islamic Republic of Iran is proclaimed following a referendum. Supporters of the Shah are executed. Fifty-two Americans are taken hostage at the US Embassy in Tehran by a group of students. Diplomatic relations are severed between Iran and the USA.

1980   Iraq invades Iran, beginning the eight-year long 'Imposed War'. The Shah dies of cancer in exile in Egypt.

1981   The American hostages are released after 444 days.

1988   The 'Imposed War' ends with a UN-negotiated truce. Thousands of left wing dissidents are executed.

1989   Khomeini declares a fatwa on novelist Salman Rushdie in response to his book, *The Satanic Verses*. Khomeini dies. Khamenei is appointed Supreme Leader.

1995   The USA imposes sanctions over alleged sponsorship of terrorism.

1997   Reformist Khatami wins the presidential election in a landslide.

2001   Khatami wins a second term.

2002   Construction resumes on Iran's first nuclear reactor. George Bush includes Iran in his 'Axis of Evil' speech.

2003   Populist radical Ahmadinejad wins the presidential election.

2009   Ahmadinejad wins a second term. The result is contested in the 'Green Revolution' protests. Protestors are beaten up, arrested, shot and killed.

2011   British Embassy in Tehran is attacked in protest over sanctions. Diplomatic ties are cut between UK and Iran.

2013   Rouhani is elected president. He speaks to President Obama – the first time American and Iranian leaders have communicated since 1979.

2015   The nuclear deal is agreed and international sanctions are to be lifted.

2016   Full diplomatic relations between the UK and Iran are reinstated.